THE EUROPEAN FREE TRADE ASSOCIATION

THE EUROPEAN FREE TRADE ASSOCIATION

An Intergovernmental Platform for Trade Relations

Georges Baur

INTERSENTIA
Cambridge – Antwerp – Chicago

Intersentia Ltd
8 Wellington Mews
Wellington Street | Cambridge
CB1 1HW | United Kingdom
Tel: +44 1223 736 170
Email: mail@intersentia.co.uk
www.intersentia.com | www.intersentia.co.uk

Distribution for the UK and
Rest of the World (incl. Eastern Europe)
NBN International
1 Deltic Avenue, Rooksley
Milton Keynes MK13 8LD
United Kingdom
Tel: +44 1752 202 301 | Fax: +44 1752 202 331
Email: orders@nbninternational.com

Distribution for Europe
Intersentia Publishing nv
Groenstraat 31
2640 Mortsel
Belgium
Tel: +32 3 680 15 50
Email: mail@intersentia.be

Distribution for the USA and Canada
Independent Publishers Group
Order Department
814 North Franklin Street
Chicago, IL 60610
USA
Tel: +1 800 888 4741 (toll free) | Fax: +1 312 337 5985
Email: orders@ipgbook.com

The European Free Trade Association. An Intergovernmental Platform for Trade Relations

First published in 2020
Second printing in 2020 with table and figure resolution improvements

Image on cover: Felix Hug / Stocksy

ISBN 978-1-78068-656-1
D/2020/7849/27
NUR 828

British Library Cataloguing in Publication Data. A catalogue record for this book is available from the British Library.

FOREWORD

The European Free Trade Association (EFTA) is the intergovernmental organisation of Iceland, Liechtenstein, Norway and Switzerland. Set up in 1960 by the Stockholm Convention for the promotion of free trade and economic integration, it offered another form of 'European integration', different to the EU – more intergovernmental, less integrated and with the capacity to allow its states to negotiate their own trade agreements. It is, however, something of a Cinderella model, forgotten by states in the rush to join the EU and integrate ever more. The countries that were and, in part still are, members of EFTA are rather like-minded and may, historically and politically, be called 'friends of the UK' (from Portugal via Switzerland to Finland). The driving force behind the original EFTA model was the UK, determined to find another way of inter-state cooperation outside the EU. Given that EFTA covers many matters the UK might need in its future 'life' outside the EU but in Europe, a closer look at EFTA might be helpful. It is unlikely that the UK would rejoin EFTA, at least in the short to medium term, but it would be a way of 'coming home'. A book analysing the EFTA Convention in depth has never been written before and there is no better person to write it than Dr Georges Baur, who worked for the EFTA secretariat for 15 years and whose deep familiarity with EFTA, the EEA and the EU means that he can provide deep insights into this subject. Now working in Liechtenstein, Georges has had the opportunity to reflect and consider the different models which he has worked with throughout his professional career, and this has helped to inform his rich legal analysis.

Professor Catherine Barnard, University of Cambridge
February 2020

PREFACE

AIM OF BOOK AND DEFINITIONS

1 This short book aims to give the reader interested in European integration beyond the dimension of mere EU membership an insight into an alternative structure that has long been overlooked and ignored. If some knew of it, then it was considered by many an outdated model and, to put it bluntly, a loose association of some economically highly specialised, small and wealthy Western European states.[1] However, the European Free Trade Association (EFTA) was once conceived as an alternative model under the United Kingdom's leadership to the then European Economic Community (EEC), now European Union (EU).

2 The lost interest in EFTA can also be shown by the (academic) writing undertaken on that subject. In the early days there were quite noteworthy publications on EFTA and the economic policy it represented.[2] Interest in the subject diminished when the UK joined the EEC. There was, however, still some academic literature produced on EFTA, notably on the free trade agreements between the EU and the EFTA states, although not much in English.[3] Then, after the inception of the European Economic Area (EEA), the interest of academia remained with that form of European integration, if at all. Most of the academic contributions dealing with EFTA either came from the EFTA Secretariat[4] or the EFTA states themselves, or these were

---

1 S. Gstöhl, 'Switzerland, Norway and the European Union – The odd ones out?' in N.M. Jovanovic (ed.), *International economic integration: Integration schemes*, Routledge, London 1998, p. 322.

2 To name but a few, see e.g.: Study Group of the Geneva Graduate Institute of International Studies, 'The European Free Trade Association and the Crisis of European Integration', Michael Joseph Ltd., London 1968; V. Curzon-Price, 'The Essentials of Economic Integration – Lessons of EFTA Experience', Macmillan, Basingstoke 1974.

3 See e.g. H.-G. Koppensteiner (ed.), 'Rechtsfragen der Freihandelsabkommen der Europäischen Wirtschaftsgemeinschaft mit den EFTA-Staaten', Orac, Vienna 1987.

4 See e.g. K. Bryn and G. Einarsson (eds.), *EFTA 1960–2010, Elements of 50 Years of European History*, EFTA, Geneva 2010.

needed as an introduction to the EEA.[5] One unfortunate consequence of this is 'that the political scientists [and other academics, G.B.], who see the "European Integration" as a synonymous with the history of the EU and its current performance, lose many opportunities for comparative research'.[6]

3 As shown by a quick look at the press, interest in EFTA has increased since the referendum of 23 June 2016, in which a slim majority of UK voters expressed their wish to leave the European Union.[7] Since the very beginning of the reporting on the so-called 'Brexit', hardly any distinction has been made between EFTA and the EEA.

4 In this book, various aspects related to EFTA will be examined in greater detail. Brexit will serve as an opportunity to introduce the subject, and there will be a chapter dealing with the question whether EFTA could be of interest to the United Kingdom (UK) when it acquires its new status outside the EU. This will, however, have to be done with the explicit proviso that at the time of the publication of this book negotiations between the UK and the EU on a future relationship have barely begun and any view on this would, therefore, be mere speculation.

5 Some concepts that will be used or which can be found in documents to which reference will be made, might be difficult to understand. The book, therefore, introduces some basic definitions. Other clarifications, such as the different forms of external trade relations or economic integration, will be further explained in the context of the respective chapters.

6 Some of the concepts in relation to the EFTA Convention might cause confusion in as far as some publications speak of the 'EFTA Convention', 'Stockholm Convention' or 'Vaduz Convention', sometimes in a rather arbitrary manner. The 'Stockholm Convention' is the EFTA Convention as it was agreed in its original form and text in 1960. The 'Vaduz Convention' is the Convention amending the 'Stockholm Convention'. This book will, however, generally use the term 'EFTA Convention' and this means the text

---

[5] See e.g. G. Baur, M. Sanchez Rydelski and C. Zatschler, *European Free Trade Association (EFTA) and the European Economic Area (EEA)*, 2nd ed., Wolters Kluwer, Alphen aan den Rijn 2018.

[6] R.T. Griffiths, 'EFTA and European Integration 1973–1984, Vindication or Marginalisation?' in K. Bryn and G. Einarsson (eds.), *EFTA 1960–2010, Elements of 50 Years of European History*, EFTA, Geneva 2010, p. 145.

[7] See e.g. The Guardian of 14 January 2017: 'Nick Clegg says May should go for Norway-style trade deal', http://www.theguardian.com/politics/2017/jan/14/nick-clegg-theresa-may-norway-style-trade-deal-brexit-eu.

currently in force, unless there is a reference to a specific text in its historic dimension. A similar problem sometimes occurs with regard to the terms 'EEC', 'EC' and 'EU'. Except in cases where the historical term matters, this book generally refers to the 'EU' as it currently is.

In the different chapters the reader may come across some repetitions. 7
These were, however, retained on purpose in order to try to facilitate access to a sometimes rather difficult subject.

STRUCTURE OF THE BOOK

Chapter 1 attempts to give an initial answer to the questions: what is 8
EFTA and what is its position among the different models of economic integration? The chapter provides a brief excursion into the specific theory, and briefly touches upon the context of global trade law, in which EFTA operates, namely the rules of the World Trade Organisation (WTO).

This is followed by Chapter 2 which offers a short historical overview of 9
EFTA. This is intended to complete the picture of economic integration in Europe.

Chapter 3 examines the EFTA Convention from a substantive point of 10
view, i.e. what subjects are covered by the cooperation amongst the EFTA states. This is also the first of the three main activities of EFTA.

Chapter 4 deals with membership of the association, its scope and 11
institutions. This will also include some words on procedures and finances.

The second main activity of EFTA, namely relations with third countries 12
and other organisations, will be dealt with in Chapter 5. The main focus will be on free trade agreements (FTAs) which EFTA and/or its member states negotiate around the globe.

Chapter 6 will focus on EFTA as a platform for its member states to base 13
their relations with the EU on. Again, as the history of European integration suggests, this is not straightforward. The four current members of EFTA chose different ways to develop their formerly loose – and from today's perspective – rather basic links with the (then) EEC into a participation in the EU's internal market, as in the case of Iceland, Liechtenstein and Norway, or a sectoral association, as in the case of Switzerland. As far as possible and required by the intimate connection between the EFTA rules and those of the EEA Agreement the chapter will also refer to the

EU's internal market and its rules. It will, however, cover neither the law of the Internal Market nor the EEA in detail as this would be outside the scope of this book. There are, however, excellent works on the subject. The chapter will proceed in the same manner with regard to the relationship between the EU and Switzerland. As mentioned before, this seems to be all the more relevant with regard to the current discussion on Brexit and the future relationship between the UK and the EU, as some of the most important elements for a functioning trading relationship between the EU and its closest neighbours can be found here. These elements will also be of importance for a future trade agreement, whatever this may be.

14 Finally, the future relationship between the UK and the EU will be at the core of Chapter 7. Given that the UK has left the EU, there will need to be a new basis for the future relationship between the UK and the EU. Even though it is currently impossible to say what form or shape it will have, that future relationship will have to be negotiated. It might therefore be worthwhile considering the EFTA Convention. This instrument might be useful for the UK, either to bridge the period until a new agreement is concluded, or to provide a base for its future relationship with the EU if the UK should eventually choose to associate itself to the internal market, or even in a long-term perspective, e.g. as a basis for its future external trade relations, or a combination of these elements.

ACKNOWLEDGEMENTS

I would like to thank Professor Catherine Barnard, Cambridge, for pushing me to write this book. The same goes for my friends and colleagues who at various stages looked over the text and provided feedback. To name but a few, with no intention to exclude anyone, my special thanks go to Professor Christa Tobler, Basel/Leiden, Stefan Barriga, Brussels, and Pascal Schafhauser, Geneva, as well as Dr. Christian Frommelt, Director of the Liechtenstein-Institute, Bendern, which supported the production of this work. My thanks also go to Intersentia. I have enjoyed working with them. In particular, Ann-Christin Maak-Scherpe and Ahmed Hegazi were extremely supportive from the very beginning to the end. Last but not least, I am grateful to Dr. Ines Brunhart for always being there and for proving to be an excellent 'mental sparring partner'.

I have tried to eliminate errors as much as possible. Any that may have remained undetected are, of course, solely mine.

CONTENTS

LIST OF TABLES AND FIGURES

FIGURES

TABLES

CHAPTER 1
WHAT IS EFTA?

1.1. ONLY A CLASSICAL FREE TRADE AREA?

1.1.1. INTRODUCTION

European integration is very much about what kind of economic integration is intended between the states involved. Since the signing of the Treaty of Rome in 1957, the EU has moved through different stages: from the European Economic Community, to the European Communities and today's European Union. And although some goals were set from the beginning[1] the next steps were seldom undisputed.[2] If we now look further back, this dispute about what kind of economic integration should be favoured amongst the (then) Western European states, is the very reason why these split into those founding the EEC on the one hand and those who favoured a lighter structure and therefore set up EFTA, on the other. These different concepts are, however, not just of historical interest. They remain relevant in today's discussions, e.g. on what model of economic integration the UK should choose after Brexit or whether, in the case of Switzerland, a 'comprehensive' FTA could replace the current regime of sectoral access to the EU's internal market.[3] In order to understand the differences between these approaches to European integration we will have to briefly examine the theory of economic integration. This will help us to better understand what is meant if these concepts are being used in national discussions. 1

1 1st preamble to the EEC Treaty: 'DETERMINED to lay the foundations of an ever-closer union among the peoples of Europe.'

2 e.g. the rejection of the Maastricht Treaty by Denmark (1992), the rejection of the Nice Treaty in a first referendum in Ireland (2001) or the rejection of the European Constitution by France and the Netherlands (2005).

3 See Ch. 7.

1.1.2. STAGES OF ECONOMIC INTEGRATION

2 The theory of economic integration categorises the degree of economic integration into seven stages.[4]

3 The basic form of economic cooperation is a **preferential trade area** or **preferential trade agreement**, if speaking of the instrument (PTA). It is a trading bloc or agreement that gives preferential access to certain of the participating countries' products. This is essentially done by reducing tariffs. These are, however, not abolished altogether. The line between a PTA and a free trade area (FTA) is not easy to draw and may be blurred. When concluding a PTA, the participating countries mostly aim at developing it into a FTA in accordance with the General Agreement on Tariffs and Trade (GATT). More generally, the term 'PTA' is also used to describe all types of economic integration since they all incorporate some degree of 'preferred' treatment.[5] In particular, 'PTA' may also mean a Regional Trade Agreement (RTA).[6]

4 A **free-trade area**, or a **free trade agreement** (FTA), which is the instrument by which member countries decide to establish such cooperation, can be seen as an enhanced form of a PTA. in addition to merely reducing tariffs, such agreements involve further cooperation between two or more countries to also reduce trade barriers like import quotas, as well as abolishing most duties and tariffs on most products originating in these territories.[7] In addition, partners in a FTA normally intend to increase reciprocal trade of goods and services. Sometimes these FTAs may also allow natural persons to move between the countries. According to some, this is considered the second stage of economic integration.[8]

5 In order to increase economic efficiency, countries often revert to a **customs union.** It is generally defined as a trading bloc which is composed

---

4 B. Belassa, *The Theory of Economic Integration*, reprint of the first edition 1961, Routledge, London 2011, p. 2, who, however, does not distinguish between PTAs and FTAs.

5 S.M. Suranovic, *International Trade Theory and Policy*: http://internationalecon.com/Trade/Tch110/T110-2.php.

6 R. Acharya, 'Regional trade agreements: recent developments' in R. Acharya (ed.), *Regional Trade Agreements and the Multilateral Trading System*, Cambridge University Press, Cambridge 2016, p. 2.

7 Art. XXIV(8)(b) GATT.

8 A. O'Sullivan and S.M. Sheffrin, *Economics: Principles in Action*, Pearson Prentice Hall, Upper Saddle River 2003, p. 453.

of a free trade area with a common external tariff.[9] The latter element requires a common external trade policy. Minor deviations such as granting different import quotas may be agreed. The main advantage is to reduce costs in cross-border trade inside the customs union and to raise the attractiveness of trade agreements with outside partners. In addition, a common competition policy is also helpful to avoid *competition deficiency*.[10] Normally, a customs union is at the basis of every economic union, monetary union or economic and monetary union.[11]

In a **single market** most trade barriers have been removed (for goods) with some common policies on product regulation, and freedom of movement of the factors of production (capital and labour) and of enterprise and services. The goal is that the movement of capital, labour, goods and services between the member states is as easy as within them. The physical (borders), technical (standards) and fiscal (taxes) barriers among the member states are removed to the maximum extent possible. These barriers obstruct the freedom of movement of goods, capital, services and workers. Sometimes the term **common market** is used. It is usually used to describe the stage of a free trade area with no tariffs for goods to which relatively free movement of capital and of services are added. Non-tariff trade barriers, however, are less reduced than in a single market which is the more sophisticated stage. The full liberalisation with regard to free movement of goods, services (including financial services), capital and people where national boundaries are of no relevance, may be known under the term **unified market**. Again, because the borders between 'single' and 'unified market' are rather blurred and because it is barely used, this book will only refer to 'single market'. To take the example of the EU, it was a common market until 1992. From then on it was a single market, which in the EU jargon is normally called the **internal market**. The European Economic Area, by which the EU's internal market is extended to the three EFTA states of Iceland, Liechtenstein and Norway, is a single market. 6

9 Art. XXIV(8)(a) GATT.

10 L.A. Winters, 'Trade and Welfare' in L.A. Winters (ed.), *Trade Flows and Trade Policy After '1992'*, Cambridge University Press, Cambridge 1992, p. 5; Ph. Nicolaides, 'The Role of Competition Policy in Economic Integration and the Role of Regional Blocks in Internationalizing Competition Policy' in M.O. Hosli and A. Saether (eds.), *Free trade agreements and customs unions*, European Institute of Public Administration, Maastricht 1997, pp. 35–49.

11 See paras. 7 and 8.

7 If the single market is added to a customs union, an **economic union** is created. The participant countries have both common policies on product regulation, freedom of movement of goods, services and the factors of production (capital and labour) and a common external trade policy.

8 If a (unified) currency is introduced in such an economic union, it becomes an **economic and monetary union** (EMU). This is, e.g., the case for those EU member states using the Euro.

9 The final stage of economic integration is that of **complete economic integration.** It leaves the integrated parts no or barely any control of economic policy. It normally includes full monetary union and far-reaching fiscal policy harmonisation. Examples for this cannot be found with modern supranational institutions (yet). It has been, however, a historic feature of the development of countries. Examples for this development are the original 13 colonies of the United States of America, the Swiss cantons or the single German states before 1871. In all these cases (quasi-) independent states formed a union that was often preceded by stages of lesser economic integration until they eventually formed a generally federalist structure of government. Some at least dream of this being the ultimate stage of the European Union.

1.1.3. FREE TRADE AREA OR CUSTOMS UNION?

10 Reverting to the core difference between the approaches the EU member states and the EFTA states respectively took, it is necessary to look a bit more closely at the reasons either had for their choice. Entering into a customs union inevitably means that there will have to be a common external customs tariff and a common external trade policy. And it will be difficult to exclude agriculture from such an area. While the EU saw this as a means to effectively remove all trade barriers and therefore complete the internal market, the EFTA states never went as far. In the early years, there were big differences between their economies, take e.g. the UK or Switzerland on the one hand and Portugal, then one of the poorest countries in Western Europe. More importantly, however, the EFTA states were not willing to give up their sovereignty with regard to external trade. Nor did they intend to have a common agricultural policy. This ultimately led to a situation where in the EEA Agreement free movement of goods was introduced, however not completely. The parties went as far as to remove all barriers as far as possible, without having to take the step into a customs union.

1.1.4. PARTICIPATION IN THE INTERNAL MARKET?

As we will see in the historical overview,[12] EFTA's second aim has always been to find a common ground with the EU, i.e. with the then member states of the EEC, to create a European free trade zone. That free trade zone was established in Western Europe in 1973, completed only a few years later. This, however, was soon no longer enough. As the EC had embarked on completing the internal market by 1992, this clearly involved more economic integration inside the EC and thus erecting barriers towards the outside world. Despite the agreements that existed between the EFTA states and the EC, the former were clearly about to lose out economically. This ultimately led to EFTA's integration into the internal market in 1994, as previously described. Only Switzerland dropped out of this project and remained at the state of a free trade relationship with both the EU and the other EFTA states, with the exception of Liechtenstein, which was part of Switzerland's customs territory. 11

Following Switzerland's refusal to join the EEA which would have allowed it to participate in the internal market, the Swiss government tried to find alternative solutions. Over six years Switzerland and the EU negotiated a package of sectoral agreements that would grant Switzerland a selective participation in some areas of the internal market, without however the politically difficult supranational institutional set-up. Ten years after Switzerland's 'no' to the EEA, the first package of bilateral agreements entered into force, followed by a second package, entering into force seven years later. This set of sectoral agreements allows Switzerland to partially participate in the internal market. In other areas, such as financial services, there may be access to the internal market through recognition of equivalence. The EU always saw this as a temporary measure to mitigate the effect of 'no deal' with regard to Switzerland's participation in the internal market. As Switzerland still considered closer integration as a 'strategic goal' and still had its application for EU membership pending until it was withdrawn in 2016, the EU had every reason to do so, despite the obvious decrease in public support for further integration. Switzerland, however, had started to grow used to this sectoral approach. But after 2006 it was clear that Switzerland did not envisage any further integration, with the exception of concluding some further useful sectoral agreements, as on energy. 12

---

[12] See Ch. 2.

13 The EU therefore started to press for the conclusion of an institutional framework agreement (IFA). This has been a politically very difficult negotiation and it is at this stage still very uncertain whether the draft agreement will ever be signed, let alone ratified. In the context of discussions in the Swiss parliament on the matter, the question had come up whether Switzerland should – instead of going down the road of the current 'bilateral approach' to at least partially participate in the internal market – try to negotiate a 'comprehensive free trade agreement' with the EU. Similar proposals have come up in the context of Brexit. It looks as if this was HM Government's preferred solution.[13] We therefore cannot put this discussion to rest as it remains of relevance to this very day and as we seem to have gone back in time. We will revert to this dilemma in Chapter 7.

1.2. IMPORTANCE OF RELATIONSHIP WITH OTHER INTERNATIONAL ORGANISATIONS

14 This book will examine EFTA's relationship with other international organisations, mainly the EU and the EEA, more closely later on. It needs, however, to be pointed out that EFTA, as with other organisations of economic integration, does not operate without any reference to globally agreed rules. Most importantly, EFTA refers to the WTO system and its main agreements, i.e. GATT, GATS and TRIPS.[14]

15 One could say that EFTA, like other organisations of economic integration, refers to the WTO system in as much as it is an exemption from one of the core principles, namely that it allows differentiation between

[13] See e.g. the UK Government White Paper, 'The Future Relationship Between the United Kingdom and the European Union', p. 7, https://assets.publishing.service.gov.uk/government/uploads/system/uploads/attachment_data/file/786626/The_Future_Relationship_between_the_United_Kingdom_and_the_European_Union_120319.pdf.

[14] GATT: The General Agreement on Tariffs and Trade (30 October 1947 and 14 April 1994) has as its main purpose to promote international trade by reducing or eliminating trade barriers such as tariffs or quotas on goods; GATS: The General Agreement on Trade in Services (14 April 1994) was created to extend the multilateral trading system to the service sector, in the same way as GATT does for goods; TRIPS: The Agreement on Trade-Related Aspects of Intellectual Property Rights (14 April 1994) sets down minimum standards for the regulation by national governments of many forms of intellectual property.

trading partners. Normally, the most favoured nation treatment (MFN) principle would apply amongst all WTO member states.[15]

All four EFTA states are members of WTO. EFTA does not entail a common external trade policy, despite the fact that EFTA states mostly act together; there is no customs union between them either, nor does a supranational body – partly – act on their behalf as the EU Commission does for the EU member states. Therefore, they are full WTO members in their own right who have formed a free trade area.[16] Countries may, however, grant their free trade (or customs union) partners more favourable conditions than other countries. This right comes with certain conditions stipulated in the relevant provisions of the WTO agreements, to ensure the complementarity of the FTA with the WTO system.[17] 16

For instance, in matters of sanitary and phytosanitary measures (SPS), the EFTA rules are essentially those of the WTO Agreement on Application of Sanitary and Phytosanitary Measures.[18] There are several more of these references, such as for state aid, public undertakings and competition rules, and public procurement.[19] Likewise, this reference to WTO rules applies not only to the EFTA Convention, hence to the relationship between the EFTA states, but also to the FTAs which the EFTA states have concluded with third countries. Normally, these will, e.g., include references to the WTO Agreement on TBT[20] or the WTO Government Procurement Agreement (GPA).[21] 17

There is also an institutional link between EFTA and the WTO. Despite it not having the competence to act on behalf of the EFTA states,[22] the EFTA Secretariat has an observer status in several WTO bodies. At ministerial conferences it regularly participates as an observer.[23] 18

15 Art. I GATT; Art. II GATS; Art. 4 TRIPS.

16 See n. 4 above.

17 Art. XXIV GATT; Art. V GATS.

18 See, however, Art. 12 in conjunction with Annex G EFTA Convention.

19 G. Baur, M. Sanchez Rydelski and C. Zatschler, *European Free Trade Association (EFTA) and the European Economic Area (EEA)*, 2nd ed., Wolters Kluwer, Alphen aan den Rijn 2018, pp. 33–34, 38 with further references.

20 Agreement on Technical Barriers to Trade, published in: *The Results of the Uruguay Round of Multilateral Trade Negotiations*, GATT Secretariat, Geneva 1994.

21 https://www.wto.org/english/docs_e/legal_e/rev-gpr-94_01_e.htm.

22 See Ch. 4.

23 Baur, Sanchez Rydelski and Zatschler (n. 19 above) p. 54.

Indeed, such forms of participation as an observer also exist with the OECD and several UN bodies. 19

1.3. CONCLUSION: FREE TRADE AREA WITH INTERNAL MARKET ELEMENTS

As we have seen, EFTA is a free trade area. It has, however, been modernised by the revision of the EFTA Convention in 2001. The four EFTA states have thereby created a free trade zone which goes beyond modern FTAs as it expressly integrates internal market elements, notably free movement of persons. In comparison with the EU's internal market or the EEA, it horizontally follows the EU 'doctrine' by covering all four freedoms, i.e. goods, services, capital and persons. Vertically, however, it falls short of the degree of integration of the EEA or the EU's internal market. Nevertheless, by extending the main features of the internal market to the relationship between the EFTA states, the multilateral effect of much of the internal market works between all EU and EFTA states. Introducing the internal market rules between the EFTA states and thus inserting a 'third leg', the effects of the EU acquis are 'triangularised'.[24] The result of this is that citizens and companies from all EU and EFTA countries have (similar to) internal market conditions in all these countries. This is, however not true with regard to access to the law: while supranational remedies exist in both the EU and the EEA, in the relationship between Switzerland and the EU and with the other EFTA states there is (with very few exceptions) only access to national authorities and courts. 20

[24] First leg: EU-EEA EFTA (Iceland, Liechtenstein, Norway); second leg: EU-Switzerland; third leg: Switzerland- EEA EFTA (Iceland, Liechtenstein, Norway).

CHAPTER 2
SHORT HISTORICAL OVERVIEW

2.1. FROM EFTA's FOUNDATION TO THE UK's ACCESSION TO THE EEC

The foundation of EFTA forms part of the movements for European integration, which were among the major political and economic developments in Western Europe after the end of the Second World War. 1

After the creation of the European Community for Coal and Steel (ECSC) in July 1951 and during the negotiations to create a European economic community as well as Euratom (European community for atomic affairs), treaties which were signed in July 1957, the United Kingdom proposed at the ministerial conference of the Organisation for European Economic Cooperation (OEEC) in July 1956 the creation of a large Western European free trade zone. It was designed to be composed of the six member states of the EEC and all other OEEC states, including the future seven EFTA states. Negotiations had been conducted very intensively in the so called 'Maudling committee'.[1] In 1958 however, negotiations had to be broken off as differences could not be overcome between the parties. 2

In June 1959, high-level officials of the seven countries, Denmark, United Kingdom, Norway, Austria, Portugal, Sweden and Switzerland, met near Stockholm to sketch a plan of how to create a free trade zone between those seven countries. In July of the same year, ministers of those countries decided to start negotiations on the basis of this plan as soon as the following autumn. These negotiations led to a finalisation of the text of the EFTA Convention on 20 November and its signature by the seven ministers on 4 January 1960. The Convention was swiftly ratified and entered into force on 3 May 1960; a separate protocol then extended the Convention to the principality of Lichtenstein, which since 1923 had formed a customs 3

1 Named after its chairman, the then Paymaster General, Sir Reginald Maudling.

union with Switzerland. Finland joined on 27 March as an associated state. The Association Agreement entered into force on 26 June 1961. Iceland joined both the EFTA Convention and the Association Agreement with Finland on 1 March 1970.

4 Following its foundation EFTA had two major goals: first, the introduction of free trade in industrial goods and several processed agricultural and fisheries products between its member states, and, second, the creation of a free trade area comprising both the seven members of EFTA and the six EEC member states.

5 The first goal was achieved by gradually lowering tariffs. After a ministerial meeting in 1963 in Lisbon this was deemed insufficient and, with the exception of Portugal, all tariffs were lowered to 0 on 31 December 1966. The first goal was therefore achieved even before the scheduled date.

6 With regard to the second goal, EFTA tried to start negotiations with the EEC straight away. At first, these negotiations aimed at bridging the differences between EFTA and the EEC. These efforts, however, were not successful. Therefore, the UK government, after discussions with the EFTA partner states, decided in 1961 to apply for membership of the EEC. Other EFTA countries followed the UK example in autumn 1961 and spring 1962 and asked either for full membership, like Denmark and Norway, or for an association with the EEC. All these attempts were unsuccessful in 1963. A second attempt by the United Kingdom to join the EEC in 1967 failed as well.

7 A breakthrough to a fundamentally new development could be seen in 1969 after the EEC summit in The Hague. In that meeting the EEC in principle agreed to enlarge the Communities through the accession of new members as well as to conclude free trade agreements with those EFTA countries which were not likely to ask for membership.

8 On 30 June 1970, negotiations started between the Council of Ministers of the EEC and the three EFTA countries which had requested membership, namely Denmark, Norway and the United Kingdom. Three months later exploratory talks started between the Commission of the EEC and the six EFTA countries that had asked for trade arrangements but not for full membership in the EEC, namely Finland, Iceland, Austria, Portugal, Sweden and Switzerland.

9 The negotiations between the EEC and the governments of Denmark, Norway and the United Kingdom were able to be concluded in a satisfactory manner in January 1972. The three countries signed the accession treaty

on 22 January 1972. They would all have become members of the enlarged EEC on 1 January 1973. Denmark and the United Kingdom effectively joined the communities on that date. The accession had been ratified by the Danish people on 2 October 1972 in a referendum. In Norway, however, the majority of voters voted against joining the communities in a referendum held on 24 and 25 September 1972. Following that, the Norwegian government had no choice but to resign.

Meanwhile, negotiations between the other EFTA states and the enlarged 10
EEC had been concluded successfully. On 22 July 1972, the EEC and five EFTA countries, namely Iceland, Austria, Portugal, Sweden and Switzerland, signed the agreements on free trade in industrial goods. These agreements entered into force on 1 January 1973, and on 1 April 1973 in the case of Iceland. In Norway, the new government had also started negotiations with the EEC on a free trade agreement. This agreement was signed on 14 May 1973 and entered into force on 1 July 1973. The free trade agreement between Finland and the EEC was signed on 5 October 1973 and entered into force on 1 January 1974. And on July 1977, after a transitional period of four and a half years, the last tariff barriers, except for very few economically sensitive products, between the EEC and the EFTA states were removed. By that date, a large Western European free trade area ('internal trading area') with a population of over 300 million people and encompassing 16 countries had been created.[2]

2.2. FROM THE WESTERN EUROPEAN FREE TRADE AREA TO THE LUXEMBOURG FOLLOW-UP PROCESS ('EUROPEAN ECONOMIC SPACE')

The date when the UK joined the EEC is seen by some as the moment 11
EFTA lost not only its competitive edge over the EEC;[3] the former key player, the UK, having left, EFTA also lost its internal cohesion.[4] The EFTA

---

2 Press release of 17 May 1977 of the Delegation of the European Communities to Canada, Nr. (77) 13.

3 R.T. Griffiths, 'EFTA and European Integration 1973–1984, Vindication or Marginalisation?' in K. Bryn and G. Einarsson (eds.), *EFTA 1960–2010, Elements of 50 Years of European History*, EFTA, Geneva 2010, p. 148.

4 W. Hummer, 'Ziele, Methoden und Ergebnisse der österreichischen Integrationspolitik' in H.G. Koppensteiner (ed.), *Der Weg in den Binnenmarkt*, Orac, Vienna 1991, p. 49.

states aimed at further developing trade and economic cooperation with the EEC. On EFTA's side, this, however, led to an increased pressure for strengthening policy cooperation amongst the EFTA states. How could they strengthen policy cooperation with the EEC if they didn't do it amongst themselves? This proved to be very difficult owing to two main factors: first, the seven countries were extremely different with regard to their economic performance, development and strength. Secondly, they had 'enshrined' national sovereignty into the EFTA Convention. This made enforcing such cooperation very difficult.[5] Nevertheless, increased exchanges between EEC (member states) and EFTA (states), among others in the 'Nordic Council', led to the first ministerial meeting in 25 years. 17[6] ministers met in Luxembourg on 9 April 1984.

12 In that so-called Declaration of Luxembourg, the ministers of the EFTA states and of the EEC and their member states explained that they 'were convinced of the importance of further actions to consolidate and strengthen cooperation with the aim of creating a dynamic European Economic Space for their countries'.[7] However, the EEC started to concentrate mainly on developing the Single European Act (SEA) and thereby completing the Treaty of Rome. The Act aimed at establishing the four freedoms, i.e. free trade in goods, free trade in services, free movement of capital and free movement of labour, by 1992. In total there were 280 decisions to be taken. To facilitate that decision-making process, the member states had even waived their right of veto. Decisions in the context of the SEA were taken by qualified majority.[8]

13 Developing the relationship with EFTA, however, had clearly become less of a priority for the EEC. In the same period, the so-called Luxembourg follow-up, a total of 9 EFTA-EC agreements were concluded.

14 These agreements were, however, of importance, mainly from a practical point of view. To mention just two which concerned border agreements: first and most importantly, the Single Administrative Document (SAD) was introduced. It served to eliminate most of the huge bureaucracy, chiefly paperwork, needed in every operation of international trade in Western Europe. A second very important issue was the rules of origin regime.

---

5 Griffiths (n. 3 above) p. 150.
6 Including Liechtenstein which had always been included in EFTA, but only became a member in its own right in 1991.
7 EFTA Bulletin 25, nr. 2 (1984), pp. 6–7.
8 Griffiths (n. 3 above) p. 152.

'Rules of origin are the criteria needed to determine the national source of a product.'[9] In cross-border trade these are needed to assess whether a product, typically combined of elements with a different country of origin, is eligible for the preferential tariffs.[10] As both EFTA and the EEC had very different sets of rules, a compromise was needed to facilitate trade in the common free trade area. These measures helped to reduce quite considerably the costs of cross-border trade between EFTA and the EEC.

Despite the fact that some important agreements were concluded, EFTA-EEC cooperation during that period was rather seen as a failure, as costly and ineffective.[11] Reasons for this were that there were no binding targets and no standard mechanisms,[12] i.e. there was no institutional set-up whatsoever. The EFTA states were forced to find common positions prior to negotiating with the EEC, partly in policy areas which were not covered by the EFTA Convention. From an economic point of view the EFTA states increasingly lost out in comparison to the EEC.[13] 15

Realising this, the EFTA states now aimed at participating to the fullest extent possible in the EEC's internal market. This should not be limited to the pre-existing bilateral EEC-EFTA states' FTAs for goods. Consequently, at a meeting between the EFTA Ministers in Geneva on 3 December 1986, a statement was issued that argued for parallelism between the EC's efforts to complete the internal market and the evolution of EEC-EFTA cooperation. 16

The Community's vision of future cooperation with the EFTA states was reflected in a speech by the then European Commissioner for External Relations and Trade Policy, Willy de Clercq, at the ministerial meeting in Interlaken in 1987. Already in 1985, the European Commission had established[14] what later became known as the 'Interlaken Principles': preserving (1) the 'Community first', (2) the autonomy of its decision-making and (3) a balance of benefits and obligations.[15] In light 17

9 https://www.wto.org/english/tratop_e/roi_e/roi_info_e.htm.

10 For an example see Ch. 3.2.1.3.

11 F. Laursen, 'The Community's Policy Towards EFTA: Regime Formation in the European Economic Space (EES)', *Journal of Common Market Studies*, 1990, 28 (4), p. 317.

12 Griffiths (n. 3 above) p. 153.

13 P. Krugman, 'EFTA and 1992' in K. Bryn and G. Einarsson (eds.), *EFTA 1960–2010, Elements of 50 Years of European History*, EFTA, Geneva 2010, p. 145.

14 COM(86) 206 final, pp. 2–3.

15 W. De Clercq, Speech at the EC–EFTA Ministerial Meeting, Interlaken, 20 May 1987, http://europa.eu/rapid/press-release_SPEECH-87-32_en.htm.

of today's discussions on the role of the Court of Justice of the EU (CJEU) in both the UK and Switzerland, it may be worthwhile noting, that by this third principle, the EEC pointed to the risk of imbalance if only the EEC and its member states were subject to legal control when implementing and applying agreements with the EFTA states. The European Court of Justice (ECJ, now: CJEU) had already held[16] that citizens and economic operators could invoke the free trade provisions of the bilateral EEC–EFTA states' FTAs before courts in the Community and that such provisions had direct effect. In contrast, no similar judicial protection was guaranteed in the EFTA states.[17] All this is, by the way, still of relevance[18] and is – even more than 30 years later – an issue in both the negotiations between the EU and Switzerland on an Institutional Framework Agreement and eventually a future agreement between the EU and the UK after Brexit.

2.3. ESTABLISHING THE EUROPEAN ECONOMIC AREA

18 On 17 January 1989, the then President of the European Commission, Jacques Delors, delivered his statement to the European Parliament on the work programme of the EEC Commission for the period 1989–92. With reference to relations with the EFTA states, he stressed that the path of pragmatic cooperation that had been taken five years ago was limited. Therefore, he proposed to seek a new form of association, which should be more institutionally structured, with joint decision-making and governance bodies. But he did make two clarifications, the full meaning of which only dawned on the EFTA negotiators in the course of the negotiations, namely: the importance of the internal structures of EFTA for future cooperation and the fact that a 'choice à la carte' from the entire EC rules was difficult to imagine.

19 The reply from the Heads of Government of the EFTA states was rather quick. After a ministerial meeting in Oslo in March of the same year, they

16 CJEU, Case C-104/81, *Hauptzollamt Mainz v C.A. Kupferberg & Cie KG*, ECLI:EU:C:1982:362.

17 See e.g. Swiss Federal Court, Case 2A.593/2005, *Physiogel*.

18 See e.g. S. Gstöhl and D. Phinnemore, 'Introduction – Privileged partnerships between the European Union and third states' in S. Gstöhl and D. Phinnemore (eds.), *The Proliferation of Privileged Partnerships between the European Union and its Neighbours*, Routledge, London & New York 2020 (2019), p. 16.

said they were 'ready to explore with the EC the possibilities of creating a more structured form of association, with the aim of creating a dynamic, homogeneous European Economic Area'.[19] At the request of Iceland, ministers also decided to fully liberalise EFTA-internal trade in fish and other marine products. Incidentally, the achievement of this objective in the framework of the EEA negotiations was to be a major obstacle to the negotiations and has regularly caused trouble since.[20]

An informal ministerial conference between the EEC, EEC member states and the EFTA states took place in Brussels on 20 March 1989. It was decided to start informal discussions immediately on the new option of global, structured integration and on the possible scope and content of this extended form of association. 20

The EFTA states had realised that, given the weak institutional structure of the EFTA Convention, they needed to strengthen the cooperation mechanism between themselves in order to facilitate a collective bargaining position. However, the EFTA Council rejected a proposal according to which the majority in the EFTA Council should have replaced the principle of consensus. 21

The first important conclusion was that the legal basis of the agreement to be negotiated must essentially be that of the EC law applicable to the internal market – the 'relevant Community law' ('acquis communautaire'). In consequence, the homogeneity of the new European Economic Area was set as a central requirement. Moreover, the principle of autonomy of the contracting parties excluded any 'superstructure' over the contracting parties. Therefore, preference was given to a 'two-pillar system' (EEC/EFTA), which – again – implied strengthening structures within the EFTA. On the question of a 'genuine, joint decision-making mechanism', extremely important to the EFTA states, the EEC replied that it was certain that permeability between the Community pillar and the pillar to be set up by EFTA had to be ensured to a certain degree, so as to take their interests into account. However, a co-decision was not acceptable to the EEC member states.[21] That could ultimately only result from accession. 22

19 L. Rye, 'EFTA's quest for free trade in Western Europe (1960–92)' in T. Grønningsæter (ed.), *EFTA Bulletin: The European Economic Area, Past, Present and Future*, EFTA, Brussels 2015, p. 14.

20 Rye (n. 19 above) p. 15.

21 H. Krenzler, European Economic Area 1994–2009, EFTA, Geneva 2009, p. 40.

23 As to the supreme institutions, a 'one-pillar' EEA structure with a joint surveillance body and an independent EEA Court, including judges from the EFTA countries, was foreseen. This had, however, to be abandoned after the CJEU's negative Opinion 1/91 on the EEA Agreement.[22] The Court essentially said an overarching court, including judges from the EFTA states, was not possible as this would encroach on the EEC's decision-making autonomy. The EFTA states therefore had to create their own EFTA Court and EFTA Surveillance Authority. The attempt to reconcile the principles of internal market homogeneity and decision-making autonomy resulted in the EFTA states renouncing any requests for permanent exceptions from the acquis and lacking a real right of co-decision.[23] This should not in fact have come as a surprise if one looks at the Interlaken Principles mentioned above.

24 The EEA Agreement was signed on 2 May 1992 in Oporto. On the same occasion, two related international agreements between the EFTA countries had been signed. One of these was to create an EFTA Surveillance Authority and an EFTA Court. The other was to create a standing committee of the EFTA countries. According to Article 108 of the EEA Agreement, which reflects the two-pillar nature of the European Economic Area, the EFTA countries establish two supranational bodies, the EFTA Surveillance Authority and the EFTA Court, which to some extent correspond with the EEC Commission and the European Court of Justice. The Standing Committee of the EFTA countries, on the other hand, is not really a new institution, but rather a successor to the existing negotiating structure of the EFTA countries, namely the High Level Negotiating Group of the EFTA, which was now called upon to coordinate the EFTA countries within the framework of the EEA.

25 The ratification of the EEA Agreement, however, did not go as smoothly. Switzerland and Liechtenstein had to pass a referendum on the matter. The Swiss people and the cantons rejected the adhesion on 6 December 1992. A week later, on 13 December, the people of Liechtenstein, however, agreed to join the EEA. Therefore, the EEA Agreement had to be adapted and references to Switzerland removed throughout the documents. The EEA Agreement could therefore only enter into force with a delay of one year on 1 January 1994. For Liechtenstein a solution had to be found which, on

---

22 Opinion 1/91 of 14 December 1991, *EEA Agreement I*, ECLI:EU:C:1991:490.

23 T. Van Stiphout, 'Homogeneity vs. Decision-Making Autonomy in the EEA Agreement', *European Journal of Law Reform*, 2007, 9 (3), pp. 431–447.

the one hand, allowed the country to participate in the EEA and, on the other, allowed it to continue its customs union with Switzerland. This was achieved in spring 1995 and Liechtenstein joined the EEA as a full member on 1 May 1995.

2.4. VADUZ CONVENTION AND GLOBAL FREE TRADE

After having rejected participation in the EEA, the Swiss government tried to negotiate a sectoral (bilateral) approach. The EC, after some hesitation, agreed to negotiate a package of sectoral agreements (Bilateral Agreements I), namely on: 26

- free movement of persons;
- technical barriers to trade (Mutual Recognition Agreement–MRA);
- public procurement markets;
- agriculture;
- land transport;
- air transport (civil aviation); and
- research.

These agreements were, however, secured by a so-called 'guillotine clause', i.e. if one agreement falls, the whole package falls. This clause was imposed by the EC as it feared Switzerland might at some point denounce the Agreement on free movement of persons, which it did not like, and continue to benefit from the other agreements which were more in Switzerland's interest. 27

Later, a second package of sectoral agreements followed (Bilateral Agreements II). This was, however, of less importance with regard to the development of the EFTA Convention. 28

Already during the negotiations between Switzerland and the EU on the sectoral agreements (Bilateral Agreements I), the Swiss Federal Council expressed its readiness to allow the negotiated results to be extended to the other EFTA states which participated in the EEA. A formal proposal to start negotiations, respecting the principles of equal treatment and reciprocity, was presented to the EFTA states after the conclusion of the sectoral negotiations. From the outset, this proposal only concerned the relationship between Switzerland and the other EFTA states, since relations 29 between Iceland, Liechtenstein and Norway were already governed by the EEA Agreement.

30 The proposal by Switzerland was subsequently taken up by the EFTA Council at ministerial level. In June 1999 it was decided to revise the EFTA Convention in order to intensify economic cooperation between the EFTA states. The envisaged improvement in cooperation should, in particular, reflect the state of relations between the EFTA states and the EC and take into account the cooperation of the EFTA states with certain non-EC member states. Finally, developments at the level of multilateral trade, notably within the framework of the WTO, should be taken into account. The sectoral agreements between Switzerland and the EU then formed the reference point in the revision of the EFTA Convention.

31 The Agreement amending the EFTA Convention was signed in Vaduz on 21 June 2001 at a ministerial level meeting of the EFTA Council. The agreement signed in Vaduz allows for a complete revision of the 1960 EFTA Convention. The revised EFTA Convention raises the contractual relations between Switzerland and the other EFTA states to a level comparable to those established by the sectoral agreements between Switzerland and the EU. The revised EFTA Convention now also provides for a basis for the negotiation of FTAs between the EFTA states and non-EU member states where that basis formerly did not exist. This refers, in particular, to the services sector, capital movements and intellectual property.

32 The following list shows the major achievements of the revised EFTA Convention:

- the existing provisions on trade in goods, the original core of the EFTA Convention, have been restructured and exempted from obsolete provisions (for example, the provisions on transitional periods for dismantling tariff measures);
- the provisions on trade in agricultural products have been updated, taking into account developments in relations between the EFTA states and non-EU member states, as well as under WTO rules. Tariff concessions on basic agricultural products have in some cases been extended (e.g. to cheese);
- the mutual recognition of conformity assessments has been newly incorporated into the EFTA Convention. The relevant provisions correspond to those of the Agreement on Mutual Recognition of Conformity Assessments between Switzerland and the EU. In addition, the notification procedure for proposed draft legislation has been

reviewed and extended to include rules on information society services to reflect recent developments within the EU and the EEA;
- the free movement of persons has now also been introduced for the EFTA area. It is accompanied by rules on the coordination of different social security systems and on mutual recognition of diplomas. The free movement of persons between the EFTA states is modelled on the regulation of the relevant sectoral agreement between Switzerland and the EU. Special provisions apply in this area between Switzerland and Liechtenstein;
- the EFTA States grant each other mutual access to their markets, which goes beyond WTO standards;
- the protection of intellectual property rights was newly incorporated into the Convention;
- the EFTA Convention now also contains provisions on trade in services and investment. However, the EFTA states have decided to maintain certain restrictions in these areas. These should be gradually reduced. The process of liberalisation also essentially depends on the conclusion of a bilateral agreement on services between Switzerland and the EU;
- finally, the EFTA Convention contains provisions on air and land transport, which copy the relevant sectoral agreement between Switzerland and the EU. In land transport, a quota system was introduced.

It now also has a 'dynamic' character. This means that it will be regularly 33
adapted to new circumstances in order to support the development of bilateral relations between Switzerland and the EU on the one hand (conclusion of new negotiations or adaptation of existing agreements in order to comply with the evolution of Community law), and those within the EEA. The notion of 'dynamic adaptation' may, however, not be seen as equal to the same notion in EEA law. Here, adaptations need to be triggered by one of the parties to the EFTA Convention, primarily Switzerland. There, adaptations essentially follow the development of EU-internal market legislation in regular meetings during the year.

CHAPTER 3
SUBSTANTIVE FIELDS OF ACTIVITY OF EFTA

3.1. INTRODUCTION

3.1.1. FREE TRADE ZONE

EFTA's first objective was to create a classical free trade zone, i.e. abolishing or at least minimising tariffs on trade between its member states.[1] At the beginning of the 1960s, trade in industrial products still dominated.[2] From the end of the 1990s, however, this was no longer sufficient. More and more services were being provided on a cross-border basis, investment required rules to protect them, and intellectual property had become increasingly important in the context of ever-growing trade relations with the then emerging markets like China and India. The establishment of the World Trade Organisation (WTO) in 1994 shows this with great clarity.[3] In order to take this development into account, the EFTA Convention was revised in the year 2000 and new areas, such as services, were added. 1

3.1.2. NEED FOR ADAPTATION

From 1972, EFTA was increasingly used as the EFTA states' basis for their relations with the EU. That development started with the conclusion of the EEC-EFTA free trade agreements and led to the conclusion of, on the one hand, the EEA Agreement in 1992 and, on the other, Switzerland's bilateral agreements in 1999 and 2002. Following this, EU nationals and 2

---

1 Arts. 2 and 3 EFTA Convention (1960).

2 R. Regul (ed.), 'EFTA', Nomos, Baden-Baden 1975, p. 10.

3 Swiss Federal Government, 'Explanatory message to the Parliament on the ratification of the GATT/WTO-Agreements (Uruguay-round)', 19 September 1994, BBl (Federal Gazette) 1994 IV 1 (German), FF 1994 IV 1 (French), pp. 10–11.

enterprises were *de facto* in a more favourable situation in either the EEA or Switzerland than citizens or enterprises from the other EFTA states respectively. For example, citizens of Iceland and Norway – Liechtenstein being a case apart[4] – were not entitled to the rights conferred by Switzerland on EU citizens in the area of the recognition of professional diplomas.

3 Already in the course of the negotiations between Switzerland and the EU on a first package of sectoral agreements (Bilateral Agreements I; BAs I),[5] the Swiss government indicated that it was ready, at the end of these negotiations, to offer equal treatment to its EFTA partners.[6] Hence, at the meeting of the EFTA Council at ministerial level on 12 and 13 December 2000, the EFTA states decided to mutually treat other's EFTA citizens and enterprises in the same way as they were treated in the context of the EFTA states' respective relations with the EU. Furthermore, and as mentioned above, developments in multilateral trade, first and foremost the WTO, had to be reflected as well. The aim was to have the amended EFTA Convention enter into force as closely as possible to the BAs I concluded between Switzerland and the EU. The revised EFTA Convention was signed at the meeting of the EFTA ministerial Council on 21 June 2001 in Vaduz. It was thus possible to establish an enlarged European market comprising all EU member states and all EFTA states, where all enjoy more or less the same rights and obligations.

4 Structurally, and in a figurative manner of speaking, 'triangularisation' has taken place, with a triangle formed by EU-Swiss relations on one side, the EU and the three EEA EFTA states on the second, and the EEA EFTA states and Switzerland on the third. This means that there is now a relationship between all states that are members of either the EU or EFTA, which is that of the single market or very similar.

3.1.3. INTERNAL MARKET ELEMENTS

5 Substantively, these amendments to the EFTA Convention were not restricted to merely updating what is generally understood to be the

---

4 Agreement of 2 November 1994 between Switzerland and the Principality of Liechtenstein concerning the amendment to the Agreement of 6 November 1963 concerning the status of foreign nationals of the other Contracting State, AS (Official Swiss Federal Law Collection [chronological]) 1995 3815.

5 See Ch. 6.

6 R. Marxer, 'Update of the EFTA Convention' in EFTA Secretariat (ed.), *EFTA Bulletin* (Geneva) September 2000, p. 8.

content of a FTA.[7] In order to grant each other rights and obligations that are analogous to those resulting from their respective relationships with the EU, such rights and obligations have been incorporated into the EFTA Convention that could be categorised as 'internal market elements'.[8] These are, in the first instance, the classical 'four freedoms' (freedom of movement of goods, persons, services and capital) and related areas, such as competition. However, they are not in every respect identical to the EU's internal market or the EEA, nor do they cover the same scope as the BAs. Although the relationship between Switzerland and the EU was the starting point, the internal market elements of the EFTA Convention go beyond the scope of the BAs and, for example, also include services.

More specifically, the EFTA states agreed to the following amendments to the EFTA Convention: 6

- the basic provisions on trade in goods were streamlined and obsolete provisions abolished;
- provisions granting persons the right to move within the entire territory of the EFTA states were introduced. This right is also facilitated by the coordination of the various social security systems and the mutual recognition of professional qualifications. Thus, qualifications obtained in an EFTA state in the form of a higher education degree and in fields such as medicine or law, architecture and trade are recognised in the other EFTA countries. The free movement of persons within the territory of EFTA is now more or less subject to the same rules as in the EU or EEA. The exceptions are mainly with regard to rights derived from the concept of Union citizenship, by reason of not having incorporated the so-called 'Union Citizenship Directive'.[9] The specific relationship between Liechtenstein and Switzerland is also taken into account;

---

7 In general terms there has been a vast updating from so-called first generation-FTAs to second generation FTAs. These would also include provisions on services, investment and government procurement; see G. Baur, M. Sanchez Rydelski and C. Zatschler, *European Free Trade Association (EFTA) and the European Economic Area (EEA)*, 2nd ed., Wolters Kluwer, Alphen aan den Rijn 2018, p. 41.

8 G. Baur, 'EFTA: eine Freihandelszone mit Binnenmarktelementen' in A. Epiney and L. Hehemann, *Schweizerisches Jahrbuch für Europarecht/Annuaire suisse de droit européen 2016/2017*, Stämpfli/Schulthess, Berne/Zurich 2017, pp. 357–370.

9 Directive 2004/38/EC of the European Parliament and of the Council of 29 April 2004 on the right of citizens of the Union and their family members to move and reside

- public procurement markets of the EFTA states were further opened up, leading to a situation where the EFTA states mutually grant each other treatment beyond WTO commitments. Sectoral coverage was extended and now also covers the purchase of products and services, including construction works, railway operators and energy companies, but excluding electricity and private utilities operating in the areas of drinking water, electricity, urban transport, ports and airports;
- the procedure for the notification of draft technical regulations was revised and, in line with recent developments in the EU and EEA, now also includes so-called 'information society services';
- the chapter on state aid, public undertakings, competition and dumping was modernised;
- the articles on trade in agricultural goods were updated and consolidated in view of EFTA FTAs and WTO developments;
- specific rules on seed, organic farming and health and plant health protection measures were introduced, with a view to the gradual abolition of technical barriers to trade in agricultural products; and
- a chapter on the protection of intellectual property, the liberalisation of investment and, as mentioned, trade in services, etc. was introduced.

7 The revision of the EFTA Convention has not only led to an extension of substantive law but has also introduced a 'dynamic'[10] procedure for legal adjustment and follow-up within the framework of the EFTA Convention. The procedure[11] can be called 'dynamic' because the changes in the legal framework are ongoing and similar to the procedure in the EEA regarding the incorporation of EU legal acts:

> 'The Member States endeavour to regularly update the Convention in order to take account of developments of the Agreement on the European Economic Area and of the bilateral agreements of 21 June 1999 between the Swiss Confederation on the one hand and the European Community and its Member States on the other. In particular the Member States shall within 3 months after the entry into

---

freely within the territory of the Member States amending Regulation (EEC) No. 1612/68 and repealing Directives 64/221/EEC, 68/360/EEC, 72/194/EEC, 73/148/EEC, 75/34/EEC, 75/35/EEC, 90/364/EEC, 90/365/EEC and 93/96/EEC; OJ L 158 of 30.4.2004, pp. 77–123.

10 G. Baur and Ch. Tobler, '„Automatische" vs. „dynamische" Rechtsübernahme' in A. Epiney and L. Hehemann, *Schweizerisches Jahrbuch für Europarecht/Annuaire suisse de droit européen 2015/2016*, Stämpfli/Schulthess, Berne/Zurich 2016, pp 347–361.

11 See Chap. 4.7 below.

force of the Agreement amending the Convention establishing the European Free Trade Association of 21 June 2001, align the Convention to common developments of the EEA Agreement and the Swiss – EC bilateral agreements.'[12]

There are, however, differences which – compared with the EEA Agreement – relate to the different context and institutions. Updating the EFTA Convention only happens by consensus between the four EFTA states. There is no procedure that provides for compulsory decision-making within a certain time frame with possible legal consequences as in the case of the EEA.[13] 8

3.2. THE SUBSTANTIVE LAW

3.2.1. FREE MOVEMENT OF GOODS

3.2.1.1. General

To liberalise trade in goods among its member states has been the main objective of the Association from its establishment.[14] The EFTA Conventions establishes a free trade area between the partners by: 9

- providing for free trade in industrial goods, including fish and other marine products;
- improved market access for agricultural products;
- including trade disciplines; and
- establishing rules on customs and origin matters.

The EFTA states have a highly developed and diversified industrial sector, and under the EFTA Convention, member states grant total elimination of customs duties for all industrial products. The fisheries sector is of major importance to both Iceland and Norway. Free trade in these products constitutes an essential element of the Convention, and as in the WTO, these products are considered industrial goods. 10

---

12 SGN 7/2001 para. 18, decided by the EFTA Council on 22 February 2002.

13 G. Baur, 'Decision-Making Procedure and Implementation of New Law' in C. Baudenbacher (ed.), *The Handbook of EEA Law*, Cham, Heidelberg etc. 2016, pp. 45–67.

14 Art. 3 EFTA Convention (1960).

11 The EFTA Convention distinguishes between basic agricultural products such as grain, milk and sugar, and processed agricultural products such as bread, chocolate and soup. In principle, the EFTA states liberalise trade in processed products. Certain measures are maintained, however, to compensate for higher costs of raw materials used by the EFTA food processing industry in the respective EFTA states. For basic agricultural products, the EFTA states grant each other preferential market access as set out in a separate Annex. The EFTA states do not, however, have a common agricultural policy.

12 With the revision of 2001, the provisions on trade in goods have been fully updated and formally adapted to the developments since the Convention entered into force.

13 As a result of the customs union established by the Treaty of 29 March 1923 between Switzerland and the Principality of Liechtenstein, Switzerland shall represent the Principality of Liechtenstein in matters covered thereby.[15]

3.2.1.2. *Customs Duties and Quantitative Restrictions*

14 The basic principle for mutually opening their markets for goods to the other EFTA states is straightforward: they prohibit customs duties on imports and exports, and any charges having equivalent effect. This also applies to customs duties of a fiscal nature.[16] With regard to measures having an equivalent effect, the EFTA Convention also addresses internal taxation. EFTA states shall not impose, directly or indirectly, on the products of other member states any internal taxation of any kind in excess of that imposed directly or indirectly on similar domestic products. Nor shall they impose on the products of other EFTA states any internal taxation of such a nature as to afford indirect protection to other products. And where products are exported to the territory of any member state, any repayment of internal taxation shall not exceed the internal taxation imposed on them whether directly or indirectly.[17]

15 Another basic principle in privileged or free trade areas is the prohibition of quantitative restrictions on imports and exports, and all measures

[15] Council Decision No. 2/2012 of 21 June 2012.
[16] Art. 3 EFTA Convention.
[17] Art. 4 EFTA Convention.

having equivalent effect between the EFTA states.[18] Hence, there shall be no quota in either direction of trade between the four states.

The EFTA states can, however, apply prohibitions or restrictions on imports, exports or goods in transit if this is justified 16

> 'on grounds of public morality; public policy or public security; the protection of health and life of humans, animals or plants and of the environment; the protection of national treasures possessing artistic, historic or archaeological value; or the protection of industrial and commercial property.'

But 'such prohibitions or restrictions shall not, however, constitute a means of arbitrary discrimination or a disguised restriction on trade between the Member States'.[19]

3.2.1.3. Rules of Origin, Administrative Cooperation and Mutual Assistance in Customs Matters

In order to assess whether goods qualify for tariff waivers or reductions, and also, whether these can be imported quota-free, it has to be assessed where these goods originate. 17

In today's interconnected economy goods are very often composed of different elements that may originate from anywhere in the world. Let's compare the two cases normally applicable in Europe: the EU Customs Union and the EFTA free trade area. For example, a car, say a 'Mini', is assembled in Oxford, but it contains many different parts that have been produced in different EU countries, leaving apart elements produced elsewhere. In this case there are no tariffs applicable as parts move (mostly) within the EU and therefore within the Customs Union. There is no customs border and therefore origin does not matter. Or a speciality plastic packing material is produced in Switzerland out of petrochemical products delivered by a Norwegian company but stemming partly from Norway and Venezuela. In order to assess whether that product can be imported into Switzerland tariff free it is necessary to know how big the Norwegian or the Venezuelan parts respectively are. If the Norwegian part does not reach a certain threshold fixed for the product to qualify as 18

18 Art. 7 EFTA Convention.

19 Art. 13 EFTA Convention; textually identical with Art. 13 EEA.

Norwegian altogether, tariffs will have to be imposed. A further feature of these principles would be the so-called 'cumulation'. This allows for multiple elements from different countries that may have contributed to a product, but are still privileged with regard to origin qualifying for preferential tariff treatment.

19 However, the amount of foreign production allowed for a product to qualify as domestic – or stemming from a partner country under preferential rules – risks being set in a somewhat arbitrary manner. In theory it could vary from country to country provided there is no customs union. That in fact creates a barrier to trade as market participants would have to assess the ratio of preferential against outside percentage of their product each time there is a cross-border trade in order to know if and possibly how much tariff they would have to pay.

20 In order to avoid this and to facilitate trade, at least in the wider trade zone of Europe, i.e. the 28 EU member states, the four EFTA states, Turkey, the Western Balkans (mostly ex-Yugoslavia) and almost all Mediterranean countries ('the Euro-Mediterranean space'), the so-called Pan-Euro-Med (PEM) Convention[20] was concluded. It establishes a single set of rules regarding origin and cumulation. This is to be implemented and applied in all bilateral or regional trade agreements among its signatories. Where it is applied it creates harmonised rules and – which is the main point for business users – allows for 'diagonal' cumulation of origin. Products will, hence, be able to be exported from, say, Egypt to Lebanon, there further processed (but less than what would be needed to obtain origin if the product came from, say, China), and exported duty free to Switzerland under the Lebanon-EFTA Agreement.

21 With regard to EFTA-internal rights and obligations concerning rules of origin, cumulation and administrative cooperation between the customs authorities, the PEM Convention has been made part of the EFTA Convention and is to be applied *mutatis mutandis*.[21] There are some special provisions applicable to basic agricultural and processed agricultural products. In order for these rules to be correctly applied the EFTA states agreed to grant mutual assistance in customs matters, regardless of whether products are covered by the EFTA Convention or not.[22]

---

20 See Ch. 6.2.2.3.

21 Art. 5(1) EFTA Convention as amended by Council Decision No. 2/2012 of 21 June 2012.

22 Art. 6 EFTA Convention and Annex B thereto.

3.2.1.4. Agriculture, Fisheries etc.

Agriculture has always been an especially contentious subject in trade 22
politics. In particular, Norway and Switzerland have a highly protected agricultural sector. In the WTO these countries – together with other like-minded countries like Japan – form the Group of 10 (G10).[23] Their agricultural protectionism is not viewed favourably by exporting nations.[24] Given that protectionist attitude, agricultural goods are generally exempted from provisions on state aid, competition and public procurement.[25]

The provisions governing agriculture have been updated and made more 23
accessible while still maintaining the special considerations affecting the sector. No substantive changes have been made to the provisions and treatment for processed agricultural products. The principle of parallelism between the treatment accorded to the EU or any other third-country partner and an EFTA state is also maintained.

The EFTA states have agreed on a number of changes that will facilitate 24
trade in agricultural products among themselves. First, the existing tariff concessions for basic agricultural products – so far covered by bilateral arrangements between individual EFTA states – have been integrated into the Convention.

Furthermore, under the revised Convention individual EFTA states have 25
agreed upon additional concessions for certain basic agricultural products such as cheese, certain vegetables (lettuce and cucumbers), live horses, and the meat of sheep or goats.

In addition, trade in seeds and organically produced agricultural products 26
will be considerably facilitated by reducing or eliminating a number of technical barriers along the same rules as under the EEA Agreement and the Swiss-EU Agricultural Agreement.

Fisheries, however, are treated quite differently and the provisions of 27
the EFTA Convention fully apply. This is noteworthy as, e.g., fisheries

---

23 A coalition of countries lobbying for agriculture to be treated as diverse and special because of non-trade concerns (Iceland, Israel, Japan, South Korea, Liechtenstein, Mauritius, Norway, Switzerland, Taiwan), https://www.wto.org/english/tratop_e/agric_e/negoti_groups_e.htm; members vary (Bulgaria dropped out after joining the EU) but term 'GIO' stands.

24 https://www.swissinfo.ch/eng/swiss-play-down-prospect-of-global-trade-deal/4837668.

25 Art. 8 EFTA Convention.

are mostly excluded from the scope of the EEA Agreement.[26] However, specific rules on trade in fish and other marine products aim at reducing or abolishing certain tariffs and quota, etc.[27]

3.2.1.5. *Sanitary and Phytosanitary Measures (SPS)*

28 All countries maintain measures to ensure that food is safe for consumers. These aim at keeping a high level of quality of food and preventing the spread of diseases. Depending on the country, its culture and other factors, these sanitary and phytosanitary measures can take many different forms. Therefore, restrictions on trade may result: 'A sanitary or phytosanitary restriction which is not actually required for health reasons can be a very effective protectionist device, and because of its technical complexity, a particularly deceptive and difficult barrier to challenge.'[28] In order to keep the free flow of trade as unhampered as possible, it is thus necessary to agree on common rules.

29 The EFTA states found an easy solution to that in the EFTA Convention: in Annex G they simply refer to the WTO Agreement on the Application of Sanitary and Phytosanitary Measures ('SPS Agreement') which aims at a coherent application of food safety and animal and plant health regulations. The SPS Agreement entered into force with the establishment of the WTO on 1 January 1995.

30 This is, however, only the basic set of rules. In reality, all four EFTA states are also bound by respective EU rules, either through the EEA Agreement[29] or the BAs[30] between Switzerland and the EU. These rules are far more detailed and also restrict the freedom to deviate from these rules in EFTA FTAs.[31]

---

26 See Art. 8(3) EEA.

27 EEA Agreement, Protocol 9.

28 https://www.wto.org/english/tratop_e/sps_e/spsund_e.htm.

29 Art. 17 EEA, particularly Annex I on veterinary and phytosanitary matters, which is constantly updated following EU legislation in that field.

30 Agreement between the European Community and the Swiss Confederation on trade in agricultural products – Final Act – Joint Declarations – Information relating to the entry into force of the seven Agreements with the Swiss Confederation in the sectors free movement of persons, air and land transport, public procurement, scientific and technological cooperation, mutual recognition in relation to conformity assessment, and trade in agricultural products, OJ L 114, 30.4.2002, pp. 132–368, in particular Annex 11 thereto.

31 See Ch. 6.

3.2.2. TECHNICAL BARRIERS TO TRADE (TBT)

3.2.2.1. General

Technical barriers to trade are impediments to the international trade of goods. They may result from different technical regulations or standards, a different application of such regulations or the non-recognition of conformity assessments carried out in another country. The term 'technical regulations' refers to the mandatory rules set out by law that must be adhered to in order for products to be offered, placed on the market, put into service, used or disposed of.[32] Technical regulations apply, for example, to the composition, the packaging or the manufacturing of a product. The term 'standards' is used to describe voluntary benchmarks 'issued by a recognized body, that provides, for common and repeated use, rules, guidelines or characteristics for products or related processes and production methods'[33] with which products comply in order to gain access to a market, while meeting the authorities and consumers' demand for safe and quality products.[34] Examples are, e.g., quality requirements for electrical tools. 31

In order to prevent such technical regulations and standards constituting a barrier to trade in global trade relations, the Technical Barriers to Trade (TBT) Agreement[35] was concluded at the level of the WTO. Essentially, partner countries need to recognise another country's technical regulations. A condition for doing so is that partner countries be informed of planned new technical regulations at an early stage. This will guarantee that the notified partner countries can prepare for such recognition on their side of the border. The same essentially applies to standards. There is no need to stress that procedures for obtaining such recognition must 32

---

32 Art. 3(b) of the (Swiss) Federal Law on Technical Barriers to Trade (TBA) of 6 October 1995; SR (German) or RS (French)(Swiss Federal Law Collection [consolidated]) 946.51.

33 TBT Agreement, Annex 1 nr. 2.

34 Regulation (EU) No 1025/2012 of the European Parliament and of the Council of 25 October 2012 on European standardisation, amending Council Directives 89/686/EEC and 93/15/EEC and Directives 94/9/EC, 94/25/EC, 95/16/EC, 97/23/EC, 98/34/EC, 2004/22/EC, 2007/23/EC, 2009/23/EC and 2009/105/EC of the European Parliament and of the Council and repealing Council Decision 87/95/EEC and Decision No 1673/2006/EC of the European Parliament and of the Council, OJ L 316, 14.11.2012, pp. 12–33, 3rd preamble.

35 https://www.wto.org/english/docs_e/legal_e/17-tbt_e.htm.

not be cumbersome or artificially block an applicant through excessive bureaucratic hurdles.

33 In order to do away with such hurdles to the circulation of goods among EFTA states, these had in 1988 concluded a convention between the EFTA states on the mutual recognition of test results and conformity assessments (Tampere Convention).[36] This has now been replaced in substance by the respective provisions of the revised EFTA Convention.

3.2.2.2. TBT in the 'Triangle' of Relations between the EU, the EEA EFTA States and Switzerland

34 At the level of the EU, in the internal market, that system was replaced by an approach that, on the one hand, issues harmonised technical regulations for the internal market. These only contain the essential requirements, mainly with regard to protecting health, the environment, consumers and safety at work.[37] On the other hand, with regard to substance, the EU legislator mostly does so by 'referring to technical standards elaborated by the European standards bodies rather than laying down technical specifications itself'.[38] This harmonised approach is applicable across the internal market and, hence, the EEA. There it is laid down in Annex II, which contains 32 chapters ranging from motor vehicles and medicinal products to cultural goods.[39] Essentially, there is no need for conformity assessment if there is a harmonised legal basis for the quality and specification of products; conformity with national technical regulations and standards of one country within the EEA is assumed by other member states. This is a big step forward for unhampered trade within the EEA, legal certainty and, of course, a relevant cost factor as conformity assessments may be expensive.

---

36 Translations of the text can be found with the Swiss administration (http://www.admin.ch) in AS 1990 1704-11 (German) or RO 1990 1704-11 (French).

37 Commission Notice – The 'Blue Guide' on the implementation of EU products rules 2016, C/2016/1958, OJ C 272, 26.7.2016, pp. 1–149.

38 H. Schepel and J. Falke, 'Legal aspects of standardisation in the Member States of the EC and EFTA', vol. 1 comparative report, European Communities, Luxembourg 2000, p. 1.

39 H. Bull, 'Commentary to Article 23, note 1' in F. Arnesen, H. Haukeland Fredriksen, H.P. Graver, O. Mestad and C. Vedder, *Agreement on the European Economic Area – A Commentary*, Beck/Hart/Nomos, Baden-Baden/Oxford/Oslo 2018.

Because of these reasons Switzerland was eager to conclude an agreement on mutual recognition of conformity assessments (MRA)[40] after the Swiss voters had rejected Switzerland joining the EEA Agreement in 1992. For ten years, until this MRA could enter into force, Swiss exporters trading with the EU faced higher costs compared to competitors in the other EFTA states because of the additional recognition procedures needed under mere WTO rules. 35

In the EFTA Convention, the chapter on TBT is divided into two parts, namely the notification of draft technical regulations[41] and the mutual recognition of conformity assessments.[42] For details, however, one has to refer to Annexes H (for notification) and I (for mutual recognition). 36

Without entering further into details, Switzerland and the EEA EFTA states grant each other mutual acceptance of reports, certificates, authorisations and conformity marks issued by the recognised conformity assessment bodies and of the manufacturer's declarations of conformity. The areas covered are the same as in the MRA between Switzerland and the EU. The same applies when Swiss and EEA requirements are deemed to be equivalent. In such cases the manufacturer's declarations of conformity shall, in particular, indicate conformity with the legislation applied in the EEA. This is, again, an example of the 'triangulation', i.e. establishing a level playing field between the EU, the EEA EFTA states and Switzerland.[43] 37

A specific feature was introduced in Annex H when the EFTA Convention was revised. In 1998, the EU consolidated its notification procedure.[44] It subsequently extended the scope of that directive, which was then 38

---

40 Agreement between the European Community and the Swiss Confederation on mutual recognition in relation to conformity assessment – Final Act – Joint Declarations – Information relating to the entry into force of the seven Agreements with the Swiss Confederation in the sectors free movement of persons, air and land transport, public procurement, scientific and technological cooperation, mutual recognition in relation to conformity assessment, and trade in agricultural products, OJ L 114, 30.4.2002, pp. 369–429.

41 Art. 14 EFTA Convention.

42 Art. 15 EFTA Convention.

43 See Ch. 1.

44 Directive 98/34/EC of the European Parliament and of the Council of 22 June 1998 laying down a procedure for the provision of information in the field of technical standards and regulations, OJ L 204, 21.7.1998, pp. 37–48.

to also cover information society services,[45] in order to prevent new obstacles to the cross-border movement of services. This extension was also incorporated into the EEA Agreement.[46] Since the EFTA Convention now also contains provisions on services, it was decided at the same time to add information society services to the notification procedure of Annex H. Hence, the scope of the obligation to notify rules under the EFTA procedure was again in line with that of EU or EEA procedures.

3.2.3. STATE AID, PUBLIC UNDERTAKINGS, MONOPOLIES AND COMPETITION RULES

3.2.3.1. State Aid

39 State aid may lead to market distortions and thereby indirectly affect trade. Therefore, the EFTA Convention refers for the rights and obligations of the EFTA states regarding state aid to Article XVI of the GATT 1994 and the WTO Agreement on Subsidies and Countervailing Measures.[47] These were made part of the EFTA Convention. There are, however, exceptions for the air transport sector,[48] especially as to certain state aid that is deemed admissible under certain conditions, such as aid to make good damage caused by natural disaster. Certain measures *may* be considered compatible like, e.g., aid to promote the economic development of areas where the standard of living is abnormally low or where there is serious under-employment. An example for such measures could be subsidies for Norwegian airlines that service areas north of the Polar Circle. The aim is to generally extend the EFTA Convention rules on state aid of the EFTA Convention to the services sector. As a general rule, the scope of the chapter on state aid is subject to a review at yearly intervals. At the same time, the EFTA member states dispense with the levying of countervailing duties in relation to each other.[49]

---

45 Directive 98/48/EC of the European Parliament and of the Council of 20 July 1998 amending Directive 98/34/EC laying down a procedure for the provision of information in the field of technical standards and regulations, OJ L 217, 5.8.1998, pp. 18–26.

46 Decision of the EEA Joint Committee No. 16/2001 of 28 February 2001 amending Annex II (Technical regulations, standards, testing and certification) and Annex XI (Telecommunication services) to the EEA Agreement, OJ L 117, 26.4.2001, pp. 16–20.

47 Art. 16 EFTA Convention.

48 Art. 6 of Annex Q to the EFTA Convention.

49 See generally Ch. XI, Art. 36 EFTA Convention on dumping.

3.2.3.2. *Public Companies and Legal Monopolies*

Under the Convention the EFTA states are obliged to ensure that public undertakings refrain from applying 40

- measures which protect domestic production where that is done by means of a duty or charge with equivalent effect, quantitative restrictions or government aid; or
- trade discrimination on grounds of nationality if that frustrates the benefits expected from the removal or absence of duties and quantitative restrictions on trade between the EFTA states.[50] Thereby the notion of 'public undertaking' is to be understood in a very broad manner and it is also to be applied in the context of air transport.[51]

3.2.3.3. *Competition*

The liberalisation of cross-border trade in goods, services and foreign investment may be hampered by restrictive business practices. For this reason, FTAs or other agreements that provide for preferential trade or the establishment of a free trade zone mostly contain trade-specific rules to protect competition. In this respect the EFTA Convention states[52] that EFTA states shall ensure that the liberalisation objectives of the agreement are not thwarted by measures like: 41

- agreements between enterprises, decisions by associations of enterprises and concerted practices between enterprises which have as their object or result in the prevention, restriction or distortion of competition; or
- abuse by one or more undertakings of a dominant position in the territories of the EFTA states as a whole or in a substantial part thereof.

Article 18 of the EFTA Convention does not create law that would be directly applicable, as expressly stated in a joint declaration by the member states: 42

> 'The Member States recognise that the provisions of Article 18 (ex Article 15) of the Convention shall not be construed so as to create any direct obligations

50 Art. 17 EFTA Convention.

51 Art. 17(4): 'Paragraph 3 shall apply to Annex Q.'

52 Art. 18 EFTA Convention.

for undertakings. They furthermore confirm that the practices referred to in Article 18 (ex Article 15) shall be interpreted in the light of the national competition laws of the Member States. (...)'[53]

Hence, the procedure is purely intergovernmental and not self-executing. The provisions of the EFTA Convention on dispute settlement[54] are, however, directly applicable. But given the limits to the judicial review of the rules on competition, any arbitration tribunal will only be in a position to examine in a very general manner whether an EFTA state has taken the necessary measures against anti-competitive practices which have a restrictive effect on trade.

3.2.4. INTELLECTUAL PROPERTY RIGHTS

43 In the last three decades, intellectual property (IP) law and policy has become a major subject of international trade agreements. Reasons for this development have been the increase in cross-border exchanges of goods, services, capital and knowledgeable persons and the fact that knowledge, data and digital content have emerged as ever more important tradable economic assets. Naturally, IP rights laws at national and international level have tried to keep pace, but have often failed.[55]

44 The provisions on the protection of IP in the EFTA Convention are divided into general rules in the main part of the agreement (and an Annex containing specific substantive obligations).[56]

45 Under the EFTA Convention, the EFTA states grant each other adequate and effective protection of IP rights. This includes combatting the infringement of such rights, be it e.g. through counterfeiting or piracy. The term 'intellectual property' encompasses copyright, including computer programs, topographies of integrated circuits and databases, as well as neighbouring rights, trade marks for goods and services, geographical indications and appellations of origin, for goods and services, industrial designs, patents and plant varieties. Undisclosed information is also understood to be protected as IP.

---

[53] Joint Declaration on Competition, para. 1.

[54] Ch. XVII, Arts. 46–48 EFTA Convention and Annex T thereto.

[55] See e.g. J. Curtis, 'Intellectual Property Rights and International Trade: An Overview', CIGI Papers no. 3, Centre for International Governance Innovation, May 2012, https://www.cigionline.org/sites/default/files/no.3.pdf.

[56] Art. 19 EFTA Convention and Annex J thereto.

The EFTA states committed themselves to grant each other national treatment and most favoured nation (MFN) treatment in this field. Exceptions thereto need to be in accordance with the TRIPS Agreement. The relevant standards are defined by reference to the following multilateral agreements: 46

- WTO Agreement of 15 April 1994 on Trade Related Aspects of Intellectual Property Rights (TRIPS Agreement);
- Paris Convention of 20 March 1883 for the Protection of Industrial Property (Stockholm Act, 1967);
- Berne Convention of 9 September 1886 for the Protection of Literary and Artistic Works (Paris Act, 1971);
- International Convention of 26 October 1961 for the Protection of Performers, Producers of Phonograms and Broadcasting Organisations (Rome Convention);
- the Geneva Act (1999) of the Hague Agreement Concerning the International Registration of Industrial Designs;
- the WIPO Copyright Treaty (Geneva 1996); and
- the WIPO Performances and Phonogram Treaty (Geneva 1996).

Those EFTA states which had not adhered to those treaties at the time of signature, undertook to do so before 1 January 2005.

With regard to technology patents, the European Patent Convention of 5 October 1973 shall determine the level of protection in Liechtenstein and Switzerland as implemented in national law, while for Iceland and Norway it is the EEA Agreement, as implemented in national law. The difference is due to the fact that Liechtenstein forms a patent union with Switzerland which is not covered by the respective rules of the EEA Agreement. Specific provisions have been inserted with regard to granting an additional term of protection for pharmaceuticals and plant protection products, designs and geographical indications. The former corresponds to Switzerland's interest in effective protection for its agrochemical and pharmaceutical industry. 47

3.2.5. (FREE) MOVEMENT OF PERSONS, SOCIAL SECURITY AND MUTUAL RECOGNITION OF DIPLOMAS

3.2.5.1. *Free Movement in International Trade Agreements*

Free movement of persons is, for many, a difficult political subject. First, some clarifications on terms are needed: free movement of persons in its 48 quite extensive meaning, encompassing workers, students, pensioners, certain non-employed people etc., is a concept of the EU. In the EEA, only workers were originally covered by free movement. This corresponds to the practice in international trade of usually restricting free movement of labour to something of an annex to services or investment. Gradually, however, through incorporation of EU secondary law (directives, regulations), it was extended further to also cover other groups (such as students, family members, retired persons etc.), like in the EU. The same happened in the relationship between the EU and Switzerland. Therefore, these days the above distinction has been abandoned and the term 'free movement of persons' is generally used, in the EFTA Convention[57] as well as in FTAs.[58]

49 Second, it has risen to a certain prominence since at European level the EU has made it an indissoluble part of the 'four freedoms'. Free movement of goods, services, capital and persons are the core liberties of the EU's internal market. And the EU has always insisted these cannot be separated or taken individually. Participation in the internal market requires subscribing to all of these or there is no participation.[59]

50 Third, in the Brexit referendum campaign it was one of the most debated issues.[60] And the Swiss example with the referendum held in 2014 on 'mass immigration'[61] seems to confirm this view. Most interestingly, opposition to immigration is an issue that is not necessarily discussed based on facts or reason. Nor does it matter whether it is about free movement within Europe or immigration from outside Europe. Supporters of a more rigid approach range from mere xenophobes to people who do not mind

57 See e.g. Ch. VIII: 'Free movement of persons'.

58 See e.g. Art. 3.9 FTA between the EFTA states and Indonesia: 'Movement of natural persons'.

59 See e.g. 'European Council (Art. 50) (23 March 2018) – Guidelines', EUCO XT 20001/18, Brussels 23.3.2018, nr. 7, https://www.efta.int/sites/default/files/documents/legal-texts/efta-convention/Vaduz%20Convention%20Agreement.pdf: 'The European Council recalls that the four freedoms are indivisible and that there can be no "cherry picking" through participation in the Single Market based on a sector-by-sector approach, which would undermine the integrity and proper functioning of the Single Market.'

60 S. Vasilopoulou, 'Campaign frames in the Brexit referendum' in D. Jackson, E. Thorsen and D. Wring (eds.), *EU Referendum Analysis 2016: Media, Voters and the Campaign*, Bournemouth University, Poole 2016, p. 114, http://www.referendumanalysis.eu/eu-referendum-analysis-2016/section-8-voters/campaign-frames-in-the-brexit-referendum/.

61 https://www.eda.admin.ch/dea/en/home/europapolitik/abstimmungen/gegen-masseneinwanderung.html.

foreigners at all but want to keep control of any form of immigration at national level; motivations for having an issue with free movement of persons are therefore manifold. This is, however, not the place to discuss this in further detail. Let's just say that this is an issue of particular political sensitivity.

At the level of international trade law, respective agreements will normally contain provisions on the movement of goods, capital and services. These may also include special rules on immigration too, but there is no 'dogma' as in EU internal market law for it to be an unconditional part of such agreements. Rather, free movement of persons has been, at that level, introduced as part of the right to trade in services. The WTO, while supporting different means for the liberalisation of services through GATS, also includes movement of persons in this framework. This is known as 'Mode 4' and refers to people providing services across borders. Essentially this covers two broad categories. On the one hand, such people are key employees who are transferred abroad within their company. This includes managers as well as technical staff. On the other hand, business visitors or independent foreign professionals in selected sectors are covered by such provisions. According to WTO statistics, the vast majority of persons moving under such 'Mode 4' rules do so for short-term visits which do not allow for gainful employment in the host country. It therefore needs to be kept in mind that the notion of free movement of persons (people) in that context has barely anything to do with the concept of free movement of persons according to EU internal market law. According to the WTO, of 288 free trade areas, 145 include specific provisions on free movement of services. Only about 40 of these agreements allow for some form of free movement of persons as service providers. In most of the FTAs that include provisions on free movement there are time limits with regard to the duration of stay and on the access to the labour market. There may also be restrictions on the sectors that citizens of the FTA partner country may work in.[62] It can thus be said that the liberalisation of free trade has not liberalised the free movement of persons around the world, and certainly nowhere close to the situation in Europe. 51

The EFTA Convention, until 2002, did not contain any provisions regarding free movement of persons, nor did it provide for such on services. Being 52

62 L. Harding, 'How the special migration rules in free trade deals work', *The Conversation*, 2 October 2018, http://theconversation.com/how-the-special-migration-rules-in-free-trade-deals-work-103709.

an agreement that first and foremost aims at creating a free trade area, one could assume that modernising it would only bring about the WTO standard, thus 'Mode 4' level. However, another reason for modernising the EFTA Convention was to bring mutual rights and duties for citizens of the EFTA states into line with those that EU citizens already enjoy in the EEA EFTA states, namely Iceland, Liechtenstein and Norway or Switzerland respectively. Therefore, after the conclusion of the Agreement between the EU and Switzerland on Free Movement of Persons (AFMP),[63] it was agreed among the EFTA states to replicate most of that agreement's content in the EFTA Convention.[64] The main exception compared to the situation in the EEA is that the so-called 'Union Citizenship Directive'[65] has to this very day not been incorporated into the EFTA Convention.

53 Hence, as in the AFMP, there are three main subjects covered in Chapter VIII of the EFTA Convention: free movement,[66] social security[67] and mutual recognition of diplomas.[68]

54 EFTA nationals are given 'a right of appeal to the competent authorities of the Member State concerned in respect of the application of the provisions' on free movement of persons. By this, the administrative authorities are targeted, which are to process such appeals 'within a reasonable period of time'. In the absence of which, or generally with respect to decisions on appeals, EFTA nationals shall be given 'the opportunity to appeal to the competent national judicial body'.[69] This is probably as far as one can go in giving individuals access to an administrative remedy and judicial review without establishing supranational bodies that could be – directly or indirectly – appealed to.

---

63 Agreement between the European Community and its Member States, of the one part, and the Swiss Confederation, of the other, on the free movement of persons – Final Act – Joint Declarations – Information relating to the entry into force of the seven Agreements with the Swiss Confederation in the sectors free movement of persons, air and land transport, public procurement, scientific and technological cooperation, mutual recognition in relation to conformity assessment, and trade in agricultural products OJ L 114, 30.04.2002, pp. 6–72.

64 Swiss Federal Government, 'Explanatory message to the Parliament on the ratification of the revised EFTA Convention', 21.6.2001, BBl 2001 4963 (German), FF 2001 4729 (French), p. 4982 (DE) and 4747-8 (FR) respectively.

65 See n. 9 above.

66 Art. 20 EFTA Convention and Annex K, app. 1.

67 Art. 21 and Annex K, app. 2.

68 Art. 22 and Annex K, app. 3.

69 Art. 11 of Annex K to the EFTA Convention.

3.2.5.2. Free Movement of Persons in the General Sense

The EFTA Convention's provisions on free movement of persons is based on the AFMP between Switzerland and the EU. The agreement will be extended virtually unchanged to the EFTA states. It covers freedom of movement for employed persons (including the self-employed) and for the economically inactive (students, pensioners and the unemployed), as well as certain aspects of the cross-border provision of services by persons. A bilateral protocol between Switzerland and Liechtenstein contains the special provisions applicable in that bilateral relationship. 55

The EFTA Convention also contains a consensual safeguard clause which corresponds to that of the AFMP. The Council is to appoint a committee responsible for the administration and the correct application of the agreement. In the occurrence of serious economic and social problems, the committee shall meet at the request of a member state to examine appropriate remedies. The Council is to decide which measures are to be taken. 56

As to the individual categories of residence, the following will apply: 57

- permanent residence: five years with an employment contract of more than one year, to be automatically renewed if the employment continues;
- short stay: 'Eurocompatible' short stay statute. The duration is linked to the duration of the employment contract (if less than a year). There is a right to family reunification as well as to changing employment geographical mobility; and
- cross-border commuters: return home weekly; no border zone.

The Protocol on free movement of persons between Switzerland and Liechtenstein forms an integral part of the EFTA Convention. It essentially provides for Liechtenstein to grant Swiss nationals equal treatment with EEA nationals. This includes restricted access to residence in Liechtenstein, notwithstanding full access to the labour market. In the subsequent legislation based on that protocol, there are also some privileges mutually granted with regard to cross-border services. 58

3.2.5.3. Social Security

The free movement of persons also covers social security issues by establishing a system of coordination between the EFTA states. The 59 objective is to apply common principles and rules so that differences in national legislation will not hinder the mobility of persons who move within the EFTA area.

60 Again, the EFTA Convention adopted the rules of the AFMP between Switzerland and the EU in the area of social security which mostly correspond to those contained in the EEA Agreement. Thus, these provisions are limited to the coordination of the social security systems of the EFTA states. Coordination means that, while applying their social security laws, individual states must accept certain common principles. Beyond that they remain free to shape their laws according to their own needs. The legal basis, borrowed from EU law, is provided by Regulations 1408/71/EEC[70] and 574/72/EEC.[71]

61 The structure of the respective provisions in the EFTA Convention is based on the model of the AFMP as well. While the EFTA Convention contains a basic provision on social security in its main text,[72] it refers for the rules in detail to the annexes.[73] Without entering too much into these details, it is worthwhile mentioning that existing bilateral agreements on social security were suspended as from the entry into force of the revised EFTA Convention, insofar as they cover the same matter.[74] Such bilateral agreements have existed for decades between Switzerland and Liechtenstein and since 1979 between Switzerland and Norway. Between Switzerland and Iceland there were no such agreements.

62 The EFTA states undertake to apply among themselves the EU legal acts with regard to the coordination of social security schemes as incorporated in the EEA Agreement, as well as in the AFMP between Switzerland and the EU, or rules equivalent to such acts.[75] Switzerland therefore had to,

---

70 Regulation (EEC) No. 1408/71 of the Council of 14 June 1971 on the application of social security schemes to employed persons and their families moving within the Community, OJ L 149, 5.7.1971, p. 2–50 (German, French, Italian, Dutch only), English special edition: Series I Volume 1971(II) pp. 416–463.

71 Regulation (EEC) No. 574/72 of the Council of 21 March 1972 fixing the procedure for implementing Regulation (EEC) No. 1408/71 on the application of social security schemes to employed persons and their families moving within the Community, OJ L 74, 27.3.1972, pp. 1–83 (German, French, Italian, Dutch only), English special edition: Series I Volume 1972(I) pp. 160–233.

72 Art. 21 EFTA Convention.

73 Annex K, Art. 8 and app. 2.

74 Art. 18 of Annex K to the EFTA Convention.

75 Art. 1 of app. 2 to Annex K to the EFTA Convention. The relevant acts are to be inserted in Section A thereto.

as in the context of the AFMP, adopt respective national law. The other three EFTA States were already adopting the relevant EU law through their membership of the EEA.

As already mentioned, the social security provisions of the EFTA Convention are based on the same provisions of EU law as the AFMP between Switzerland and the EU and the EEA Agreement. This, however, does not allow for 'cross-agreement' coordination between all states covered – in substance – by the same EU legal acts. This could only be achieved by institutionally linking the social security legislation of the three agreements involved. And that can only be done in the politically difficult context of further integration, especially of Switzerland. 63

3.2.5.4. Recognition of Diplomas

Additionally, the mutual recognition of professional diplomas[76] will be introduced under the EFTA Convention, which will further facilitate the free movement of persons. Qualifications obtained in an EFTA state under so-called general systems for the recognition of higher education diplomas and of professional education or training in the following specialised areas will be recognised in the other EFTA states: legal professions, medical and paramedical activities, architecture, commerce and intermediaries. 64

With regard to the mutual recognition of diplomas, the agreement provides that Switzerland and the other three EFTA states apply among themselves the EU legal acts as incorporated in the EEA Agreement as well as in the AFMP between Switzerland and the EU. This – again – leads to recognition of diplomas in accordance with the relevant EU legal acts. 65

3.2.6. INVESTMENT, CAPITAL MOVEMENTS, SERVICES

As part of the revision work, the EFTA states have decided to also include regulatory areas that previously were not covered by the EFTA Convention. This was the case, for example, with regard to investment and trade in services. 66

During the preparatory phase it became apparent that the Nordic countries, on the one hand, and Switzerland (and Liechtenstein as an accessory as 67

[76] Art. 22 EFTA Convention; app. 3 to Annex K to the EFTA Convention.

far as trade relations with third countries outside the EEA are concerned), on the other hand, had different ideas about what new regulatory areas to include, and how. Norway and Iceland advocated the development of an ambitious services and investment chapter. They argued that the EFTA Convention should be as comprehensive as possible and should govern the whole of economic relations between the EFTA states. Switzerland and Liechtenstein, however, wanted to establish a common platform for the four countries to negotiate EFTA's third-country relations (FTAs) and thereby strengthening EFTA's position in such negotiations.

68 There was another difficulty to be addressed: Iceland, Liechtenstein and Norway were already linked to each other by the respective rules of the EEA Agreement and thus part of a deeply integrated preferential system. The relationship between Switzerland and the other EFTA member states, by contrast, was based on the commitments regarding trade in services entered into under the WTO regime. Consequently, the Swiss trade legislation regarding services reflected the commitments Switzerland has entered into in the WTO. Any substantial concession will therefore result in a change in Switzerland's internal legislation. On the other hand, the legislation of the other three EFTA states reflects commitments made under the EEA, which gives these countries more room for manoeuvre in shaping their preferential trade policy, as far as this is covered by the EEA Agreement.

69 The final agreement confirmed the increased willingness of all four EFTA states to cooperate in the field of investment and services. In essence, the agreement is based on the principles of European law, but also contains provisions which can be found international trade law.

3.2.6.1. Investment and Capital Movement

70 The provisions of Chapter IX of the updated EFTA Convention are contained in section 1 (establishment) and section 2 (capital movement). Not least with regard to EFTA-third-country relations, it was important to broadly unify the EFTA states' legal framework with regard to investment and capital. Such agreements, as far as they are concluded with overseas countries, as a rule, also contain corresponding provisions on establishment. If the EFTA states want to gain anything from negotiating as a group they also need to offer a more or less coherent legal framework with regard to investment and capital movement.

The core of the material scope is the right of establishment for companies incorporated under the legislation of an EFTA state and having its registered office, head office or main establishment in the territory of the EFTA states. The right of establishment applies equally to the establishment, acquisition and management of agencies, branches or subsidiaries of one EFTA state's companies in the territory of another EFTA member state. 71

Therefore, a company or firm formed in accordance with the laws of an EFTA state may set up and operate its business in another EFTA state. Companies of other EFTA states shall be granted national treatment and MFN treatment. An important principle was to ensure that the same legal conditions apply to all forms of companies. However, the EFTA states were able to invoke derogations that are listed in the annexes to the Convention.[77] There is a so-called 'standstill clause' that prohibits expanding or toughening these exceptions.[78] The most important exception from the above principle of equal treatment and non-discrimination is the reservation with regard to business activities involving the exercise of public authority.[79] Furthermore, it is possible to derogate from national treatment if the special treatment applied is justified by legal and technical differences between companies registered in different EFTA states, subsidiaries, branches and agencies. However, the difference in treatment must not go beyond what is strictly necessary for legal and technical reasons.[80] In the financial services sector, EFTA states may take measures necessary for prudential reasons to, e.g., ensure the protection of investors, account holders, policyholders or persons subject to a fiduciary liability, or the integrity and stability of the financial system. These measures may, however, not disadvantage companies of the other EFTA states vis-à-vis their own companies. 72

The movement of capital shall be free of any restrictions in so far as it concerns establishment. The rules on capital movements are subject to a review within two years after the entry into force of the updated Convention with a view to their further liberalisation.[81] 73

77 Annexes L, M, N and O for reservations from Iceland, Liechtenstein, Norway and Switzerland respectively to Ch. IX (investment) and Ch. X (trade in services).

78 Art. 23 EFTA Convention.

79 Art. 27 EFTA Convention.

80 Art. 24 EFTA Convention.

81 Art. 28 EFTA Convention.

3.2.6.2. *Trade in Services*

74 The chapter on trade in services has a similar structure to the chapter on investments. It covers all areas of trade in services with the exemptions for land and air transport.

75 Regarding cross-border supply of services between EFTA citizens, i.e. the consumption of services of citizens from one EFTA state in another, and the supply of services by local presence, the revised Convention opens up this sector subject to some minor reservations. It must be remembered that the supply and the consumption of services by individuals are also governed by the rules regarding the movement of persons.

76 Any benefits that an EFTA state may grant to the European Union in the future in terms of liberalisation of trade in services will have to be extended to the other EFTA states.[82] This was seen as being of particular importance if Switzerland were to take further steps in this area vis-à-vis the EU. This undertaking was, however, not followed up when the Services Directive[83] was integrated into the EEA Agreement.

77 In principle, any restriction of cross-border provision of services is prohibited.[84] This involves having a service provider in one EFTA state provide services to another EFTA state without restriction, even without physical presence in that EFTA state. Furthermore, the provision allows unrestricted provision of services over on the basis of a temporary residence of the provider or consumer in another EFTA state. Therefore, there is essentially national treatment.

78 There are, however, country reservations by which the EFTA states had the option to declare in which areas they wanted to deviate from the principle of freedom to provide services.[85] This chapter also contains a 'standstill clause' according to which the restrictions in force on the entry into force of the (revised) Convention may neither be extended nor toughened. Furthermore, the chapter provides for a MFN clause, under which the EFTA states pledge to not treat each other less favourably than a third country. There is an exception with regard to the member states of the EU due to the respective agreements of Iceland, Liechtenstein and Norway as

82 Art. 29(5) EFTA Convention.

83 Directive 2006/123/EC of the European Parliament and of the Council of 12 December 2006 on services in the internal market, OJ L 376, 27.12.2006, pp. 36–68.

84 Art. 29 EFTA Convention.

85 See n. 77 above.

well as Switzerland. With a view to future agreements between the EFTA states and the EU, the former undertake to open negotiations in order to mutually grant each other the benefits of such agreements.

Again, in the financial services sector, EFTA states may take measures 79
necessary for prudential reasons to protect investors, account holders, policyholders or beneficiaries of a fiduciary transaction, or to ensure the integrity and stability of the financial system. These measures are, of course, subject to not disadvantaging companies of the other EFTA states compared to their own companies.

The EFTA Convention does not contain any obligation for the EFTA states 80
to disclose information on transactions and accounting documents of individual customers or other confidential or proprietary information held by public authorities.[86] Mutual recognition should not be made in a way that equates to a means of discriminating between different countries when applying standards or criteria for the approval, licensing or certification of service providers.[87]

As regards audio-visual services, the Council of Europe Convention on 81
Transfrontier Television[88] remains applicable between Switzerland and the other EFTA states. This convention is similar to the respective EU directive which was also incorporated into the EEA Agreement.[89] With regard to further discussions in this area in the EFTA framework, it seems that Switzerland was able to commit its EFTA partners to the line followed by Switzerland in the Council of Europe. However, due consideration is to be given to negotiations with the European Union and results thereof.[90]

---

86 Art. 31 EFTA Convention.

87 Art. 32 EFTA Convention.

88 European Convention on Transfrontier Television of 5 May 1989, ETS 132, as amended according to the provisions of the Protocol (ETS 171) which entered into force, on 1 March 2002.

89 At the time of entry into force of the revised EFTA Convention this was Council Directive 89/552/EEC of 3 October 1989 on the coordination of certain provisions laid down by Law, Regulation or Administrative Action in Member States concerning the pursuit of television broadcasting activities, OJ L 298, 17.10.1989, p. 23–30. This directive has since been replaced by Directive 2007/65/EC of the European Parliament and of the Council of 11 December 2007 amending Council Directive 89/552/EEC on the coordination of certain provisions laid down by law, regulation or administrative action in Member States concerning the pursuit of television broadcasting activities, OJ L 332, 18.12.2007, pp. 27–45.

90 This somewhat astonishing statement can be found at: Swiss Federal Government, 'Explanatory message to the Parliament on the ratification of the revised EFTA Convention' (n. 64 above), p. 4995 (DE) and 4760 (FR) respectively.

Subsidies and (state) aid to the audio-visual sector remains unchallenged within EFTA, in particular as regards radio and television fees.

82 This chapter also includes country exceptions,[91] which allow EFTA states to derogate from certain obligations set out in this chapter. These exceptions may be applied in the context of surveillance activities or concern measures for the protection of public order, public health or protection of the environment. Measures to avoid double taxation as well as those for correct application of tax law are equally subject to such derogations. Finally, it is not possible to invoke the provisions of this chapter for the exercise of rights in the field of public procurement.

3.2.7. LAND AND AIR TRANSPORT

83 As mentioned above,[92] special rules apply to transport services. The reciprocal liberalisation of access to transport markets was introduced in the EFTA Convention with its revision.[93] To that end, essential elements of the Swiss-EU bilateral agreements have been transposed into the EFTA Convention, including references to EU rules regarding road, rail and air transport.

84 In the field of land transport, the EFTA Convention now provides for a gradual reciprocal opening of the markets for the transportation of both persons and goods by road and by rail between all the EFTA states.

85 The rules on civil aviation lay down the terms on which an air transport company of an EFTA state will have access to the air transport markets of another EFTA state.

86 It is worth noting that existing bilateral treaties granting air traffic rights between individual EFTA states remain in force if the traffic rights they grant are not covered by the revised EFTA Convention and further that there is no discrimination on the grounds of nationality.

---

91 These are, as is the case with regard to the country exceptions to the GATS Agreement, not published. They can normally be obtained with the national administration or the WTO Secretariat or at https://www.wto.org/english/tratop_e/serv_e/serv_commitments_e.htm.

92 See para. 73 above.

93 Art. 35 EFTA Convention. Annex P regulates the modalities of liberalisation in the land transport sector.

The unrestricted freedom of establishment, with the exception of Swiss operators in Iceland, is the core of the new provisions on air transport in the EFTA Convention. Other provisions that aim at creating open and equal market conditions in air transport concern the granting and surveillance of state aid, fares and rates, the conduct of computer reservation systems, environmental regulations, licensing issues, the slot allocation, ground handling, air carrier liability, technical harmonisation and air safety. 87

3.2.7.1. *Land Transport*

The substantive rights and duties of the Land Transport Agreement between the EU and Switzerland (LTA)[94] were extended to the other EFTA states, keeping the wording as far as possible identical to that of the sectoral agreement. The central components are mutual market access in the road and rail sectors for passenger and freight transport, as well as the allocation of quotas for 40-tonne journeys and empty and light journeys. 88

The EFTA Convention's scope expressly covers bilateral, transit and three-country traffic ('cabotage') in the freight and passenger sectors of the road and international rail transport for goods and persons as well as combined transport. Railway companies which operate exclusively in regional, suburban or city traffic are, however, excluded. The principles of non-discrimination, reciprocity, territoriality, transparency and freedom of choice of the mode of transport, as well as the objectives of sustainable mobility and a coordinated transport policy in the Alpine Space, apply. 89

Within the framework of the EFTA Convention, Switzerland transposes the acquis of the EU, which is also mentioned in Annex 1 of the Land Transport Agreement with the EU, into equivalent Swiss law. However, before doing so, the adaptation of Swiss law to developments in EU law, for example in railway law, must first be clarified within the framework of the Swiss-EU joint committee (on the LTA) before adjustments can be made under the EFTA Convention. A special feature of the LTA is an exemption 90

94 Agreement between the European Community and the Swiss Confederation on the Carriage of Goods and Passengers by Rail and Road – Final Act – Joint Declarations – Information relating to the entry into force of the seven Agreements with the Swiss Confederation in the sectors free movement of persons, air and land transport, public procurement, scientific and technological cooperation, mutual recognition in relation to conformity assessment, and trade in agricultural products, OJ L 114, 30.4.2002, pp. 91–131.

from free transit: lorries with an axle weight of 40 (metric) tonnes and above may only travel on dedicated transit roads and are subject to a quota allocation. It would, however, lead too far to expand on this.

91 As a reminder: the other three EFTA states incorporate the relevant EU acquis within their membership of the EEA. Respective proposals to formally amend the EFTA Convention are to be made by a dedicated committee.[95] Finally, existing bilateral agreements between EFTA member countries, such as between Switzerland and Liechtenstein,[96] have precedence over these provisions with regard to the interests of international freight and passenger transport.[97]

3.2.7.2. Air Transport

92 Prior to the revision of the EFTA Convention there was among the EFTA states only an aviation agreement between Norway and Switzerland. That agreement only contained rules on regular services. It was limited to key issues such as traffic rights, capacity and tariffs. The relations between Switzerland and Liechtenstein with regard to aviation were regulated in an exchange of notes.[98] This provided for a general delegation of almost all supervisory tasks by Liechtenstein to Switzerland.

93 The liberalisation of air transport between the EFTA states is regulated in Annex Q to the EFTA Convention.[99] In principle, the substance of the Annex is based on the provisions of the Agreement on Air Transport (AAT) between the EU and Switzerland,[100] with the exception of the rules

---

95 The procedures applicable to that Committee are laid down in Art. 29 of Annex P to the EFTA Convention.

96 Treaty between Switzerland and Liechtenstein on the annexation of the Principality of Liechtenstein to the Swiss customs territory of 29 March 1923 (SR 0.631.112.514).

97 Art. 4 of Annex P to the EFTA Convention.

98 Notenaustausch zwischen der Schweiz und Liechtenstein betreffend die Zusammenarbeit der schweizerischen und der liechtensteinischen Behörden im Bereich der Zivilluftfahrt vom 27 Januar 2003, LGBl. (Liechtenstein Law Gazette) 2003 Nr. 40; LR (Liechtenstein Law Collection [consolidated]) 0.748.091.011.

99 Art. 35 EFTA Convention.

100 Agreement between the European Community and the Swiss Confederation on Air Transport – Final Act – Joint Declarations – Information relating to the entry into force of the seven Agreements with the Swiss Confederation in the sectors free movement of persons, air and land transport, public procurement, scientific and technological cooperation, mutual recognition in relation to conformity assessment, and trade in agricultural products, OJ L 114, 30.4.2002, pp. 73–90.

on competition and institutional provisions. These two areas have been excluded because all horizontal regulations are contained in the main text of the EFTA Convention and for all sectors. However, a Committee on Air Transport was established through the Annex.

3.2.8. PUBLIC PROCUREMENT

In the area of public procurement, the revised EFTA Convention builds on the EFTA states' commitments under the WTO's Agreement on Government Procurement (GPA), to which all EFTA states are parties. Moreover, the Convention goes beyond the WTO rules by extending the sectoral coverage. This extended coverage includes: purchases of products and services including construction services, by railway operators, entities active in the field of energy other than electricity and private utilities active in the fields of drinking water, electricity, urban transport, ports and airports in the EFTA states. 94

The chapter on public procurement applies to contracts awarded by railway operators, entities active in the field of energy (other than electricity) for which the estimated value exceeds EUR 400,000 for supplies/services and EUR 5,000,000 for works. When awarded by private utilities, the thresholds are SDR[101] 400,000 for supplies/services and SDR 5,000,000 for works. 95

This section also lays down the basic principles governing public procurement such as non-discrimination, transparency and reciprocity. 96

The bilateral agreement between Switzerland and the EU on aspects of public procurement (APP)[102] aimed to extend the scope of application 97

101 Definition by the International Monetary Fund: 'The SDR is an international reserve asset, created by the IMF in 1969 to supplement its member countries' official reserves. So far SDR 204.2 billion (equivalent to about US$291 billion) have been allocated to members, including SDR 182.6 billion allocated in 2009 in the wake of the global financial crisis. The value of the SDR is based on a basket of five currencies – the U.S. dollar, the euro, the Chinese renminbi, the Japanese yen, and the British pound sterling.' https://www.imf.org/en/About/Factsheets/Sheets/2016/08/01/14/51/Special-Drawing-Right-SDR.

102 Agreement between the European Community and the Swiss Confederation on certain aspects of government procurement – Final Act – Joint Declarations – Information relating to the entry into force of the seven Agreements with the Swiss Confederation in the sectors free movement of persons, air and land transport, public procurement, scientific and technological cooperation, mutual recognition in relation to conformity assessment, and trade in agricultural products, OJ L 114, 30.4.2002, pp. 430–467.

of the GPA[103] to the Swiss-EU relationship in order to achieve a level of mutual market access between suppliers from the contracting parties that is comparable to the EEA. After Iceland had joined before the entry into force of the revised EFTA Convention as well, all EFTA countries were members of the GPA. With the revision of the EFTA Convention, the mutual market access of the APP, comparable with the EEA, was extended to all EFTA states.

98 The additional[104] mutual market access[105] of the EFTA Convention is based – like the APP – on the GPA. In addition, the EFTA Convention also sets out the basic principles of non-discrimination, transparency and mutual market access. The substance of the extended scope of application is stated in the Annex (R) and the appendices thereto. The scope of the GPA rules is to be extended to areas and providers not subject to the GPA. As in the APP, in sectors where public service providers are already covered by the GPA, private service providers are covered as well. The respective sectors are water, electricity and transport. In addition, providers in the field of energy, except for electricity, and rail transport are to be covered.[106] In the energy sector there is a special regime for Norwegian procurements in the oil and gas sector. Following a decision by the EFTA Surveillance Authority, more flexible procedures are applicable to these areas.[107] However, the principles of non-discrimination, transparency and competition apply to these kinds of procurement as well.

99 Unlike in the APP, providers in the telecommunications sector were not included because of the ongoing liberalisation of that particular market. Indeed, developments in this area suggested that, when the revised EFTA Convention entered into force, providers operating in that market would benefit from the provision that a body is not subject to procurement rules (any longer) when it operates in a geographically defined area, under substantially the same conditions and provides the same services as its competitors.[108]

100 Mutual market access for local government procurement, as in the APP, is to be ensured within the framework of the GPA. Since with the entry into force of the APP Switzerland has placed its municipalities under the GPA,

---

[103] https://www.wto.org/english/docs_e/legal_e/rev-gpr-94_01_e.htm.

[104] i.e. beyond the benefits granted by the GPA.

[105] Art. 37 and Annex R to the EFTA Convention.

[106] Art. 2 of Annex R to the EFTA Convention.

[107] Fn. 1 to Art. 2 (b) [ii] of Annex R to the EFTA Convention.

[108] Art. 3 of Annex R to the EFTA Convention.

and the other EFTA partners had previously done so as well, there was no need to retain this principle in the revised EFTA Convention.

Essentially, all procuring entities – whether subject to the GPA, the APP, the EEA Agreement or the EFTA Convention – should apply the same principles and rules. To facilitate application, it is the rules of the GPA that apply.[109] The thresholds are the same as in the APP,[110] the provisions cover the same services[111] and the same exceptions apply.[112] 101

The APP provides for a complaints procedure and a special regime for monitoring compliance with its obligations. This provision was, however, not included in the EFTA Convention as the other three EFTA states seemed not to have shown any particular interest in adopting such a provision.[113] 102

Market participants should, as a principle, not discriminate below the thresholds either. This is enshrined in the APP. However, this provision lacks enforceability because the application of respective remedies provided by national law – here Swiss law – was expressly excluded. This was mirrored in the EFTA Convention.[114] Therefore, only the general non-discrimination provision provided for by the EFTA Convention, as well as Article 7, remain as a legal basis to prevent discriminatory behaviour below the thresholds. 103

3.3. ECONOMIC AND MONETARY POLICY COOPERATION

For the sake of completeness, it should be mentioned that with the revision of the EFTA Convention the EFTA states also included a legal basis for economic and monetary policy cooperation. According to that provision, the EFTA states 104

> 'shall exchange views and information concerning the implementation of this Convention and the impact of the integration on economic activities and on the

---

109 Arts. 6 and 9 of Annex R to the EFTA Convention and app. 14 thereto.

110 Art. 5 APP.

111 Art. 4 of Annex R to the EFTA Convention and apps. 10 and 11 thereto.

112 Art. 8 of Annex R to the EFTA Convention and apps. 10 and 13 thereto.

113 Swiss Federal Government, 'Explanatory message to the Parliament on the ratification of the revised EFTA Convention' (n. 64 above), p. 5000 (DE) and 4764 (FR) respectively.

114 Art. 7 of Annex R to the EFTA Convention, last sentence, and app. 12 thereto.

conduct of economic and monetary policies. Furthermore, they may discuss macro-economic situations, policies and prospects. This exchange of views and information shall take place on a non-binding basis.'[115]

Strictly speaking, the content of this article merely confirms what the 105
EFTA states regularly do in the context of their Council meetings.[116] It also mirrors in some way the respective exchanges within the EEA in EEA Council meetings or in joint committee meetings. However, given the intragovernmental nature of the EFTA Convention it seems nonetheless useful to have such a provision. It helps the EFTA Secretariat exercise its duty to prepare the necessary information on behalf of the member states and gain access to the member states' data that is needed. Furthermore, it also provides for a formal basis in case the effects of an economic or financial crisis, such as that of Iceland after 2008, need to be discussed.

115 Art. 42 EFTA Convention.

116 See Ch. 4.

CHAPTER 4

EFTA INSTITUTIONS, MEMBERSHIP, SCOPE AND OTHER GENERAL PROVISIONS

4.1. INTRODUCTION

1 After having dealt with the substantive provisions of the EFTA Convention in the previous chapter, there are, of course, other provisions that it is worthwhile describing. This chapter will begin with the more general provisions, such as the nature of EFTA and its territorial scope, but also those provisions on accession and association and withdrawal. Finally, this chapter will look at EFTA's institutions and procedures.

4.2. NATURE AND TERRITORIAL SCOPE

2 The nature of EFTA is that of an intergovernmental organisation.[1] Hence, it is quite different in scope from, e.g., the EU. It was deliberately chosen to be different as many of its members could not agree with the then EEC's supranational tendency and political aims. The EFTA states have not surrendered any of their sovereignty to the Association or any institutions thereof. EFTA does not have legal personality like the EU.[2] Nevertheless, it enjoys diplomatic immunity and so do part of the staff of the EFTA Secretariat, the EFTA Surveillance Authority and the EFTA Court according to seat agreements with Switzerland, Belgium and Luxembourg.

1 See also G. Baur, M. Sánchez-Rydelski and C. Zatschler, *European Free Trade Association (EFTA) and the European Economic Area (EEA)*, 2nd ed., Wolters Kluwer, Alphen aan den Rijn 2018, p. 24.

2 Art. 47 TEU.

3 The Convention is applicable to the territories of the EFTA states,[3] thus defining the territorial scope. Exceptions are mentioned in Annex U. According to that protocol the Kingdom of Norway was given the right to exempt the territory of Svalbard (Spitzbergen) from the application of the Convention with the exception of trade in goods when ratifying the Agreement amending the Convention establishing the European Free Trade Association of 21 June 2001.

4 Norway exercised its right. Therefore, the EFTA Convention does not apply to the territory of Svalbard, with the exception of Articles 3 through 11.[4] Given the special status of the archipelago under international law, the respective provision further states:

> '2. In the event of a conflict between the Treaty Regulating the Status of Spitzbergen and Conferring the Sovereignty on Norway, done at Paris, 9 February 1920 (the "Spitzbergen (Svalbard) Treaty") and this Agreement, the Spitzbergen (Svalbard) Treaty shall prevail to the extent of the conflict, without prejudice to the positions of the Parties in respect of the Spitzbergen (Svalbard) Treaty. In the event of such conflict or a dispute as to whether there is such conflict or as to its extent, the dispute settlement provisions of this Agreement shall not apply.'

4.3. ACCESSION

4.3.1. GENERAL

5 During its existence, EFTA saw various changes in membership.[5] The last accession to EFTA took place in 1991 when Liechtenstein joined as a full member, essentially for the purpose of participating in the EEA in its own right. Before that, Liechtenstein was part of the geographical scope and a *de facto* member, represented by Switzerland. This was due to the Customs Treaty between Switzerland and Liechtenstein[6] and reflected in

3 Art. 58 EFTA Convention.

4 Annex A to Art. 2 of the EFTA Convention.

5 See Ch. 2.

6 Art. 8 of the Customs Treaty between Switzerland and Liechtenstein of 29 March 1923, https://www.eda.admin.ch/eda/en/home/representations-and-travel-advice/liechtenstein/switzerland-liechtenstein.html. With regard to the UK, this was followed by an exchange of letters of 26 April 1924 regarding the extension of commercial treaties between Switzerland and the UK to Liechtenstein.

the Protocol to the EFTA Convention (1960) with Liechtenstein and again in the Protocol to the EFTA-Finland Association Agreement. In both cases the signatories to the EFTA Convention and Liechtenstein agreed that the Convention shall apply to Liechtenstein as long as it forms a customs union with Switzerland and Switzerland is a member of the Association, and that for the purposes of the Convention, Liechtenstein shall be represented by Switzerland.[7] With Liechtenstein's accession in 1991, that country became a party in its own right as a party to the EFTA Convention and with regard to its participation in the EEA Agreement. However, with regard to EFTA's third-country relationships and although Liechtenstein participates in the negotiations, it is still Switzerland which concludes the Agreements on behalf of both countries.

Since the entry into force of the EEA Agreement and the subsequent recast 6
of the EFTA Convention in 2001, no new member has been admitted to EFTA. There, have been potential candidates though.[8] Criteria for membership of EFTA would in such a case have to be found. There are essentially three groups of criteria: first, legal criteria as mentioned in the EFTA Convention. Secondly, if needed, further criteria could be developed by analogy, drawn from the needs of the Association in political, economic, financial and structural respects as well as by comparison to similar organisations. Thirdly, political criteria would need to be taken into account as well.

If one were to look for criteria to compare with, of course, the so-called 7
'Copenhagen Criteria' of the EU come to mind.[9] These criteria need to be fulfilled by countries that wish to adhere to the EU. The Copenhagen Criteria contain three sub-criteria: First, *political criteria* seek to assess the stability of institutions guaranteeing democracy, the rule of law, human rights and the respect and protection of minorities. Secondly, *economic criteria* assess whether there is a functioning market economy capable of competition within the EU and, thirdly, the *criteria regarding the adoption of acquis* examine a country's capacity to accept the Community acquis

---

7 P.J.G. Kapteyn, R.H. Lauwaars, P.H. Kooijmans, H.G. Schermers and M. van der Leeuwen Boomkamp (eds.), 'European Free Trade Association' in *International Organization and Integration, Volume IIB-J*, Martinus Nijhoff, The Hague, Boston, London 1983, p. 1.

8 See paras. 10, 27 and 28 below.

9 TEU (Maastricht), Art. 49; European Council Presidency Conclusions, Copenhagen 22.6.1993, at 7(A)(iii).

(i.e. its ability to fulfil membership obligations and adhere to the aims of political, economic and monetary union).[10]

4.3.2. LEGAL CRITERIA

4.3.2.1. 'Open' Criteria

8 The accession procedure is set out in Article 56 of the EFTA Convention:

> 1. Any State may accede to this Convention, provided that the Council decides to approve its accession, on such terms and conditions as may be set out in that decision.
> 2. The Council may negotiate an agreement between the Member States and any other State, union of States or international organisation, creating an association embodying such reciprocal rights and obligations, common actions and special procedures as may be appropriate. Such an agreement shall be submitted to the Member States for acceptance and shall enter into force provided that it is accepted by all Member States.
> 3. Any State acceding to this Convention shall apply to become a party to the free trade agreements between the Member States on the one hand and third states, unions of states or international organisations on the other.

9 From the text of the aforementioned article it seems quite clear that there is no specific procedure, hence accession to EFTA depends widely on negotiations. Quite logically, barely any criteria for the qualification of a candidate can be found. Conditions and terms are to be defined by the EFTA states and the candidate country, subject to approval by the EFTA Council.

10 Besides the will to adhere to the objectives of the Association,[11] there are only four 'hard' legal criteria, two of which are spelled out in the respective Article 56 on accession and association, namely that only a state may become a member of EFTA and that 'any State acceding to this Convention

---

10 For more details, see Ch. Hillion, 'The Copenhagen Criteria and their Progeny' in Ch. Hillion (ed.), *EU Enlargement: A Legal Approach*, Hart Publishing, Oxford 2004, p. 2; N. Wammen, 'Enlargement Remains a Driver of Change' in *20 Years that Changed Europe – The Copenhagen Criteria and the Enlargement of the European Union*, conference report, Danish Presidency of the EU, Copenhagen 2013, p. 5.

11 Art. 1 EFTA Convention.

shall apply to become a party to the free trade agreements [FTAs] between the Member States on the one hand and third states, unions of states or international organisations on the other'.

Strictly speaking, the first legal criterion ('state') excludes dependent territories (for example the Faroes, Guernsey and the Aaland Islands), the logic of which becomes more apparent if applied to potential membership of the EEA. Taking the example of the Faroes: as long as Denmark remains in charge of their foreign policy, EFTA membership would lead to a situation where 'Copenhagen' could, for example in an EEA Joint Committee meeting, sit on both sides of the table. However, in 2016 the Faroes applied for membership in EFTA; the issue remaining pending.[12] 11

As to the second legal criterion, namely the obligation to apply to become a contracting party to EFTA's FTAs,[13] this could create problems for countries having concluded a (full) customs union with the EU, i.e. if the UK were to remain, after Brexit or in a new trade relationship, in the EU's Customs Union. Because by entering into such a customs union, these countries have waived their sovereign rights to an external trade policy of their own and submitted to the EU's external trade policy. It might, however, be less problematic in cases such as Turkey or Andorra, Monaco and San Marino. These are not fully integrated into the EU's Customs Area or only participate with regard to certain products. That would leave them free to at least join EFTA's FTAs in parts. 12

This criterion for candidates for EFTA membership to also apply to join EFTA's FTAs may, for economically less attractive states, also create problems with regard to their administration and renegotiation because this would require the third countries to agree to the FTAs being amended. However, many of EFTA's newer FTAs already contain provisions that allow the inclusion of further partners on EFTA's side.[14] 13

The very provision, however, only obliges candidate countries to *apply* to become a party; it does not say anything about the respective outcome being conditional upon membership of EFTA. Therefore, and because accession to EFTA depends considerably on negotiations and the interests of the parties, this requirement might also be waived. 14

---

12 H. Spongenberg, 'Faroe Islands seek closer EU relations', *EUObserver*, https://euobserver.com/foreign/24907.

13 Art. 56(3) EFTA Convention.

14 See e.g. Art. 10.4 of the FTA between the EFTA states and the Republic of Korea.

15 Another option might be an associated status[15] as this might make it easier for parties to waive the obligation of applying to become a party to EFTA's FTAs. An example of such an association, however not excluding that country from participating in FTAs, was Finland's status between 1960 and 1986. This was on some occasions advocated as a solution for the UK should it choose to (re-)join EFTA and either remain as part of the EU Customs Union or prefer to conclude its own trade agreements.[16] It would, at this point in time be mere speculation to enter further into this argument.

4.3.2.2. 'Hidden' Criteria

16 From the above it is obvious that the main text of the EFTA Convention does not really give much indication about what criteria parties interested in accession to EFTA would need to fulfil. The 'void' would thus have to be filled by indications in the preamble to the EFTA Convention. Some of these are, however, not very clear and will thus rather be used as indicators for analogous criteria in other treaties, agreements or conventions,[17] such as the Copenhagen Criteria.

17 Further to the two aforementioned criteria, the preamble to the EFTA Convention hides two criteria which could be seen as legally binding. One of them includes 'relations with the European Union, which are based on proximity, long-standing common values and European identity'.[18] While the latter two elements are less clear to define (see below), proximity seems to be one such legal criterion that would have to be taken into account in the case of a request for accession or association. This also fits with the criterion 'European State' in Article 128(1) EEA. As to the concrete delimitation of proximity it would be reasonable to refer to the respective definitions, including their uncertainties, in the context of the EU, particularly Article 8 TEU,[19] as this preamble of the EFTA Convention refers in any case to relations with the EU.

---

15 Art. 56(2) EFTA Convention.

16 D. Phinnemore and C. Najy, 'The Option of Association: The United Kingdom Post-Brexit and the European Free Trade Association, in *foraus-Policy Brief*, June 2017.

17 M. Paparinskis, 'Analogies and Other Regimes of International Law' in Z. Douglas, J. Pauwelyn and J.E. Viñuales (eds.), *The Foundations of International Investment Law: Bringing Theory into Practice*, Oxford University Press, Oxford 2014, p. 2.

18 6th preamble to the EFTA Convention.

19 K. Schmalenbach, 'Commentary to Article 8 TEU' in: Ch Calliess and M. Ruffert (eds.), *Kommentar zum EUV/AEUV*, 4th ed., Beck, Munich 2011, p. 163.

The question would therefore be whether e.g. Canada, otherwise clearly a like-minded country,[20] could become a member of EFTA. In principle, the relevant provision on accession says that 'any State may accede (…)'.[21] In contrast, the condition according to the EEA Agreement is that 'any European State becoming a member of EFTA may (…)'. If one, however refers to the 'hidden' criteria, the picture is less clear. One could stretch the meaning of 'proximity' as not needing to be understood in a strict geographic sense. The 'European identity', however, is a more delicate sub-criterion. That could, in turn, be dismissed as standing in the way because it rather refers to EFTA's aims than to an applicant's qualification. And the CETA[22] would clearly represent a 'privileged relationship (…) with the European Union'. In conclusion, given the generally flexible attitude of the current EFTA states it could at least not be excluded that the 'European identity' criterion would be an unsurmountable one. 18

A second preamble, again added with the revision of Vaduz in 2001, refers to the EFTA states' 'rights and obligations under the Agreement establishing the World Trade Organization' (WTO),[23] which implies that candidates for accession or association would have to abide by the same rules and, hence, be members of the WTO themselves.[24] 19

Such references to inter alia 'opening up the public procurement markets', 'appropriate protection of intellectual property rights', 'fair conditions of competition',[25] 'environmental policies' and 'the objective of sustainable development',[26] as well as 'recognised core labour standards',[27] suggest certain expectations with regard to potential partners. They should have a certain degree of economic development and, hence, the ability to show 20

---

20 M-P. Kothbauer-Liechtenstein and M. Kongshem, 'The Group of Like-Minded Countries within the OSCE' in IFSH (ed.), *OSCE Yearbook 2005*, Baden-Baden 2006, p. 89.

21 Art. 56(1) EFTA Convention.

22 Comprehensive Economic and Trade Agreement (CETA) between Canada, of the one part, and the European Union and its Member States, of the other part, OJ L 11, 14.1.2017, p. 23–1079.

23 8th preamble to the EFTA Convention.

24 Given that in 2014 the EFTA countries suspended negotiations on a FTA with the Russian-led customs union between Russia, Belarus and Kazakhstan because, among other reasons, only Russia was currently a WTO member, membership of the WTO must be all the more relevant in case of accession.

25 7th preamble to the EFTA Convention.

26 9th preamble to the EFTA Convention.

27 10th preamble to the EFTA Convention.

that there is a functioning market economy capable of competition: Does the country have a viable market economy? Is its economic structure of such a nature to allow it to become a full partner within the (internal) market(s), at least within a reasonable time? Is there enough economic stability to overcome a crisis?

21 This criterion is a complex one, especially when it becomes mixed up with a political point of view. In many cases where this issue has been raised in the political context in the past, membership of EFTA with a view to becoming a member of the EEA was envisaged because the potential candidate countries were not (yet) seen as fit to participate in the EU's internal market. However, the EEA essentially consists of the internal market. Hence, as long as participation in the internal market is the main characteristic feature of the EEA, and depending on the importance given to this very criterion, there is a lack of compatibility between the aspirant country and the agreement that the country aims to join.

22 Then, in view of a country's ability to fulfil EFTA/EEA membership obligations, the question of whether there is sufficient financial stability to share the costs and sufficient administrative capacity to sustain institutional participation in the EEA might be of relevance.

23 Finally, 'common values'[28] could be seen as also encompassing the stability of institutions guaranteeing democracy, the rule of law, human rights and respect for and protection of minorities. Hence, membership of organisations of which the EFTA states are members, such as the Council of Europe and the Organisation for Security and Cooperation in Europe, will inevitably require that certain standards are met. For example, fundamental rights should be safeguarded, stable institutions should be in place and the rule of law observed.

24 As mentioned above, this clearly reminds us of the 'Copenhagen Criteria'.[29] These apply, however, rather by analogy. In practical terms, such an approach is, for example and *a priori*, likely to exclude some, if not most of the southern Mediterranean countries, if the 'European identity' criterion

---

[28] 6th preamble to the EFTA Convention; 'They recognised that Ukraine as a European Country shares a common history and common values with the countries of the European Union' (European Council 2008: 5); currently Art. 1(2)(a) of the new EU-Ukraine Association Agreement, ratified in June 2014, states the aim 'to promote gradual rapprochement between the Parties based on common values'.

[29] See para. 7 above.

were to be seen as a compulsory one and, currently, certainly Belarus if we consider among others the 'WTO criterion'.

4.3.3. POLITICAL CRITERIA

Quite naturally, national interests of countries vary in terms of political criteria.[30] In the case of the EEA EFTA states it is fairly obvious: there is one comparably big country (Norway), a small country (Iceland) and a very small country (Liechtenstein). That already sets the tone as to who might not wish to be hampered by the smaller countries. While international law generally boils down to 'one country, one vote', international politics is rather about power politics. This may also explain Norway's interest in preserving its own predominance[31] within the EFTA pillar of the EEA, with the EEA thus becoming Norway's 'preserve' or *chasse gardée*. Two reasons may account for this: first, Norway pays about 90 per cent or more of the EEA institutions' budget and for cohesion and programme participation.[32] Secondly, it becomes much easier in a domestic discussion to support a view of a quasi-bilateral but non-EU way of integration. Therefore, Norway would like to see as little interference as possible from other countries, especially small ones. From this it also follows that Norway has no wish to include further small, or for that matter big, countries that would have a say without contributing as much. This might have been different if Iceland joined the EU, however, as maintaining the EEA EFTA pillar in its current form would have proved to be very challenging with only two members. 25

Moreover, in case of an accession to EFTA, perhaps with the aim of joining the EEA, Switzerland forms part of the equation even though it is not a member of the EEA. In recent discussions Switzerland seems to rather value its relations with its EFTA partners, particularly Norway, higher than the interest in having another (small) country join EFTA and 26

---

30 With reference to Hans Kelsen, see M. García-Salmones Rovira, 'The Politics of Interest in International Law', *European Journal of International Law*, 2014, 25, pp. 782–783.

31 It is, however, interesting to note that Norway does, in the context of the G20, oppose larger nations behaving in a comparable manner. See interview of J. Gahr Støre (Norwegian foreign minister), 'One of the Greatest Setbacks Since World War II', *Spiegel Online*, 2010, https://www.spiegel.de/international/europe/norway-takes-aim-at-g-20-one-of-the-greatest-setbacks-since-world-war-ii-a-702104.html.

32 See Ch. 6.

therefore generally does not appear to contradict the Norwegian position, also because it does not want to be involved in matters ultimately affecting the EEA.

27 There have not been many requests to join EFTA. The request by Algeria announced in the Swiss press[33] to our knowledge did not go further than being evoked alongside a Swiss ministerial visit to Algiers. More seriously, in 2005 the Faroe Islands did enquire about EFTA membership, a request that was renewed in 2016.[34] However, with the only clear legal criterion being that an applicant must be a state, the Islands face the problem of an unclear situation (to outsiders) regarding its sovereignty and the possibility of representing itself in foreign policy matters.

28 Another candidate that could not be dismissed as easily was Slovenia, which applied for EFTA membership soon after its independence. However, the EFTA states were ultimately not ready to go beyond the conclusion of a simple FTA[35] and rejected its application in autumn 1995. Slovenia ultimately became a full member of the EU in 2004.

4.3.4. 'SOFT' CRITERIA

29 Under the heading of political criteria, 'soft' criteria also need to be mentioned. The problem is that these are, by nature, difficult to define precisely and the countries to which they are attributed might not even want to admit that such criteria exist. However, the discussion about Turkey with regard to its EU membership and the image of the EU as a 'club of Christian nations' can be presupposed as a known fact.[36] There is also the talk of prejudices[37] or 'national identity'[38] and, finally, the size of

---

33 See interview of P. Couchepin (Swiss minister of economy), 'Couchepin unterstützt EFTA Beitritt Algeriens', *news.ch 2007*, http://www.news.ch/Couchepin+unterstuetzt+EFTA+Beitritt+Algeriens/276756/detail.htm.

34 See n. 12 above.

35 FTA between the EFTA states and Slovenia of 13 June 1995, since 2004 replaced by the respective agreements between the EFTA States and the EU.

36 E. Shakman Hurd, 'What is Driving the European Debate about Turkey?', *Insight Turkey*, 2010, 12, p. 185.

37 A. Zick, T.F. Pettigrew and U. Wagner, 'Ethnic Prejudice and Discrimination in Europe', *Journal of Social Issues*, 2008, 64, pp. 233–251.

38 A. Von Bogdandy and St. Schill, 'Die Achtung der nationalen Identität unter dem reformierten Unionsvertrag', *Zeitschrift für ausländisches öffentliches Recht und Völkerrecht*, 2010, 70, pp. 711–715; T.H. Eriksen, *Immigration and national identity in Norway, Migration Policy Institute*, Washington D.C. 2013, pp. 4, 8.

the country.[39] Based on that argument, Norway's then Minister of Foreign Affairs, reacting to the Commission's praise of the EEA Agreement as a model for other non-EU Western European countries, including Andorra, Monaco and San Marino, responded that 'the EEA framework was negotiated and established among states having more diverse economies and with larger administrative capacity'.[40] His Icelandic counterpart supported him on this. That more or less ended the discussion. Since 2015, Andorra, Monaco and San Marino have been negotiating 'one or several' association agreement(s) with the EU.[41] Negotiations are ongoing.

4.4. ASSOCIATION

Next to membership, there is also the possibility of an association. Hence, 30
'the Council may negotiate an agreement between the Member States and any other State, union of States or international organisation, creating an association embodying such reciprocal rights and obligations, common actions and special procedures as may be appropriate'.[42] This association can take more or less any form from 'lesser' membership to a FTA. It was, however, not intended to be the basis for the EEA Agreement, as some argue.[43] The provision, already contained in the original EFTA Convention of 1960,[44] aimed at giving a legal basis for politically delicate cases, such as Finland. It may later be used as the basis for the EFTA state's FTAs, although normally no mention is made thereof. The same may be true with the EEA Agreement, although it was rather the EFTA states joining the EU's internal market and not the other way around.

---

39 See G. Baur, 'Who can join the European Economic Area?' in S. Gstöhl (ed.), *The European Neighbourhood Policy in a Comparative Perspective*, Routledge, London and New York 2016, p. 65.

40 EEA Council, 'Draft minutes of the 38th meeting of the EEA Council', Council document EEE 1609/12, Brussels, 26.11.2012, p. 31.

41 For a recent overview, see F. Maiani, 'Unique, yet archetypal: relations between the European Union and Andorra, Monaco and San Marino' in S. Gstöhl and D. Phinnemore (eds.), *The Proliferation of Privileged Partnerships between the European Union and its Neighbours*, pp. 84–101.

42 Art. 56(2) EFTA Convention.

43 E.D. Stratenschulte, 'Die europäische Einbahnstrasse – in beide Richtungen gesperrt! Der Europäische Wirtschaftsraum als Möglichkeit der Integration Osteuropas?' in H. Høybraaten and J. Hille (eds.), *Northern Europe and the Future of the EU/Nordeuropa und die Zukunft der EU*, Berliner Wissenschaftsverlag and Intersentia, Berlin and Cambridge 2011, pp. 143–159.

44 Art. 41(2) EFTA Convention (1960).

31 As to Finland's case, one has to see this in the context of the Cold War where Finland had managed, with difficulty and bravery, to remain independent after 1945, however, at the price of not daring to antagonise the Soviet Union. On the one hand, it thus had to remain neutral in a sense that fully joining EFTA was difficult in the light of the UK being its driving force and at the same time one of the Soviet Union's major antagonists. On the other hand, the UK was Finland's prime export market. Or as the Swiss government put it at the time:

> 'De fait, la Finlande était placée devant l'alternative suivante: Ou bien elle s'associait à l'AELE, sous une forme ou sous une autre, ce qui la mettait en mesure de se présenter à armes égales avec les pays Scandinaves sur le marché britannique, son principal débouché; ou bien elle restait en dehors de l'AELE, réduisait son commerce avec l'Europe occidentale et dépendait de plus en plus étroitement des marchés des pays de l'Est.'[45]

32 In reality, EFTA Council meetings and those of 'FIN-EFTA' were held jointly. The agendas were virtually identical. There were certain substantial differences with regard to trade issues covered. It would, however, go beyond the remit of this introduction to extend on this. In 1986, the relations with the Soviet bloc having started to thaw, Finland was able to drop its reservations and fully joined EFTA.

4.5. WITHDRAWAL

33 The provisions on withdrawal from EFTA are quite straightforward: any EFTA state may withdraw from the Convention provided that it gives 12 months' notice in writing to the Depositary, currently Norway, which shall notify the other EFTA states.[46] Major withdrawals happened in 1972/1973, when Denmark and the UK joined the EU and in 1994/1995, when Austria, Finland and Sweden joined the EU. Portugal left in between, in 1986. When Denmark and the UK left, a problem with regard to timing occurred: Denmark (and Norway, where a referendum did not go favourably and the government had to withdraw its wish to join the EEC)

---

[45] Message of the Swiss Federal Council to the Parliament on the Association Agreement between the EFTA states and Finland of 9 May 1961, FF 1961 1039 (French); BBl. 1961 1048 (German).

[46] Art. 57(1) EFTA Convention.

could not keep to the notice period for constitutional reasons and had to ask the other EFTA states for a shortening of the delay according to the Convention.[47] This was, of course, granted. This serves only to demonstrate the relative flexibility the EFTA states usually apply when applying the provisions of the Convention. This is, however, not to say they would not keep their commitments. But in cases such as the one just described, EFTA states often seem rather willing to apply common sense.

Of course, before leaving, the bill must be settled. This not only applies when the UK leaves the EU. Hence, 'before the withdrawal takes effect, the Member States shall agree on appropriate arrangements and equitable cost-sharing relating to the withdrawal'.[48] This may be fairly easy as long as there is no complicated budgetary structure due to a high degree of integration. Already the departure of Austria, Finland and Sweden was quite complicated, given their engagement in EU programmes they had participated in as EFTA states. It was even more complicated to take them out of the commitments in the Financial Mechanism, the EEA EFTA states' cohesion fund, as this happened in the middle of an ongoing period. But nothing compares to extricating the UK from its commitments as an EU member state. 34

4.6. EFTA INSTITUTIONS

4.6.1. INTRODUCTION

EFTA is an intergovernmental organisation. By definition, there is little room for any political organs or institutions which might exercise any sovereign rights on behalf of the EFTA states. Supranational elements are therefore missing. This is in contrast to the EEA, where the EFTA Surveillance Authority and the EFTA Court provide such services. These are EFTA bodies but only in the context of the EEA. They do not have a bearing on the running of EFTA as an organisation. Nevertheless, there is the need for certain institutions to run smoothly even an organisation such as EFTA. 35

---

47 Message of the Swiss Federal Council to the Parliament on the Agreements between Switzerland and the EU (Free Trade Agreement etc.) of 16 August 1972, FF 1972 706 (French); BBl. 1972 717 (German).

48 Art. 57(2) EFTA Convention.

36 Generally, the structure can be described as the EFTA Council, i.e. the EFTA states, at the centre with a set of committees of different kinds tasked by it and some advisory bodies, around it. The EFTA Secretariat, which coordinates the work of EFTA, not only with regard to the EFTA Convention, but also on EEA matters, acts on the orders of the Council.

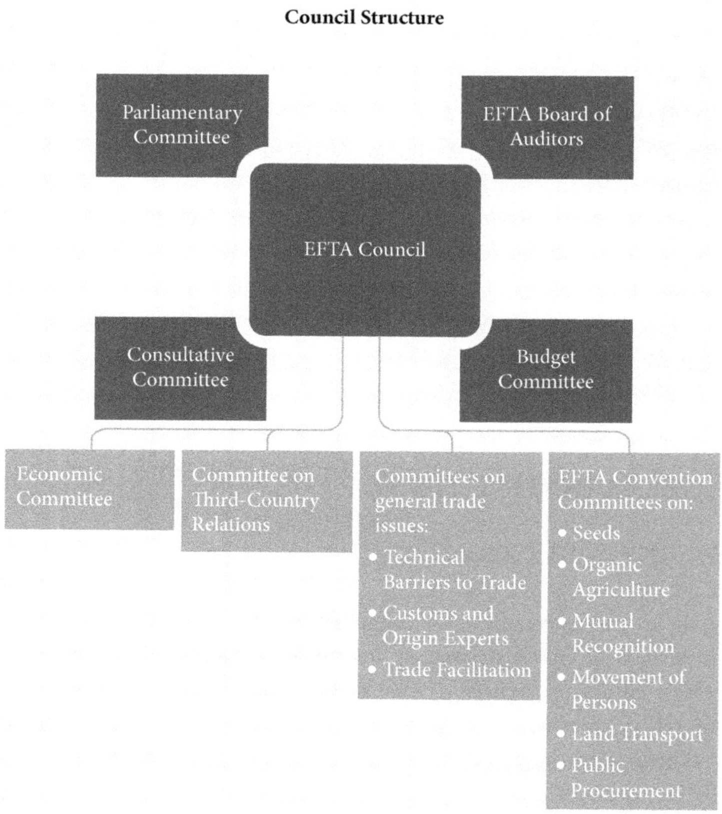

Figure 4.1. Council structure
Source: EFTA Secretariat.

4.6.2. THE EFTA COUNCIL

37 The EFTA Council normally works at two levels: at ministerial level it meets twice a year and decides major issues, often of a political nature.

The regular work of the Council is done at ambassadors' level in about eight meetings throughout the year. The EFTA Council is responsible for the correct application and functioning of the EFTA Convention. In particular, it is the Council's responsibility:

- to exercise the powers and functions conferred on by the EFTA Convention;
- to decide on amendments to the EFTA Convention;
- to supervise the application of the EFTA Convention and keep its operation under review;
- to consider whether further action should be taken by the EFTA states in order to promote the attainment of EFTA's objectives;
- to facilitate the establishment of closer links with other states and unions of states;
- to seek to establish relationships with other international organisations to facilitate the attainment of EFTA's objectives;
- to negotiate trade and cooperation agreements between the EFTA states and any other state, union of states or international organisation;
- to endeavour to resolve disputes that may arise regarding the interpretation or application of the EFTA Convention; and
- to consider any other matter that may affect the operation of the EFTA Convention.[49]

Furthermore, the Council has the power to amend the provisions regarding the Annexes[50] as well as the substance of the following Annexes, unless otherwise provided for therein: 38

- A on rules of origin;
- H on the procedure for the provision of information in the field of technical regulations and of rules on information society services;
- S on organs committees and other bodies set up by the Council; and
- T on Arbitration.

This competence also includes amendments to the Appendices to the following Annexes:

- E on seeds;
- F on organic agriculture;

[49] Art. 43(1) EFTA Convention.
[50] Art. 53(2) EFTA Convention.

- K on the (free) movement of persons;
- P on land transport;
- Q on air transport; and
- R on public procurement.

This leaves Annex B (on mutual administrative assistance in customs matters), C and D, both repealed,[51] G (on SPS), I (on TBT: mutual recognition of conformity assessments), J (intellectual property rights), L, M, N, O (national reservations on investment and services) and U (territorial application). These mostly contain provisions that depend on international or European law or that need to be decided by parliaments at national level, as they touch upon constitutional rights, and can therefore not be amended by the national executives or their representatives in the EFTA Council.

39 The Council also has a role as facilitator, mediator or platform for discussions as it shall facilitate the mutual exchange of information and consultations between the EFTA states, between the EFTA states and third states, international associations or international organisations. It is called to settle disputes submitted to it prior to an eventual arbitration procedure.[52]

40 The Convention authorises the Council to set up bodies, other committees or working groups, in addition to the committees provided for by the Convention.[53]

41 It follows from EFTA's qualification as an intergovernmental organisation that in principle every member state is represented, has one vote and decisions are to be taken 'by unanimous vote'. This, however, is to be understood as decision taking by consensus[54] because 'decisions or

51 Council Decision No. 2/2012.

52 Art. 47 EFTA Convention.

53 Art. 43(3) EFTA Convention and Annex S thereto.

54 As to the difference between unanimous and by consensus, see G. Baur, 'Will New Developments in Global Economic and Financial Policy Erode International Law and the Sovereignty of States? – the Example of Liechtenstein' in M. Kohen (ed.), *Promoting Justice, Human Rights and Conflict Resolution through International Law / La promotion de la justice, des droits de l'homme et du règlement des conflits par le droit international – Liber Amicorum Lucius Caflisch*, Brill-Nijhoff, Leiden 2007, pp. 1015–1036.

recommendations shall be regarded as unanimous unless any Member State casts a negative vote'.[55]

The Council as such can only issue recommendations. Its decisions are those of the EFTA states according to their own internal procedures. The same applies to any amendment to the EFTA Convention.[56] The execution of the decisions is ensured by the individual EFTA states. 42

4.6.3. COMMITTEES AND OTHER BODIES ASSISTING THE COUNCIL[57]

As mentioned above,[58] the Council has the power to set up organs, committees and other bodies, as it considers necessary to assist it in accomplishing its tasks. This competence was used generously and a large number of committees and expert groups have been established which report directly to the EFTA Council.[59] 43

There are, e.g., the following expert groups: Group of State aid experts; Group of experts on public procurement; Group of experts on intellectual property; Group of experts on price compensation; Group of experts on services, investment and establishment; Group of experts on efficient trade procedures; and Group of legal experts. These expert groups may also work across EFTA and EEA matters. 44

The Council is assisted by, essentially, two categories of committees: first, there are those entrusted with specific tasks within the scope of EFTA. Secondly, there are committees entrusted with updating the annexes to the EFTA Convention. The latter were introduced after the EFTA Convention was amended in 2001. 45

With that amendment, a certain 'dynamic' adaptation of law was introduced. The term 'dynamic' in this context describes the fact that whenever there 46

---

55 Art. 43(5) EFTA Convention.

56 Art. 59 EFTA Convention.

57 Baur, Sánchez-Rydelski and Zatschler (n. 1 above) pp. 25–29 apply a slightly different structure to those committees. This, however, is rather a matter of where one puts the emphasis and, thus, of taste. With regard to substance this description mostly follows the former.

58 See para. 40 above.

59 See Annex S to the EFTA Convention.

is a development in the relationship between Switzerland and the EU, or between the EEA EFTA states and the EU respectively, the annexes of the EFTA Convention are, in principle, to be amended accordingly.[60] The term 'dynamic' stems from EEA law. However, given the different context and institutional set-up, the procedures of amending the annexes are not the same.[61] In the context of EFTA, one should therefore rather speak of 'quasi-dynamic' adoption of new law.

4.6.3.1. Committees Entrusted with Specific Tasks

47 The committees having specific tasks, which are not related to the updating of the EFTA Convention, are, e.g.:

- the Committee on TBT;[62]
- the Committee of Origin and Customs Experts;[63] and
- the Committee on Trade Facilitation.[64]

These committees essentially make reports and proposals to the Council which is then to take respective decisions.

48 There are three cases that merit particular attention due to their more horizontal roles. First, the Committee on Third-Country Relations[65] has a coordinating role with regard to the negotiation of FTAs and matters related to their functioning. It also prepares joint committee meetings under declarations of cooperation, recommendations on other third-country matters and other issues that the EFTA Council might task it with.

49 The second in this category is the Budget Committee.[66] It is in charge of establishing EFTA's annual budget.[67] Furthermore, it carries out tasks

---

60 G. Baur, 'EFTA: eine Freihandelszone mit Binnenmarktelementen' in A. Epiney and L. Hehemann, *Schweizerisches Jahrbuch für Europarecht/Annuaire suisse de droit européen 2016/2017*, Stämpfli/Schulthess, Berne/Zurich 2017, pp. 366–7.

61 See Ch. 6.

62 Council Decision No. 10/84, as amended by Council Decision Nos 8/88 and 4/94. The Committee on Technical Barriers to Trade discusses standardisation and conformity assessment policies.

63 Council Decision No. 8/74, as amended by Council Decision No. 4/92.

64 Council Decision No. 1/2010.

65 Council Decision No. 2/96.

66 Council Decision No. 10/60.

67 See para. 40 below.

assigned to it either by the Financial Regulations[68] or the EFTA Council. Each EFTA state is represented on the Budget Committee. The EFTA Budget covers not only the projected costs of running the Association according to its tasks set out in the EFTA Convention. It also includes the figures regarding costs likely to be incurred in the three EEA EFTA states' participation in the EEA. Hence, the two parts also divide costs – based on GDP figures – in a different manner: once between all four EFTA states, once between Iceland, Liechtenstein and Norway only.

The third case is the Economic Committee.[69] It normally exchanges views on economic policy in the EFTA states and conducts a dialogue on such matters with the EU on economic and monetary problems and policies. In the latter case it also prepares the annual EFTA ECOFIN ministerial meeting. That meeting serves to exchange information and views between the EFTA and the EU ministers of finance and/or economy. It was, in October 2014, exceptionally used to agree between the EEA EFTA states and the EU on a political way forward on how to incorporate the new financial supervisory structure into the EEA.[70] This also shows that distinctions between EFTA and the EEA can sometimes be blurred. 50

4.6.3.2. *Committees Entrusted with Updating the EFTA Convention*

Certain committees have been tasked, since 2002, with regularly updating the EFTA Convention. These are the committees responsible for: 51

- air transport;
- land transport;
- (free) movement of persons;
- conformity assessment;
- organic agriculture;

---

68 EFTA's Financial Rules and Regulations contain the rules applicable to setting up EFTA's budget as well as to its auditing.

69 Council Decision No. 16/64, as amended by Council Decision No. 11/73 and replaced by EFTA/C.SR 9/95 (EFTA/EC 1/95).

70 See http://data.consilium.europa.eu/doc/document/ST-14178-2014-REV-1/de/pdf. Printed (English) in the Annex to G. Baur, 'Les autorités de surveillance européennes et les Etats EEE-AELE' in C. Kaddous and S. Matthey (eds.) *Services financiers*, Schulthess, Geneva 2016, pp. 363–378.

- public procurement; and
- seeds.[71]

52 These committees normally elaborate recommendations to the Council to amend certain provisions of the annexes according to the development either in the respective BAs between Switzerland and the EU or the EEA Agreement. It will then be up to the Council to take the respective decision (or not). The Committee on Mutual Recognition in Relation to Conformity Assessment, however, has a decision-making competence of its own: it is entitled to decide itself on certain amendments to the annex on mutual recognition in relation to conformity assessment.[72] Of course, it has to notify the EFTA Council of its decisions without delay.

4.6.4. THE EFTA BOARD OF AUDITORS

53 The Board of Auditors (EBoA)[73] is as the supreme auditing authority of EFTA and reports directly to the EFTA Council. It is responsible for the audit of the accounts of the EFTA Secretariat, the EFTA Surveillance Authority and the EFTA Court. Furthermore, it is the EU Court of Auditors' equivalent for the control and auditing of the EEA EFTA states' contributions in the context of their participation in EU programmes.

54 The composition of the EBoA varies depending on the body to be audited. If the EFTA Secretariat is being audited, all four EFTA states will be represented on the board. If, however, the EFTA Surveillance Authority or the EFTA Court is being audited, the EBoA only consists of the three members from the EEA EFTA states. In reality, however, the Swiss representative will in such cases act as an observer.

55 The members of the EBoA are independent in the performance of their duties. Their work is, however, defined by a mandate as well as terms of reference governing the audits. These are different depending on whether

[71] See respectively Council Decision Nos. 5/2002; 6/2002; 7/2002; 8/2002; 9/2002; 10/2002 and 11/2002 of 18 June 2002 (copies of these decisions can be requested from the EFTA Secretariat in Geneva).

[72] Annex I to the EFTA Convention.

[73] EFTA/C.SR 14/92 (EFTA/EEA 46/92 para. 14) and Council Decision No. 6/98.

it is the EFTA Secretariat, the EFTA Surveillance Authority or the EFTA Court that is to be audited according to their respective Financial Regulations.

4.6.5. POLITICAL ADVISORY COMMITTEES

Another category of committees includes those advising the EFTA Council from a political point of view. These are, as will soon become clear, not acting under its orders as they have a political mandate. These are the Committee of Members of Parliament (CMP)[74] and the Consultative Committee (CC).[75] 56

The CMP has up to five members from the national parliament of each EFTA state. They elect one of their peers as their Chair by a simple majority of the members present for a term of one year. The CMP normally holds four meetings per year, in addition to the two customary joint meetings with EFTA ministers. They discuss issues of general interest with regard to EFTA and they may issue resolutions or ask the Council for information. Recently the CMP, e.g., repeatedly asked the Council for information on the implications of Brexit for EFTA and its relationship with the UK. A further task is to support the Council in its FTA negotiations with third countries, especially to convey the parliamentary perspective to their counterparts in the FTA-partner countries' parliaments. 57

The entry into force of the EEA Agreement in 1994 formally led to the existence of two EFTA Parliamentary Committees. Next to the CMP there is also the EEA Joint Parliamentary Committee which, on the EFTA side, is composed of the same members from Iceland, Liechtenstein and Norway. These essentially discuss EEA matters with their colleagues from the European Parliament that form the EU part of the EEA Parliamentary Committee. They normally issue resolutions on issues that are debated in the EU and/or the EFTA states and which are of relevance to the EEA. Switzerland's representatives in the CMP may 58

[74] Council Decision No. 11/77.

[75] Council Decision No. 5/61, as amended by Council Decision Nos 10/68, 11/88, 1/94 and 2/94.

take part as observers in the meetings of the EEA Joint Parliamentary Committee and the Committee of Members of Parliament of the EFTA Countries, which deals with all other matters, including relations with third countries.

59 The Consultative Committee is the second of these advisory bodies. Representatives of industry and labour (trade unions and employers' organisations as well as industry representatives) in the EFTA states exchange views as well among themselves and with the EFTA Council. Normally, six members from Norway, four members each from Iceland and Switzerland and two from Liechtenstein participate in meetings of the Committee. The CC elects a Chair and two Vice-Chairs, chosen from among its members, with a term of office of two years. The European organisations – to name but the largest of these: ETUC (European Trade Union Confederation) and BusinessEurope (Confederation of European Business) – may send one observer each.

60 The CC usually holds three to four internal meetings per year, in addition to the annual joint meeting with the Standing Committee of the EFTA states. Biannually, the EFTA social partners meet with the EFTA Council at ministerial level: in the spring with ministers from all four EFTA states and in the autumn with the 'Ministerial Chair'. Annual meetings with the Committee of Members of Parliament ensure an exchange of views between social partners and parliamentarians of the EFTA states.

61 Again, the entry into force of the EEA Agreement led to the establishment of a respective Joint EEA Consultative Committee. In addition to the CC members from Iceland, Liechtenstein and Norway, social partners' representatives from the EU's Economic and Social Council (ECOSOC) discuss relevant matters with regard to the EEA. The Swiss representatives may participate as observers in this EEA body as well.

62 The third and least-known advisory body, the so-called EEA EFTA Forum, was set up by a decision of the Standing Committee of the EFTA states[76] as an informal body to involve elected representatives from local and

[76] Decision of the Standing Committee of the EFTA States No. 10/2009/SC of 3 December 2009 establishing a Forum of Elected Representatives of Local and Regional Authorities of the EEA EFTA States.

regional authorities in EEA matters. The Forum works closely with other EEA EFTA bodies and has established links with the Committee of the Regions of the European Union, an EU advisory body that was established in 1994 just after the signing of the EEA Agreement. It has 12 full members, six from Iceland and six from Norway. Switzerland is currently participating as an observer and Liechtenstein has decided not to take part for the time being.

4.6.6. THE EFTA SECRETARIAT

The administration of the Agreement, together with the preparation of meetings and documents, is the responsibility of the EFTA Secretariat. This includes the main EFTA activities, such as the relationship between the EFTA states and their support for the negotiation of FTAs, and also the bulk of the management of the EEA Agreement. 63

The EFTA Secretariat, from a legal point of view, only provides services to the EFTA states, comparable for example to the Council Secretariat for the EU. It does not – formally – have an active role or act, e.g. as 'guardian of the treaties', such as the EU Commission. Nevertheless, the EFTA Secretariat is, of course, expected to have a 'proactive' attitude, which will allow the EFTA states to make their decisions. For this reason, the EFTA Secretariat regularly draws up notes to the EFTA states, which contain analyses of legal or political problems and, where appropriate, proposals to resolve them. In the context of the EEA Agreement, however, the EFTA Secretariat's role is more extensive, although it is not even mentioned in the EEA Agreement. It is, for instance, tasked with preparing in detail the incorporation of EU law into the EEA Agreement. In all cases it normally serves as the Secretariat of the different committees and bodies in both EFTA and EEA EFTA matters.[77] The respective officer is inter alia to prepare agendas, draft the minutes, coordinate with other bodies as may be necessary and report to the Council or the Standing Committee if invited to. 64

[77] See G. Baur, 'Decision-Making Procedure and Implementation of New Law' in C. Baudenbacher (ed.), *The Handbook of EEA Law*, Cham, Heidelberg etc. 2016, p. 53.

65 There are about 90 staff employed with the EFTA Secretariat in Geneva, Brussels and Luxembourg. Nominally, also the staff of the Financial Mechanism Office (FMO) in Brussels, managing the EFTA- and Norwegian Financial Mechanisms ('EEA Grants' and 'Norway Grants'), are part of the EFTA Secretariat. These additional 80 people or so, however, are in reality 'governed' by the Financial Mechanism Committee (FMC), which consists of representatives of Iceland, Liechtenstein and Norway. The odd structure was chosen to allow the FMO to be covered by EFTA's seat agreement with the Belgian government.

4.7. PROCEDURES

4.7.1. INTRODUCTION

66 The decision-making procedure in EFTA is quite straightforward. As mentioned before, it is, with very few exceptions,[78] the EFTA Council that is competent to take decisions.[79] However, with the amendment of the EFTA Convention in 2001, a 'quasi-dynamic' way of adopting new law has been introduced.[80] Hence, procedures concerning how new law is to be introduced in the annexes of the EFTA Convention needed to be developed.

67 Another procedure of interest is that for dispute resolution. This has been introduced with the amended EFTA Convention as well. In the 40 years before that there was only very light dispute resolution between the EFTA states, i.e. political discussion and mediation by the Council, but no proper arbitration.

4.7.2. LEGISLATION AND/OR ADOPTION

68 The introduction of a procedure to adopt new law into the EFTA Convention depending on developments in the bilateral relationship

[78] See para. 52 above.
[79] See 4.6.2 above.
[80] See para. 46 above.

between Switzerland and the EU or the EEA respectively is based on the following declaration by the EFTA Council:

> 'The Member States endeavour to regularly update the Convention in order to take account of developments of the Agreement on the European Economic Area and of the bilateral agreements of 21 June 1999 between the Swiss Confederation on the one hand and the European Community and it's Member States on the other. In particular the Member States shall within 3 months after the entry into force of the Agreement amending the Convention establishing the European Free Trade Association of 21 June 2001, align the Convention to common developments of the EEA Agreement and the Swiss – EC bilateral agreements.'[81]

From a substantive point of view this means 'autonomous re-enactment' of 69
EU law by own volition. This is well known to the Swiss from their practice of introducing EU law into national law – beyond the obligations under the BAs – although not being forced to do so.[82] Hence, the legal development within the respective framework for the transfer of substantive EU law, either into the BAs or the EEA Agreement,[83] is reflected in the relationship between the four EFTA states. For example, Regulation (EC) No. 883/2004 on the coordination of social security schemes[84] was incorporated into the EEA-Agreement as well as into the AFMP between Switzerland and the EU.[85] It has therefore been incorporated into Appendix 2 of Annex K to the EFTA Convention.[86]

However, the EFTA states are not obliged to incorporate any EU law, 70
unless they decide so by common accord. Therefore, e.g., in the chapter on

---

81 SGN 7/2001 para. 18, adopted by the EFTA-Council on 22.2.2002.

82 See e.g. F. Maiani, 'Legal Europeanization as Legal Transformation: Some In-sights from Swiss "Outer Europe"', EUI Working Papers MWP 2008/32; M. Oesch, 'Switzerland and the European Union', Dike/Nomos, Zurich/St. Gallen 2018; A. Heinemann, 'Rechtliche Transplantate zwischen Europäischer Union und der Schweiz' in L. Fahrländer et. al. (eds.), *Europäisierung der schweizerischen Rechtsordnung*, Dike, Zürich, St. Gallen 2013, pp. 21–24.

83 i.e. including, as the case may be, adaptions, exceptions etc., see Baur (n. 77 above) pp. 57–60.

84 Regulation (EC) No. 883/2004 of the European Parliament and of the Council of 29 April 2004 on the coordination of social security systems, OJ L 166, 30.4.2004, pp. 1–123.

85 Agreement between the European Community and its Member States and the Swiss Confederation on the free movement of persons, OJ L 114, 30.4.2002, pp. 6–72.

86 Council Decision No. 5/2015.

services there was very little adoption of new law. Although services are clearly covered by the EFTA Convention,[87] the EFTA states are less keen to follow the development in EU law in order to apply it among themselves than in other sectors. On the one hand, this can be seen from the different reservations they made,[88] on the other this shows in the fact that, e.g., neither the so-called Services Directive[89] nor major parts of the financial services acquis were incorporated into the EFTA Convention. This may perhaps also be explained by the fact that these are – unlike in the EEA – not covered by the BAs between Switzerland and the EU. However, this seems in practice not to have harmed economic relations between the EFTA states in any way.

71 In procedural terms, the steps usually followed for the amendment of the annexes to the EFTA Convention are as follows:

- Switzerland, by way of a contact point in the Swiss administration, informs EEA EFTA experts, the EFTA Secretariat and the Council, as the case may be, on developments under the BAs between Switzerland and the EU.
- The EFTA Secretariat informs the relevant committees about developments regarding EU legal acts to be incorporated into the EEA Agreement and the BAs.
- Meetings of the committees are to be called and prepared by the EFTA Secretariat following instructions of the committees' chairpersons.
- The Secretariat prepares draft reports from the committee meetings as well as any draft recommendations on acts being considered for integration into the EFTA Convention, including any proposed adjustments or any problems otherwise encountered.
- After having received comments from the committee, the EFTA Secretariat finalises the report including any draft decision and puts these on the agenda of the forthcoming meeting of the Council.
- The committees may perform their aforementioned tasks by written procedure.
- The Council normally adopts such decisions as 'A points', i.e. without further discussion. The amendments to the annexes are then to be published by the EFTA Secretariat.

[87] Arts. 29–35 EFTA Convention; see Ch. 2.
[88] Annexes L-O to the EFTA Convention.
[89] Directive 2006/123/EC of the European Parliament and of the Council of 12 December 2006 on services in the internal market, OJ L 376, 27.12.2006, pp. 36–68.

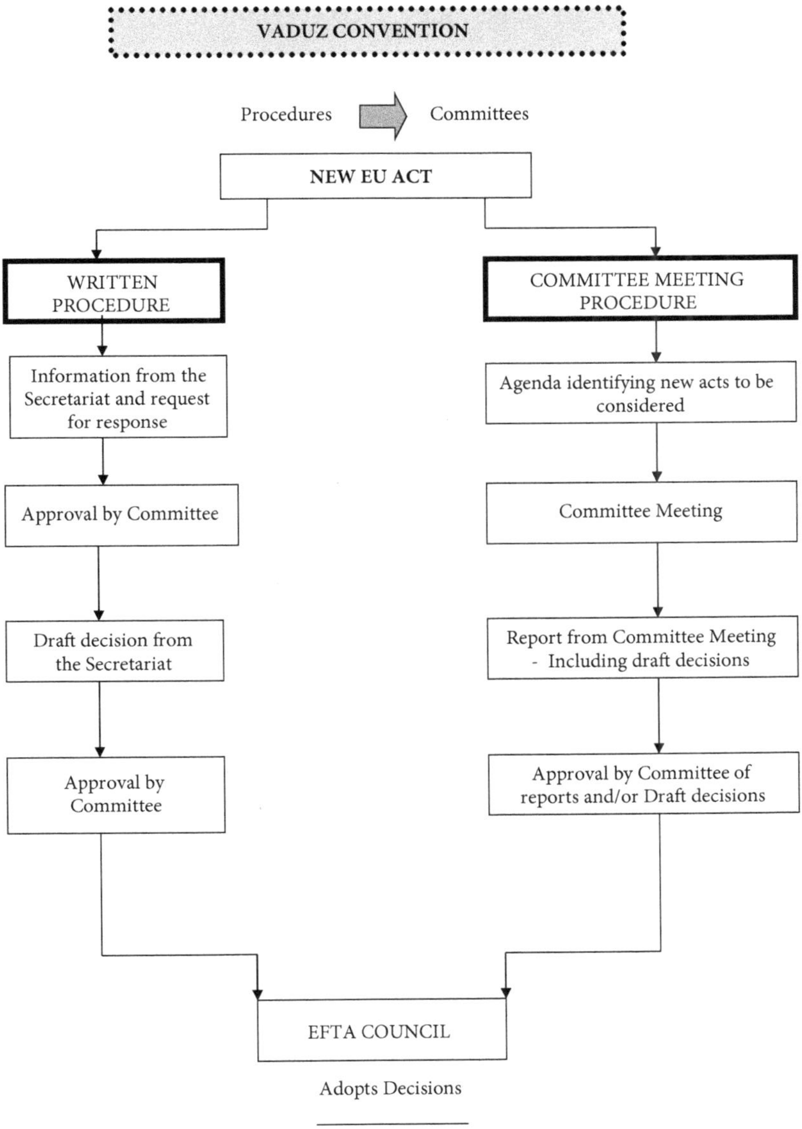

Figure 4.2. Vaduz Convention
Source: EFTA Secretariat.

4.7.3. DISPUTE RESOLUTION AND ENFORCEMENT

72 As mentioned before, the EFTA Convention, up to its revision, did not provide for a proper dispute resolution mechanism. This is, up to a certain point, a logical consequence of the fundamentally intergovernmental nature of EFTA. Furthermore, as long as the substantial scope of EFTA focused on trade in goods and related items, not many disputes were likely to arise. During the first 40 years of EFTA's existence, there were only very few disputes. Given the much broader scope of the revised EFTA Convention and the introduction of the triangular relationship[90] with regard to the incorporation of new legal acts, the introduction of a dispute settlement mechanism was called for.[91] The scope of this mechanism generally extends to all issues covered by the EFTA Convention.[92]

4.7.3.1. Consultation

73 Before resorting to arbitration, the EFTA states must hold consultations.[93] These are to be held between the parties to the dispute, and, where appropriate, in the Council, in order to settle the dispute at an early stage. Those states that are not involved in the dispute must be notified. The Council will not deal with a matter until this has been requested by an EFTA state.

4.7.3.2. Arbitration

74 Arbitration may be initiated by any EFTA state if the dispute cannot be resolved by consultation within 45 days.[94] Any EFTA state not involved in the dispute will be notified. It may choose to be a party to the proceedings so that it can make known its views.[95] A three-party arbitral tribunal shall first determine whether there is any merit to the claim and, if appropriate, propose measures to remedy the situation. The judgments of the arbitral tribunal are binding and final for all EFTA states involved in the dispute.[96]

---

90 See Ch. 3.
91 Ch. XVII, Arts. 46–48 EFTA Convention.
92 Art. 46 EFTA Convention.
93 Art. 47 EFTA Convention.
94 Art. 48 EFTA Convention.
95 Art. 48(2) EFTA Convention.
96 Art. 48(3) EFTA Convention.

If declared unlawful, the contested measures set by the defendant are either to be annulled or compensated.[97] If the defendant EFTA state continues to fail to comply, this can ultimately lead to the suspension of advantages provided for in the EFTA Convention or by related agreements. This could, for instance, be the withdrawal of preferential tariffs (or the application of duties where they were actually discontinued) because, e.g., the prerequisites for preferential accumulation are not fulfilled (anymore). 75

Contrary to the EEA Agreement and in accordance with its intragovernmental character, the EFTA Convention does not provide for any procedure in favour of individuals. Claims which persons or companies may have are to be brought before the national courts of the EFTA states. 76

4.8. FINANCES

Every organisation needs to be properly funded to attain its objectives. For EFTA, it is the Council which holds the respective competence and responsibility to set out the necessary financial arrangements.[98] This includes establishing a budget and fixing the appropriate shares of those expenses between the EFTA states. The respective procedures have been laid down in EFTA's Financial Regulations and Rules 77

Every year, the Secretary General submits a budget proposal to the EFTA Council at least six months before the beginning of the financial year. That is accompanied by a performance plan, which describes the main aims and expected results of the services provided by the EFTA Secretariat. Upon receipt of these documents, the Council will forward that proposal to the Budget Committee. The Budget Committee, composed of the EFTA states' experts, will then examine the proposal and make – not later than two months before the beginning of the financial year – a recommendation to the Council who will then adopt the budget. 78

Given that EFTA has offices in three countries – Switzerland (Geneva), Belgium (Brussels) and Luxembourg (Luxembourg) – the budget is drawn up in Euros and Swiss Francs. It is financed by contributions by member states. Their shares are normally determined on the basis 79

97 Art. 2(2) of Annex T to the EFTA Convention.
98 Art. 44(c) EFTA Convention.

of their respective GDP figures. Of the total budget in 2018, Iceland covered 3.12 per cent, Liechtenstein 1.02 per cent, Norway 53.26 per cent and Switzerland 42.60 per cent. The reason for the lower contribution from Switzerland in comparison to its relative size in EFTA is to be found in the fact that Switzerland is not a contracting party to the EEA Agreement. However, with regard to most expenses, notably the costs of the EFTA Secretariat, whose staff predominantly service the EEA Agreement, Switzerland does fully participate in the costs. It does not do so, however, with regard to the costs incurred for the publication of the EEA Supplement to the Official Journal of the European Union. The latter contains the Icelandic and Norwegian language versions. The respective translation and publication costs, which are quite substantial, are borne by the EEA EFTA states alone. This, in turn, includes Liechtenstein which, strictly speaking, would not need most of these services as its respective publications are taken care of by the German language services of the EU.

80 EFTA's total budget for the year 2018 amounted to CHF 23,307,000. Of that sum, CHF 2,260,000 were set aside for the negotiation of FTAs and CHF 757,000 for maintaining the current ones; CHF 4,434,000 for servicing the EEA and CHF 1,128,000 for translation and publication, mainly the EEA supplement to the Official Journal of the EU, i.e. its Icelandic and Norwegian language versions. While costs related to Brexit were in 2018 still covered under the general budget parts of the divisions involved, EFTA set aside a dedicated amount of about CHF 500,000 for 2019 to deal with preparations for the UK leaving the EEA etc.

CHAPTER 5
TRADE RELATIONS WITH THIRD COUNTRIES AND GROUPS OF COUNTRIES

5.1. INTRODUCTION

5.1.1. HISTORICAL NOTE

1 Today, the EFTA states have a considerable network of free trade agreements (FTAs) and other types of agreements with different kinds of partners, i.e. countries, special administrative regions (Hong Kong, China) and groups of countries all over the world. This was, however, not part of the original (main) scope of EFTA. Originally, free trade was to be established, first, among EFTA states and, second, with the EU (originally the EEC, later EC).

2 Naturally, there was, also, the perspective to conclude FTAs with close neighbours that were – at the time – members of neither EFTA nor the EU. Such a case was Spain or, later, Turkey. Then, after the collapse of communism and the respective economic bloc (COMECON),[1] FTAs were concluded with the Central and Eastern European countries. There was, already then, a certain parallel development with that of the EU which had concluded so-called 'Europe Agreements' with these countries to allow them to eventually join the EU.[2]

---

1 'Council for Mutual Economic Assistance' of the then USSR, the communist Central and Eastern European states and some others; see e.g. R. Bideleux and I. Jeffries, 'A History of Eastern Europe: Crisis and Change', Routledge, London 1998; M. Kaser, 'Comecon: Integration Problems of the Planned Economies', Royal Institute of International Affairs/Oxford University Press, Oxford 1967.

2 'The Europe Agreements create an association between the EU and a number of countries in Central and Eastern Europe. To date they have been signed with Poland, Hungary, the Czech and Slovak Republics, Bulgaria and Romania. They set out the framework for political dialogue and the promotion of the expansion of trade and

3 Around the same time, in the second half of the 1990es, the EU started to negotiate FTAs at a global level.[3] In order not to lose competitiveness in comparison with the EU, EFTA started to build a similar network of FTAs.

4 In this context FTAs means agreements on free trade with third countries, i.e. excluding trade relations in substance between the EFTA states or with the EU.

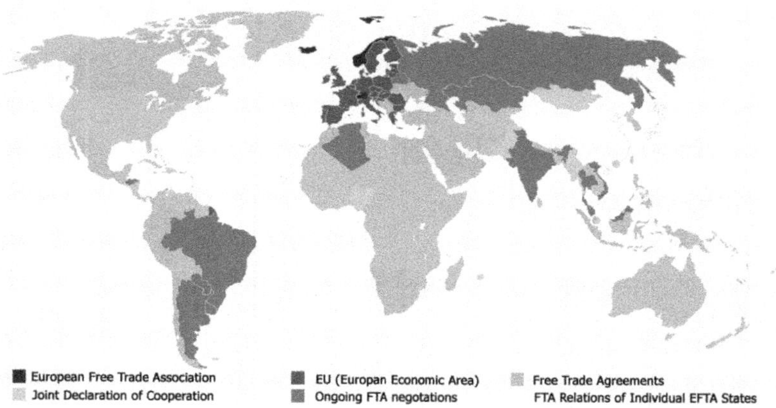

Figure 5.1. EFTA's worldwide network (as at 1 January 2020)
Source: EFTA Secretariat.

5 In 2018, 29 FTAs were in place with 40 partner countries and customs territories: Albania, Bosnia and Herzegovina, Canada, the Central American states of Costa Rica and Panama (entry into force pending for Guatemala), Chile, Colombia, Ecuador (entry into force pending), Egypt, Georgia, the Gulf Cooperation Council (GCC, comprising Bahrain, Kuwait, Oman, Qatar, Saudi Arabia and the United Arab Emirates), Hong Kong China, Indonesia (entry into force pending), Israel, Jordan, the Republic of Korea, Lebanon, North Macedonia, Mexico, Montenegro,

economic relations with a view to contributing to the economic development and prosperity of the signatories.' https://europa.eu/rapid/press-release_MEMO-94-7_en.htm.

3 S. Woolcock, 'The Role of the European Union in the International Trade and Investment Order', Dahrendorf Forum IV, Working Paper No. 10, 11 April 2019, pp. 2–3, 11–12.

Morocco, Palestinian Authority, Peru, the Philippines, Serbia, Singapore, the Southern African Customs Union (SACU, comprising Botswana, Lesotho, Namibia, South Africa and Eswatini), Tunisia, Turkey and Ukraine.[4]

5.1.2. LEGAL BASIS AND INTERNATIONAL LAW (WTO) CONTEXT[5]

The legal basis for EFTA's third-country relations can be found in Article 56(2) of the (revised) EFTA Convention. According to that provision, 6

> 'the Council may negotiate an agreement between the Member States and any other State, union of States or international organization, creating an association embodying such reciprocal rights and obligations, common actions and special procedures as may be appropriate.'

Preferential or free trade agreements, however, must also conform with the rules of the World Trade Organization (WTO). A key principle of the multilateral trading system is the most favoured nation (MFN) treatment. In practice, this means that a lower customs duty offered by one member of the WTO to another country must be extended to all other members of the WTO. However, a country may grant more favourable treatment to partner states in comparison to the other WTO members if it enters into a FTA or customs union. In order to do so, certain conditions stipulated in the relevant provisions of the WTO agreements, to ensure the compatibility of the FTA with the WTO system, must be observed.[6] For example, FTAs must be comprehensive in order to be compliant with the WTO's requirements. It would not suffice to conclude an agreement about, say, just financial services. 7

In order to establish transparency with regard to such agreements, a respective mechanism was introduced in 2006 (Transparency Mechanism 8

---

4 EFTA Secretariat, *58th Annual Report of the European Free Trade Association 2018*, Geneva 2019, p. 9.

5 https://www.efta.int/free-trade/fta-and-wto.

6 See Art. XXIV of the GATT, for trade in goods, and Art. V of the GATS, for trade in services.

for Regional Trade Agreements [RTAs][7]). Thus, WTO member states must announce in a timely manner and subsequently notify any such agreement to the WTO. This also applies to any subsequent changes affecting the implementation or the operation of an agreement. The WTO maintains an electronic database including relevant tariff and trade-related information on all notified FTAs. There is an EFTA Committee which prepares notifications of new EFTA FTAs to the WTO and EFTA is represented by the EFTA Secretariat in the WTO Committee on Regional Trade Agreements (CRTA) as an observer.

5.1.3. TYPES OF EFTA's THIRD-COUNTRY RELATIONS

9 Third-country relations may either take the form of joint declarations on cooperation, FTAs or agreements on technical cooperation.

Table 5.1. EFTA's Joint Declarations and FTAs

Partner	Joint Declaration	Free Trade Agreement	
	Signing	Signing	Entry into Force
Albania	10 December 1992	17 December 2009	1 November 2010
Algeria	12 December 2002		
Bosnia and Herzegovina		24 June 2013	1 January 2015
Canada		26 January 2008	1 July 2009
Central American States	20 July 2010 (Panama)	24 June 2013 (Costa Rica and Panama)	19 August 2014
Chile		26 June 2003	1 December 2004
Colombia	17 May 2006	25 November 2008	1 July 2011
Ecuador	22 June 2015	25 June 2018	
Egypt	8 December 1995	27 January 2007	1 August 2007
Georgia	28 June 2012	27 June 2016	1 September 2017 (for Georgia. Iceland and Norway)
Guatemala		22 June 2015	

continued

[7] The term 'RTA' is used by the WTO, while EFTA always uses 'FTA'. These terms are used synonymously.

Table 5.1. *continued*

Partner	Joint Declaration	Free Trade Agreement	
	Signing	Signing	Entry into Force
Gulf Cooperation Council (GCC)*	23 May 2000	22 June 2009	1 July 2014**
Hong Kong China		21 June 2011	1 October 2012
Indonesia		16 December 2018	
Israel		17 September 1992	1 January 1993
Jordan	19 June 1997	21 June 2001	1 September 2002
Kosovo	23 November 2018		
Republic of Korea		15 December 2005	1 September 2006
Lebanon	19 June 1997	24 June 2004	1 January 2007
North Macedonia	29 March 1996	19 June 2000	1 May 2002
Malaysia	20 July 2010		
Mauritius	9 June 2009		
Mexico		27 November 2000	1 July 2001
Mercosur***	12 December 2000		
Moldova	24 November 2017		
Mongolia	28 July 2007		
Montenegro	12 December 2000	14 November 2011	1 September 2012
Morocco	8 December 1995	19 June 1997	1 December 1999
Myanmar	24 June 2013		
Nigeria	12 December 2017		
Pakistan	12 November 2012		
Palestinian Authority	16 December 1996	30 November 1998	1 July 1999
Peru	24 April 2006	24 June 2010	1 July 2011
Philippines	24 June 2014	28 April 2016	1 June 2018****
Serbia	12 December 2000	17 December 2009	1 October 2010
Singapore		26 June 2002	1 January 2003
Southern African Customs Union (SACU)*****		26 June 2006	1 May 2008

continued

Table 5.1. *continued*

Partner	Joint Declaration	Free Trade Agreement	
	Signing	Signing	Entry into Force
Tunisia	8 December 1995	17 December 2004	1 June 2005
Turkey		10 December 1991 Comprehensive update: 25 June 2018	1 April 1992
Ukraine	19 June 2000	24 June 2010	1 June 2012

*Bahrain, Kuwait, Oman, Qatar, Saudi Arabia and the United Arab Emirates.
**The Member States of the GCC informed EFTA that the EFTA-GCC FTA is applied by their authorities as of 1 July 2015.
***Argentina, Brazil, Paraguay and Uruguay.
****The Philippines informed EFTA that the EFTA-Philippines FTA is applied by their authorities as of 24 October 2018.
*****Botswana, Lesotho, Namibia, South Africa and Eswatini.

Source: EFTA Secretariat.

5.2. JOINT DECLARATIONS ON COOPERATION

10 Joint declarations on cooperation:

- can be a first step towards free trade relations with the partners concerned;
- examine ways and means of expanding and liberalising the trade relations between the trading partners;
- address cooperation on trade-related issues such as information on foreign trade, customs and origin matters, technical barriers to trade, intellectual property rights, trade in services, public procurement markets and competition;
- aim to improve conditions for the implementation of private sector cooperation; and
- serve as a basis for offering scholarships and extending technical assistance in areas such as customs and origin matters and statistics.

11 From an institutional point of view, there is a joint committee, which acts as a forum for the parties to review their cooperation, discuss any other issue of mutual interest and formulate appropriate recommendations. The secretariat services for the joint committees are performed jointly by the EFTA Secretariat and the respective ministries in the partner countries.

5.3. FREE TRADE AGREEMENTS

5.3.1. GENERAL

EFTA's FTAs establish free trade areas between the trading partners, which cover substantially similar areas to those of the EFTA Convention.[8] The terms 'EFTA free trade agreement' or 'EFTA third-country relations' are misleading because it is in fact not EFTA that is a party to a FTA with a partner country or partner countries, but the EFTA states themselves. Within EFTA, the EFTA states have not relinquished their foreign trade policy competence and EFTA is not a customs union. Therefore, the EFTA states are in principle free to unilaterally conclude FTAs with third countries as well. Furthermore, as will be shown below,[9] there is also some leeway for differentiations between the EFTA states even though they negotiate together. 12

EFTA has set out four principles for choosing partners to conclude FTAs with: 13

- the economic relevance of the partners, as measured by trade or the potential for trade;
- the potential risk of discrimination against EFTA exporters compared to exporters from main competitors, such as the EU, the US, Canada, Japan and others;
- the likelihood of concluding an agreement based on EFTA's offensive and defensive[10] interests compared to those of the potential partner; and
- political considerations, such as a favourable political context in the partner country or a desire to contribute positively to the partner country's stability and inclusion within the framework of European or global economic cooperation.

The conclusion of the first FTAs was triggered by the last of the above principles and happened after the transition that took place in Eastern Europe between 1989 and 1991. The EFTA states, like the EU, wanted 14

---

8 See Ch. 3.

9 See para. 54.

10 International trade jargon, stands for positive or negative interests in FTA negotiations, i.e. what the parties would like to achieve or prevent from having to agree to. An offensive trade interest of the UK would be e.g. pharmaceuticals, while dairy products rather constitute a defensive trade interest.

to assist some of the Central and Eastern European countries in moving from a centrally administered economy (COMECON) to a free market economy. In addition, the EFTA states tried to prevent their economies from suffering competitive disadvantages in these countries after the EU had concluded the so-called Europe Agreements preparing the former communist states for eventual EU membership. It was, essentially, about levelling 'the playing field in Europe'.[11] Most of the Central and Eastern European countries having joined the EU, or being about to do so, nowadays only the second purpose remains: trying to create a level playing field in comparison to EU free trade agreements.[12]

15 Just for the sake of completeness, it seems appropriate to mention that between the two main purposes, there were also very concrete reasons that triggered the EFTA states to negotiate certain FTAs. One was related to the EU's 'Barcelona Process', establishing the Euro-Mediterranean Partnership.[13] By this means, the EU tried to implement several policies with the countries of the southern rim of the Mediterranean Sea, such as market access, energy supply (petrol) and migration. The EFTA states, which did not wish to be left behind economically, joined the trade part. Here the main issue was to join a regional zone of rules of origin that allows for diagonal cumulation[14] through the 'Pan-Euro-Med (PEM) Convention'.[15]

---

11 D. Rao, 'Past Achievements and Future Challenges of the European Free Trade Association – Twenty Years of Trade Relations and Beyond (1991–2011), World Trade Institute, Bern 2011, p. 35, https://www.wti.org/media/filer_public/8c/30/8c303fcb-1a1d-443f-a83b-1f87f5099a16/masters_thesis_darius_rao.pdf.

12 G. Weder, 'EFTA's Third-Country Relations Adapting to New Realities' in K. Bryn and G. Einarsson (eds.), *EFTA 1960–2010, Elements of 50 Years of European History*, EFTA, Geneva 2010, p. 197.

13 See e.g. M. Pace, 'Rethinking the Mediterranean: Reality and Re-Presentation in the Creation of a "Region"' in F. Laursen (ed.), *Comparative Regional Integration: Theoretical Perspectives*, Ashgate, Aldershot 2003, pp. 174–177; E. Adler and B. Crawford, 'Normative Power: The European Practice of Region Building and the Case of the Euro- Mediterranean Partnership (EMP)', UC Berkeley, Berkeley 2004; European Commission website on the Euro-Mediterranean partnership, https://ec.europa.eu/trade/policy/countries-and-regions/regions/euro-mediterranean-partnership/.

14 See definition by the Swiss Federal Customs Administration: 'Diagonal cumulation makes it possible to use input materials originating in different free trade parties, provided that all parties taking part in the process have free trade agreements with one another using the same rules of origin.' https://www.ezv.admin.ch/dam/ezv/en/dokumente/archiv/a5/ursprung/die_kumulation_indenfreihandelsabkommen.pdf.download.pdf/cumulation_in_freetradeagreements.pdf.

15 See Ch. 3.

Another trigger for EFTA to engage in a new quality of third-country relations was the blossoming of FTAs at the turn of the last century. This, again, was partly a reaction to the WTOs 'Doha Round' being stuck.[16] 16

5.3.2. SUBSTANTIVE SCOPE COVERED IN FTAs[17]

FTAs always cover a certain range of topics, subject to the political willingness of the parties. These topics have gradually increased over time with the development of subsequent 'generations' of FTAs.[18] They are regularly adapted and upgraded in consideration of three main objectives: 17

- make them as effective as possible;
- ensure that they take into account developments at WTO level; and
- make them compatible with the evolution within the wider European economic integration framework.[19]

In practice, FTAs primarily deal with customs and origin matters, as well as processed agricultural products. Furthermore, they contain evolutionary clauses or 'in-built agendas allowing the partners to develop or deepen their relationship in certain fields',[20] mostly with respect to services and investment. Generally speaking, FTAs offer third countries a trade regime similar to the one existing amongst the EFTA states. In more detail, the following topics are normally covered by EFTA's FTAs: 18

5.3.2.1. Industrial Products

The EFTA states have a highly developed and diversified industrial base. EFTA FTAs therefore normally grant total elimination of import duties for all industrial products upon entry into force of a FTA, while accepting that their FTA partners still request import duties on their side or transitional periods for lifting these. 19

16 Rao (n. 10 above) p. 37.

17 https://www.efta.int/Free-Trade/Topics-FTAs-502455; G. Baur, M. Sánchez-Rydelski and C. Zatschler, *European Free Trade Association (EFTA) and the European Economic Area (EEA)*, 2nd ed., Wolters Kluwer, Alphen aan den Rijn 2018, pp. 43–44.

18 See para. 50 below.

19 Baur, Sánchez-Rydelski and Zatschler (n. 16 above) p. 42.

20 Ibid., p. 41.

5.3.2.2. *Agricultural Products, Fish and Other Marine Products*

20 EFTA FTAs generally distinguish between 'basic' and 'processed' agricultural products. Unlike the EU, the EFTA states do not have a common agricultural policy. Basic agricultural products, such as grain, milk or sugar, were therefore originally dealt with in bilateral arrangements concluded between each EFTA state and the partner country. An example would be the bilateral agreements on agriculture between Canada and Iceland, Canada and Norway as well as Canada and Switzerland, including Liechtenstein. These are negotiated in parallel with the FTA.[21] In more recent agreements the EFTA states have moved away from separate agreements on agriculture and now include agriculture within the main agreement, in the goods chapter, and deal with the country specifics in the annexes thereto. An example would be the FTA between the EFTA states and the Central American states (currently Costa Rica, Guatemala and Panama while negotiations with Honduras are on hold).[22]

21 For processed agricultural products, such as soup, yoghurt or chocolate, EFTA in principle grants preferential access. However, in order to compensate for higher costs of raw materials used by EFTA's food processing industry, certain measures, e.g., price compensation systems, may be maintained.[23] Such arrangements on processed agricultural products are normally contained in separate protocols to the FTAs. Under these protocols each country has its own table listing the products for which it grants concessions to its partner countries.

22 As the fisheries sector is of major importance to Iceland and Norway, free trade in fish and other marine products is an essential element of EFTA FTAs. These products are treated as industrial products in accordance with the WTO framework.

5.3.2.3. *Rules of Origin*

23 In a context of multiple product chains where products increasingly contain inputs from several countries, and where production processes extend

[21] Entry into force: 1 July 2009.

[22] Entry into force for Costa Rica and Panama: 19 August 2014 (Norway), 29 August 2014 (Liechtenstein and Switzerland) and 5 September 2014 respectively (Iceland). Entry into force for Guatemala is still pending (January 2020).

[23] Such duties normally reflect the difference between the domestic market price and the world market price of the basic agricultural component of the product.

over several economies, simple and liberal rules of origin are required for economic operators. These determine the country of origin of products and thus which products may benefit from preferential conditions under a FTA. The FTAs normally allow for the use of up to 50 per cent of non-originating input in the production of certain products. However, each FTA contains specific rules of origin and product specific rules (PSR).[24]

5.3.2.4. *SPS/TBT*

24 There are two very important groups of measures that could severely hamper international trade: sanitary and phytosanitary (SPS) measures, and technical regulations and standards that may lead to technical barriers to trade (TBT). Generally, respective clauses in EFTA FTAs build on the respective agreements of the WTO, namely the WTO Agreement on TBT[25] and the WTO Agreement on SPS.[26] Some of the EFTA FTAs, however, feature additional elements aimed at avoiding such barriers.

25 Most importantly and due to the EFTA states' close relations with the European Union, SPS provisions in EFTA FTAs need always to be compatible with EU standards. These are relevant for the EFTA states due to the respective provisions of the EEA Agreement,[27] the Agricultural Agreement between the EU and Switzerland[28] and the Additional Agreement extending the latter to Liechtenstein.[29] If the EFTA states were to allow for different rules to be applied in their FTAs, any exports into the

24 'Even if the materials from third countries (non-originating materials) are used in the production, goods are considered as originating when the goods satisfy the requirement set out in the product-specific rules (PSR)', https://www.customslegaloffice.com/global/what-is-product-specific-rules-psr/.

25 (WTO) Agreement on Technical Barriers to Trade. The Agreement is published in 'The Results of the Uruguay Round of Multilateral Trade Negotiations', GATT Secretariat, Geneva 1994.

26 (WTO) Agreement on the Application of Sanitary and Phytosanitary Measures (SPS Agreement).

27 Annex I, Chapter I of the EEA Agreement (veterinary issues), Annex I, Chapter II of the EEA Agreement (feedingstuffs), Annex II, Chapter XII of the EEA Agreement (foodstuffs) and Annex II, Chapter XIII of the EEA Agreement (MRLs [maximum residue levels]).

28 Agreement between the European Community and the Swiss Confederation on trade in agricultural products, OJ L 114, 30.4.2002, pp. 132–368, especially Annex 11.

29 Additional Agreement between the European Community, the Swiss Confederation and the Principality of Liechtenstein extending to the Principality of Liechtenstein the Agreement between the European Community and the Swiss Confederation on trade in agricultural products, OJ L 270, 13.10.2007, pp. 6–11.

EU might be prohibited. This is true for any country that is part of or has access to the EU's internal market.[30]

5.3.2.5. *Intellectual Property Rights*

26 EFTA FTAs provide for high standards of protection of intellectual property rights (IPR), including measures to enforce such rights against infringement, counterfeiting and piracy. IPR provisions in EFTA FTAs build on the principles of national and MFN treatment as set out in the TRIPS Agreement.[31] In some FTAs the level of protection in certain areas goes beyond that.

5.3.2.6. *Competition and State Aid*

27 EFTA's FTAs also include rules on competition and state aid. These aim at ensuring that trade liberalisation under the FTA is not hampered by practices of private and public enterprises as well as monopolies which may prevent, restrict or distort competition.

28 The competition rules foresee cooperation and exchange of information in order to ensure and facilitate the enforcement of the FTA parties' respective competition laws.

29 The state aid rules refer in principle to the respective WTO provisions.[32] These are based on notification requirements and annual reporting.

5.3.2.7. *Trade in Services and Investment*

30 Earlier FTAs, essentially before the year 2000, only contain so-called evolutionary clauses on services and investment. By these, the parties to the FTA expressed their will to achieving gradual liberalisation and mutual opening of markets for investments and trade in services. More recent EFTA FTAs include proper provisions on the liberalisation of trade in services. These cover all modes of supply and also contain specific provisions on sectors of particular importance, such as financial,

---

[30] See Ch. 7 for the consequences for the UK post-Brexit.

[31] (WTO) Agreement on Trade-Related Aspects of Intellectual Property Rights.

[32] Art. XVI GATT 1994 and WTO Agreement on Subsidies and Countervailing Measures.

telecommunications or maritime services. They, again, build on the WTO General Agreement on Trade in Services (GATS) and normally follow a similar approach, complemented by enhanced provisions and specific commitments (so-called 'WTO+' or 'WTOx').[33]

On investment, EFTA FTAs follow different patterns as far as coverage 31
is concerned. They mostly focus on rules liberalising the establishment of investments and/or on the promotion of investments. There may, however, be different structures in different FTAs. For example, as Norway was not interested in participating in negotiations on investments with the Republic of Korea,[34] the respective chapter was not included in the FTA, but a separate investment agreement concluded between Iceland, Liechtenstein and Switzerland on the one part and the Republic of Korea on the other. A different example is the FTA with Singapore, which not only contains an investment chapter, thus all EFTA states participating, but also a rather broad coverage of investment: the FTA with Singapore 'also foresees the possibility of direct dispute settlement between a Party to the Agreement and an investor of another Party. Such disputes may be submitted to binding arbitration provided both parties to the dispute agree upon this'.[35] All of the later FTAs also contain provisions regarding the establishment of foreign investors.

5.3.2.8. *Public Procurement*

Several recent EFTA FTAs have included commitments concerning 32
access to the parties' government procurement markets on the basis of reciprocity, non-discrimination and transparency. Such provisions either build on the plurilateral WTO Government Procurement Agreement (GPA) or substantially replicate its structure and content and mostly include a clause that the parties should aim to accede to it.

---

33 'WTO+' (World Trade Organisation-plus) means that commitments in an agreement go beyond the normal provisions of the WTO agreements while a 'WTOx' agreement means that an agreement covers issues for which there are no WTO agreements within specific areas. This is, however, a distinction not made by EFTA which only uses the term 'WTO+'.

34 Ch. Etter, 'Les accords préférentiels, partie de la politique économique extérieure suisse: l'exemple de l'ALE avec la Corée du Sud', *La vie économique – Revue de politique économique*, 2000, 6, p. 57.

35 https://www.efta.int/free-trade/free-trade-agreements/singapore#anchor-7.

5.3.3. 'POLICY TOOLS'

5.3.3.1. Trade Facilitation

33 Trade facilitation aims at simplifying and accelerating the clearance of imported and exported goods, thereby reducing costs for the business community. Reflecting the increasing importance of this topic, EFTA has started to include provisions in its FTAs aiming to implement the main trade facilitation principles of transparency, simplification and cooperation. It also refers in its FTAs to relevant agreements, such as the Revised International Convention on the simplification and Harmonisation of Customs Procedures (Revised Kyoto Convention). Since its entry into force on 22 February 2017, there has also been a topical WTO instrument which is increasingly going to be referred to in FTAs, namely the WTO Trade Facilitation Agreement (TFA).

5.3.3.2. Trade Remedies

34 EFTAs FTAs should limit the possibility of taking trade remedy measures between the parties, and in particular prohibit anti-dumping measures. They should also exclude originating products from global safeguard measures if such products do not cause or threaten to cause serious injury, in accordance with WTO rules and practice. Furthermore, EFTA aims at FTAs including certain WTO+ elements, such as notifications and consultations. These provisions, again, build on WTO law and seek to complement it to reflect the spirit of the special relations established between free trade partners.

5.3.3.3. Different Levels of Economic Development

35 EFTA FTAs take into account the different levels of economic development of partner countries. While the EFTA sates normally abolish all tariffs and other restrictions on industrial products upon entry into force of the FTA, less economically developed partners may benefit from a transitional period.[36] Technical cooperation[37] is another means of addressing different levels of development in EFTA FTAs.

---

[36] See para. 19 above.

[37] See para. 68 et seq below.

5.3.4. SUSTAINABLE DEVELOPMENT

One might see sustainable development as another policy tool. However, given its increasing importance and because it has a horizontal impact on all kinds of subjects covered in FTAs, sustainable development deserves to be covered a bit more extensively. 36

Since 2010, EFTA systematically includes chapters on trade and sustainable development (TSD) in its FTAs and in updates of existing FTAs. This is the result of international trends, strongly pushed by the EU, and of respective discussions in both the EFTA Parliamentary Committee and the EFTA Consultative Committee. For national parliaments of the EFTA states to approve newly negotiated FTAs, the inclusion of substantial provisions on TSD has become a *de facto* prerequisite. This also applies to processes aiming at modernising existing FTAs. A revised agreement containing no or substandard TSD provisions is likely to fail to obtain the necessary support from legislators and the wider public given the constantly rising expectations in this regard. 37

EFTA's approach in negotiations of new FTAs, or the revision of existing FTAs, is based on a model chapter which builds on well-established international standards and instruments in the field of the environment and labour. First, it reaffirms the parties' existing obligations deriving from membership of the International Labour Organisation (ILO) and as parties to the ILO conventions and the multilateral environmental agreements (MEAs) which they have ratified. Regarding labour standards, the chapter also reaffirms the two main ILO instruments which are of a particular relevance in a trade context, namely the Declaration on Fundamental Principles and Rights at Work (1998) and the Declaration on Social Justice for a Fair Globalisation (2008). There are, however, more such instruments, depending on the particular subject. 38

As to the content, the provisions of the TSD chapter do not, however, create new environmental or labour standards and do not seek to harmonise domestic standards between the parties. The chapter recognises each party's right to regulate while encouraging high levels of protection for the environment and labour standards. It contains obligations for the parties not to fail to effectively implement their environmental and labour laws and not to lower or waive labour or environmental protection in order to attract or encourage trade and investment. 39

40 The TSD chapter normally contains a commitment whereby the parties aspire to promote trade in and the dissemination of goods and services contributing to sustainable development. In particular, EFTA proposes a commitment to sustainable forest management and associated trade and to sustainable management of fisheries and aquaculture. In both provisions, EFTA foresees a general recognition of the importance of these issues and the role of trade in pursuing these objectives. Both provisions are complemented by a list of targeted measures that the parties commit to undertake in this regard. The measures either refer to existing commitments or are of a promotional nature.

41 Given that EFTA follows an approach of cooperation, particularly with regard to TSD, any matters arising under this chapter are not subject to arbitration under the FTA. The parties are rather called upon to settle any matters arising under the chapter in an amicable manner. Accordingly, the possibility of imposing sanctions or suspending concessions granted in case of a breach of an obligation under the chapter is not foreseen either.

42 An example of such a chapter on TSD can be found in the FTA between the EFTA states and the Central American states.[38] The FTA between the EFTA states and Indonesia contains even more specific provisions, particularly on trade in palm oil:

> 'With a view to ensuring economically, environmentally and socially beneficial and sound management and operation of the vegetable oils sector, the Parties commit to, inter alia:
>
> (a) effectively apply laws, policies and practices aiming at protecting primary forests, peatlands, and related ecosystems, halting deforestation, peat drainage and fire clearing in land preparation, reducing air and water pollution, and respecting rights of local and indigenous communities and workers;
> (b) support the dissemination and use of sustainability standards, practices and guidelines for sustainably produced vegetable oils;
> (c) cooperate on improving and strengthening government standards where applicable;
> (d) ensure transparency of domestic policies and measures pertaining to the vegetable oils sector; and
> (e) ensure that vegetable oils and their derivatives traded between the Parties are produced in accordance with the sustainability objectives referred to in subparagraph (a).'[39]

---

38 FTA, Ch. 9.
39 FTA, Art. 8.10(2).

The respective preferential treatment for palm oil produced in such a sustainable manner can then be found in the respective concessions by the EFTA states, i.e. the schedules on tariff commitments on goods between each of the EFTA states and Indonesia.[40] 43

5.3.5. INSTITUTIONAL SET-UP UNDER THE FTAs

EFTA's FTAs all contain a joint committee, composed of representatives of the EFTA states and the respective partner country. It supervises the implementation and further development of the FTA. Disputes that may arise regarding the interpretation or application of the FTAs may also be brought before the joint committee. It can take decisions, e.g., for the adoption of its rules of procedure, the establishment of subcommittees, for amendments of the annexes and protocols to the FTA and, subject to subsequent ratification and approval procedures, amendments to the FTA as such. Joint committees usually meet every year unless an urgent issue needs to be addressed, for instance, to provide a forum for consultations between parties to a dispute. To facilitate its work, a joint committee may establish subcommittees. Such subcommittees have been established in the field of customs and origin matters or trade in goods more generally. 44

5.3.6. DISPUTE SETTLEMENT UNDER THE FTAs

Earlier EFTA FTAs only foresee that any differences between the parties should be resolved through a consultation. More recent EFTA FTAs also contain provisions on dispute settlement between the parties. Dispute settlement starts with consultations. The consultations take place before the joint committee, established under the FTA, unless the party or parties making or receiving the request for consultations disagree. 45

If the matter has not been resolved during the consultations, it may be referred to arbitration by one or more parties involved. The procedure is carried out before an arbitration panel. Other parties can intervene in the 46

40 FTA, Annex III (Iceland), Annex IV (Norway) and Annex V (Liechtenstein and Switzerland).

procedure. The arbitration panel is to render its ruling within 90 days from the date of its establishment. Such rulings are final and binding on the parties to the dispute; they cannot be appealed against.

47 The parties to the dispute are bound by the ruling and must comply with the ruling. The party complained against shall notify the other party within 30 days after the ruling has been transmitted of:

- the specific measures required for complying with the ruling;
- the reasonable period of time to do so; and
- a concrete proposal for temporary compensation until the full implementation of the specific measures required for compliance with the ruling.

48 If the parties to the dispute disagree on such notification, the complaining party may request a ruling on whether the proposed measures are in compliance with the original ruling. It may also request an opinion on the duration of the period of time and on whether the compensation proposal is manifestly disproportionate. In case a party concerned fails to notify the implementing measures, or if the implementing measures are not in compliance with the ruling, a mutually acceptable compensation can be agreed. Failing such agreement, the complaining party is entitled to suspend the application of benefits granted under the agreement equivalent to those affected by the measure found to be inconsistent with. Such suspension of benefits shall be temporary and shall only be applied by the complaining party until the measure found to be inconsistent with this agreement has been withdrawn or amended, so as to bring it into conformity with the agreement, or the parties to the dispute have reached agreement on a resolution of the dispute.

49 Of course, conciliation and mediation procedures can be undertaken voluntarily if the parties involved so agree.

5.3.7. 'GENERATION-TYPES' OF FTAs

50 As we have previously seen, a distinction was made between 'earlier' and 'newer' FTAs. There are indeed different types ('generations') of FTAs. While the notion of 'generations' may not be widely used by practitioners, it has certainly its advantages from a didactic point of view. With regard to EFTA and generally speaking, FTAs concluded before the year 2000 were

so-called first-generation agreements.[41] Such first generation FTAs mainly covered free trade in goods, including basic and processed agricultural products. As to rules of origin, those partner countries participating in the PEM Convention normally agree the latter being applied directly. In other cases, the EFTA states strive to have a standardised model based on the PEM Convention incorporated into the FTA.[42] With regard to services and investment, only a non-binding evolutionary clause was usually incorporated. The parties to the FTA agreed to aim to gradually liberalise and mutually open their respective markets, should they consider this to be useful in the future. Furthermore, these type of FTAs covered IPRs as well as trade remedies and disciplines. These may include anti-dumping, SPS and TBT.

The FTA with Mexico, EFTA's first transatlantic agreement, was also the 51
first second-generation agreement. In addition to the matters normally covered by first-generation agreements, as described above, that agreement, with regard to substance, also contains substantive provisions in the field of services, investment, competition rules and government procurement. In addition, second-generation agreements also include dispute settlement provisions which correspond to those of the revised EFTA Convention. Another feature of these newer FTAs are sustainable development clauses as well as, mostly in FTAs with developing countries, clauses on economic cooperation or technical assistance.

Despite the standard clauses as shown above and depending on the 52
'generation' it belongs to, every FTA has individual features depending, inter alia, on the economic interests involved or the degree of economic development of EFTA's FTA partner. It would be beyond the scope of this book to analyse the different FTAs and compare these.[43] However, in order simply to provide an overview, Table 5.2 is intended to also show the complexity of such a network of FTAs.

---

41 This also includes the FTA with Canada which the partners stated to negotiate in 1998 and which was concluded in 2008. Attempts, essentially by the EFTA states, to upgrade that agreement have, so far, been unsuccessful.

42 Rao (n. 10 above) p. 52.

43 A brief description of 'flagship models of EFTA Free Trade Agreements' can be found at Rao (n. 10 above) pp. 57–62.

Table 5.2. Substantive scope of EFTA's FTAs

Free Trade Agreements concluded	Signing	Entry into force	Relations established	JDC	WTO membership	SCM	AD measures	Safeguards	SPS measures	TBT	Government procurement	Competition	IPR	Services	Investment	Dispute settlement	JC Decisions/ Amendments	Other areas included/notes
Turkey	1991	1992	1991	–	✓	SCM basis	GATT Art VI reference	elaborated	SPS basis	TBT reference	basic	basic	TRIPS basis	–	–	–	33	–
Israel	1992	1993	1992	–	✓	SCM basis	GATT Art VI reference	elaborated	very basic	TBT reference	basic	basic	TRIPS basis	very basic	very basic	very basic	21	–
Morocco	1997	1999	1995	✓	✓	SCM basis	ADP reference	elaborated	very basic	TBT reference	basic	basic	TRIPS basis	very basic	very basic	very basic	16	technical assistance
Palestine	1998	1999	1996	✓	-	elaborated	ADP reference	elaborated	very basic	very basic	very basic	basic	basic	very basic	very basic	very basic	6	political references in the Preamble; technical assistance
Macedonia	2000	2002	1996	✓	✓	SCM basis	ADP reference	elaborated	very basic	TBT reference	basic	basic	TRIPS basis	very basic	very basic	very basic	12	technical assistance
Mexico	2000	2001	2000	–	✓	SCM basis	ADP basis	elaborated	SPS basis	TBT basis	comprehensive	elaborated	TRIPS basis	comprehensive	elaborated	comprehensive	9	–
Jordan	2001	2002	1997	✓	✓	SCM basis	ADP reference	elaborated	very basic	TBT reference	basic	basic	TRIPS basis	very basic	very basic	very basic	8	–
Croatia	2001	2002	2000	✓	✓	SCM basis	ADP basis	elaborated	SPS reference	TBT reference	basic	basic	TRIPS basis	very basic	very basic	very basic	7	technical assistance
Singapore	2002	2003	2001	–	✓	SCM basis	prohibited	elaborated	SPS reference	TBT basis	GPA basis	basic	TRIPS basis	very comprehensive	comprehensive	comprehensive	8	–
Chile	2003	2004	2000	–	✓	SCM basis	prohibited	elaborated	SPS basis	TBT basis	comprehensive	elaborated	TRIPS basis	comprehensive	elaborated	comprehensive	6	–
Lebanon	2004	2007	1997	✓	-	SCM basis	ADP reference	elaborated	SPS reference	TBT reference	basic	basic	elaborated	very basic	very basic	very basic	3	technical assistance
Tunisia	2004	2005	1995	✓	✓	SCM basis	ADP basis	elaborated	SPS basis	TBT basis	basic	basic	TRIPS basis	very basic	very basic	very basic	0	technical assistance
South Korea	2005	2006	2004	–	✓	SCM basis	ADP basis	elaborated	SPS basis	TBT basis	GPA basis	basic	TRIPS basis	comprehensive	comprehensive	comprehensive	8	side Agreement on Investment (excluding Norway)
SACU(1)	2006	2008	2003	–	✓	SCM basis	ADP basis	elaborated	SPS basis	TBT basis	basic	basic	basic	very basic	very basic	very basic	1	special treatment for BW, LS, NA and SZ; technical assistance
Egypt	2007	2007	1995	✓	✓	SCM basis	ADP basis	SG basis	SPS basis	TBT basis	basic	basic	TRIPS basis	basic	basic	very basic	2	technical assistance
Canada	2008	2009	1998	–	✓	SCM basis	ADP basis	elaborated	SPS basis	TBT basis	GPA basis	basic	TRIPS basis	basic	basic	comprehensive	1	trade facilitation
Colombia	2008	2011*	2006	✓	✓	SCM basis	ADP basis	SG basis	SPS basis	TBT basis	comprehensive	elaborated	TRIPS basis	elaborated	elaborated	very comprehensive	0	e-commerce; biodiversity clause in IPR; trade facilitation
GCC(2)	2009	pending	2000	✓	✓	SCM basis	ADP basis	SG basis	SPS basis	TBT basis	comprehensive	basic	basic	elaborated	basic	comprehensive	0	Customs Valuation Agreement included; e-commerce; trade facilitation
Albania	2009	2010	1992	✓	✓	SCM basis	prohibited	elaborated	SPS basis	TBT basis	basic	basic	TRIPS basis	GATS reference	basic	basic	0	trade facilitation
Serbia	2009	2010	2000	✓	-	SCM basis	prohibited	elaborated	SPS basis	TBT basis	basic	basic	TRIPS basis	GATS reference	basic	basic	0	trade facilitation
Ukraine	2010	pending	2000	✓	✓	SCM basis	prohibited	elaborated	SPS basis	TBT basis	elaborated	basic	TRIPS basis	very comprehensive	elaborated	comprehensive	0	review clause on sustainable development; trade facilitation
Peru	2010	2011**	2006	✓	✓	SCM basis	ADP basis	SG basis	SPS basis	TBT basis	comprehensive	elaborated	TRIPS basis	basic	elaborated	very comprehensive	0	e-commerce; biodiversity clause in IPR; trade facilitation
Hong Kong	2011	pending	2010	–	✓	SCM basis	prohibited	SG basis	SPS basis	TBT basis	GPA basis	basic	TRIPS basis	comprehensive	elaborated	comprehensive	0	side Agreement on Labour; trade and environment; trade facilitation
Montenegro	2011	pending	2000	✓	-	SCM basis	prohibited	SG basis	SPS basis	TBT basis	basic	basic	TRIPS basis	basic	basic	basic	0	trade and sustainable development; trade facilitation
ongoing negotiations																		
Bosnia-Herzegovina			2011	–	–													
Central America(3)			2010	only Panama	✓													
Rubeka(4)			2007	–	–													
India			2007	–	✓													
Indonesia			2005	–	✓													
negotiations on hold																		
Algeria			2002	✓	–													
Thailand			2005	–	✓													
potential negotiations																		
Malaysia			2010	✓	✓													
Mauritius			2009	✓	✓													
Mercosur(5)			2000	✓	✓													
Mongolia			2007	✓	✓													
Vietnam			2010	–	✓													

* Colombia: entry into force not yet implemented by Iceland and Norway
** Peru: entry into force not yet implemented by Norway

(1) Southern African Customs Union (Botswana, Lesotho, Namibia, South Africa, Swaziland)
(2) Gulf Cooperation Council (Bahrain, Kuwait, Oman, Qatar, Saudi Arabia, United Arab Emirates)
(3) Central America (Costa Rica, El Salvador, Guatemala, Honduras, Nicaragua, Panama)
(4) Customs Union of Belarus, Kazakhstan and Russia
(5) Mercado Común del Sur (Argentina, Brazil, Paraguay, Uruguay)

First generation FTA
Second generation FTA

very basic = simple reference or very limited provisions
basic = provisions with limited coverage
elaborated = provisions with extensive coverage
comprehensive = provisions with comprehensive coverage
very comprehensive = provisions with highly comprehensive coverage
*** reference = the policy area is referred to or partially based on its related WTO provisions
*** basis = the policy area is governed by its related WTO agreement and often contains WTO+ elements

Source: D. Rao (n. 10 above) p. 49.

5.3.8. SPECIFICITIES OF EFTA's FTA POLICY

EFTA is not a customs union. Its member states therefore formally do not have a common trade policy as, e.g., the EU. It is rather a 'trade policy that is co-ordinated in a flexible and case-by-case manner'.[44] Thus, Iceland, Liechtenstein, Norway and Switzerland are neither obliged to negotiate FTAs jointly. This gives those countries the 'external flexibility' to either negotiate through EFTA or alone. This will in most cases result in an EFTA-third country free trade area with identical provisions, at least for the essential content except for agriculture.[45] However, although FTAs may have been negotiated jointly through EFTA and in one document, the result will *legally* always be a FTA between the third country and the respective EFTA state.[46] EFTA is, hence, rather a platform for trade negotiations[47] and for concentrating market power. 53

The EFTA states do have some bilateral FTAs negotiated outside EFTA. The most noteworthy ones are those between China and both Iceland and Switzerland individually. Another is that between Switzerland and Japan. And it seems that Switzerland's attempts to engage in negotiations with the US, a first attempt having been unilaterally aborted by Switzerland in 2006, are undertaken on a purely bilateral basis. 54

The reference above to 'external flexibility'[48] dictates that there must also be 'internal flexibility'. As a consequence of the fact that, in effect, the EFTA states – even though negotiating together as EFTA – will eventually end up with a FTA between themselves and the third country, these FTAs may contain variations or even apply to some only of the EFTA states. Two examples shall suffice to show this. For instance, in the FTA between the EFTA states and Singapore[49] the chapter on investments is part of the main text of the FTA. A variation of the above example is that of the EFTA-Korea FTA.[50] The set-up is substantially the same as in the EFTA-Singapore FTA. However, as Norway did not participate in the negotiations 55

---

44 WEDER (n. 11 above) p. 200.
45 See para. 20 above.
46 G. WEDER (n. 11 above): 'in each member's own right, i.e. without surrendering their treaty-making power.'
47 T. COTTIER, 'EFTA Free Trade Agreements: Past, Present and Future' in D. Bratanov (ed.), *EFTA Bulletin, EFTA Free Trade Relations*, EFTA, Geneva 2013, p. 43.
48 See para. 53 above.
49 Entry into force 1 January 2003.
50 Entry into force 1 September 2006 for Korea, Norway, Liechtenstein and Switzerland, and 1 October 2006 for Iceland.

Table 5.3. The EFTA states' bilateral FTAs

Bilateral Free Trade Agreements concluded	Partner	Entry into force or relations established	Scope of the agreement and particularities
Iceland	Greenland	1985	Information not available
	Faroe Islands	1993	Second generation FTA named the Hoyvik Agreement: single market with the Faroe Islands; language is very basic but the Agreement covers the four freedoms of goods, services, capital and persons; free trade in agriculture (excepted in fish and marine products); provides a cooperation framework for culture, education, energy, environment health services, research and development, resource management, telecommunication tourism and transport.
	China	ongoing since 2007	Second generation FTA
Norway	Greenland	1985	Information not available
	Faroe Islands	1993	Basic first generation FTA with basic elements on competition, subsidies, IPR, public procurement, dumping, safeguards and dispute settlement
	China	ongoing since 2008	Second generation FTA
Switzerland Liechtenstein	Faroe Islands	1995	Extremely basic first generation FTA; only covers industrial goods without any trade discipline apart from safeguard measures based on the GATT
	Japan	2009	Second generation FTA; arguably the most comprehensive Swiss FTA outside the EU; in addition to classical policy areas of second generation FIAs, it also includes comprehensive obligations on electronic commerce and movement of persons (without being comparable to CH-EU free movement of persons)
	China	ongoing since 2011	Second generation FIA

Source: D. Rao (n. 10 above), p. 50.

on investments,[51] the respective chapter was not included in the FTA, but a separate investment agreement concluded between Iceland, Liechtenstein and Switzerland, on the one part, and the Republic of Korea, on the other. Both the FTA with Singapore and the investment agreement between Korea and Iceland, Liechtenstein, and Switzerland, contain provisions on investor-state dispute settlement (ISDS).

5.3.9. COMPARISON WITH THE EU

5.3.9.1. General

For obvious reasons, comparison is normally made with the EU. With regard to trade, both the EU and EFTA have large FTA networks. That is quite natural as both try to create a certain level playing field with regard to their respective access to third-countries' markets. Over time of course the EU became number one, given a change in ratio of member states of EFTA and the EU respectively that went from 7:6 to 4:28 (2019). Even though the EFTA states are among the richest in the world and maintain a comparatively large FTA network, particularly taking into account their relative smallness, the EU's is probably the largest in terms of countries covered, value and depth. 56

The EU sees itself as the largest economy in the world 'with a GDP per head of €25 000 for its 500 million consumers'. It certainly is the world's largest trader of manufactured goods and services and 'it ranks first in both inbound and outbound international investments'. With regard to preferential trade agreements (PTAs), 'the EU is the top trading partner for 80 countries. By comparison the US is the top trading partner for a little over 20 countries'.[52] 57

As the EU is a customs union, it lacks EFTA's flexibility with regard to negotiating variations between the member states with regard to such FTAs. And the EU member states have no possibility of negotiating individual trade agreements. On the other hand, the sheer size of the market combined with an access to all of its different economies and their large variety of products and services often gives the EU an advantageous negotiating position in comparison with EFTA. Furthermore, 'EU agreements are more elaborate and comprehensive. (…) In the long run, EU association 58

51 See n. 34 above.
52 https://ec.europa.eu/trade/policy/eu-position-in-world-trade/index_en.htm.

agreements offer deeper relations and are likely to marginalise the current generation of EFTA agreements to the extent that they exist'.[53]

5.3.9.2. *Different Types of Agreements and Motivations for Negotiating These*

59 EFTA's FTAs are rather straightforward with regard to their aim and 'typology'. There is a network of FTAs and joint declarations on cooperation are rather precursors to FTAs than a special type of agreement. However, EFTA now also has its 'Comprehensive Economic Partnership Agreement' (CEPA), concluded between the Republic of Indonesia and the EFTA states.[54]

60 By contrast, the EU counts the following 'types' of agreements in their 'trade portfolio':

- 'First-generation' preferential trade agreements.
- 'New-generation' preferential trade agreements.
- Deep and Comprehensive Free Trade Areas (DCFTAs).
- Economic Partnership Agreements with African, Caribbean and Pacific (ACP) states.[55]

61 The first category, unlike in the case of EFTA, not only contains 'standard' type FTAs, but also encompasses such different agreements as the EU-Turkey Customs Union (1963), the EU-Switzerland or EU-Norway FTAs (1972 and 1973), the EU-Chile Association Agreement (2003), the EU North Macedonia Stabilisation and Association Agreement (SAA; 2001) or the EU-Kosovo SAA (2016). These agreements do not even share the same legal basis in the EU Treaties.[56]

62 The second category, 'new-generation PTAs', however, essentially corresponds to the 'second-generation FTAs' in EFTA's case. The EU

---

[53] Cottier (n. 47) p. 45.

[54] Signed on 16 December 2018; ratification procedures ongoing (January 2020).

[55] European Commission, *Report from the Commission to the European Parliament, the Council, the European Economic and Social Committee and the Committee of the Regions on Implementation of Free Trade Agreements 1 January 2018–31 December 2018*, COM(2019) 455 final, 14.10.2019, pp. 2–3.

[56] For 'classical' FTAs: Art. 2017 TFEU, for other agreements involving a form of association: Art. 8 TEU and Art. 217 TFEU; see also P. Van Elsuwege and M. Chamon, 'The meaning of "association" under EU law', research paper for the European Parliament's AFCO Committee, European Union, Brussels 2019, pp. 15–17.

introduced these in a clear shift after 2006 towards more bilateral PTAs with an increased protection of the EU's trade interests, while remaining committed to multilateral trade negotiations.[57] These agreements negotiated with selected third countries typically go beyond tariff cuts and trade in goods and also cover services and public procurement. 'Solid provisions on trade and sustainable development (TSD) are a core part of all "new generation" trade agreements concluded since 2010.'[58]

The DCFTAs, currently with Georgia, Moldova and Ukraine, go beyond mere FTAs. They also contain an integration component aiming at gradually leading these countries closer to the EU. They 63

> 'provide for deepening of political association and gradual economic integration between the EU and its three partners, based on shared values and principles i.e. democracy and the rule of law, good governance, respect for human rights and fundamental freedoms, as well as a free market economy which would facilitate the participation in EU policies.'

The main thrust of these agreements is twofold:

- gradual, reciprocal market opening, i.e. elimination/reduction of tariffs and elimination of non-tariff barriers to trade; and
- far-reaching and dynamic regulatory approximation to the EU law.[59]

The EU of course thinks its integration model should serve as a booster for other regional integration zones.[60] This is mainly the case in region-to-region agreements such as with ECOWAS (Western Africa) or CARICOM (Caribbean). The Economic Partnership Agreements with the ACP states rather serve a development purpose. These have, however, also to be seen in a post-colonial context.[61] 64

---

57 European Commission, *Communication from the Commission to the Council, the European Parliament, the European Economic and Social Committee and the Committee of the Regions – Global Europe: Competing in the World*, COM(2006) 567 final, 4.10.2006, pp. 8–12.

58 European Commission, *Individual reports and info sheets on implementation of EU Free Trade Agreements*, SWD(2018) 454 final, 31.10.2018, p. 15.

59 European Commission (n. 35 above) p. 71.

60 S. Woolcock, 'European Union policy towards Free Trade Agreements', ECIPE Working Paper, No. 03/2007, pp. 3–4.

61 See Art. 131 EEC Treaty: 'The Member States hereby agree to bring into association with the Community the non-European countries and territories which have special

5.3.9.3. *Practical Examples*

65 Thus, although EFTA FTAs tend to cover similar ground as for instance EU FTAs, they do not always have the same depth in areas such as public procurement, IPRs and sometimes market access for goods and services. EFTA member states are considerably smaller than the EU and therefore have narrower trade interests, which means that in some cases concessions obtained by the EU may not be relevant for EFTA.

66 However, there are also cases where EFTA economic operators are disadvantaged compared to EU competitors. As a concrete example, the Comprehensive Economic and Trade Agreement (CETA) and the EU-Korea FTA have led to a comparative disadvantage for Swiss dairy exporters to Canada and Korea compared to their EU counterparts. Similarly, EFTA does not have the same access to government procurement and services in Canada as the EU does since the older EFTA-Canada Agreement only covers trade in goods. And negotiations on revising that agreement met with little enthusiasm on the Canadian side because of the protective attitude of the EFTA states with regard to agricultural products, particularly dairy products.

67 In some cases, as with Canada and Korea, EFTA was able to get an agreement early and benefit from a first-mover advantage for several years compared to European competitors. The same is true for individual EFTA states' FTAs like the one between Switzerland and Japan. However, once the European Union reached an agreement with these countries, they were able to obtain a higher level of concessions resulting in advantages for EU competitors. Similarly, EFTA now has an FTA with the Philippines while the EU does not, giving economic operators in EFTA an advantage. But if the EU ever concludes negotiations with the Philippines it is likely to produce more concessions in a number of areas. While EFTA has been able to conclude agreements more quickly in a number of cases, the EU tends to get deeper and more comprehensive agreements.[62]

---

relations [read: were formerly colonies of; *note by the author*] with Belgium, France, Italy and the Netherlands.' Based on the provisions of Arts. 131 to 136 the EU subsequently concluded the Lomé, Cotonou and ACP Agreements, then, as from 1975, also including former British colonies.

62 EFTA Background Note for the EFTA Advisory Bodies, 15.11.2018, p. 10.

5.4. TECHNICAL COOPERATION

EFTA technical assistance covers a series of programmes and projects funded under EFTA's budget. Its main purpose is to support existing and possible future FTAs. More to the point, such projects on trade policy issues shall help to assist free trade partners in the implementation of the FTAs and assist partners within the framework of the declarations of cooperation to prepare for free trade relations. EFTA, for instance, arranges seminars, workshops and study visits adapted to the particular needs of individual countries. These may cover areas such as customs and origin matters, TBT, trade facilitation, IPRs, competition rules, state aid and public procurement. In a similar vein, the EFTA Statistical Office participates in technical cooperation on statistics, often in cooperation with Eurostat. 68

5.5. STRENGTHS AND CONSTRAINTS OF EFTA's FTA POLICY

5.5.1. STRENGTHS

Despite their relative smallness in size and population, the EFTA states have a number of advantages with regard to negotiating FTAs. They are highly prosperous, capital-rich economies with high purchasing power. That, on the one hand, makes them attractive markets for potential partners. On the other, EFTA states are also a significant source of foreign direct investment. In addition, the EFTA states have stable economies and politics and trade policies that are consistent over time. 69

These strengths have enabled EFTA to create a worldwide network of FTAs. Figures indicate that there are clear benefits to be had from these FTAs as between 2006 and 2015 the share of exports that went to FTA partners increased by three percentage points more than exports to the rest of the world. This is the combined effect of additional FTAs and intensification of trade following the conclusion of FTAs and represents a value of almost EUR 10 billion.[63] 70

63 EFTA Background Note (n. 61 above) p. 9.

71 In some cases, the EFTA states – as a group or bilaterally – were able to get an agreement early and benefit from a first-mover advantage for several years compared to larger competitors. Examples would be the EFTA FTA with Canada or the FTAs between Iceland or Switzerland and China, as well as the FTA between Switzerland and Japan.

5.5.2. CONSTRAINTS

72 EFTA faces challenges due to constraints both in terms of offensive and defensive interests: for instance, EFTA countries are among the most protective of their agricultural markets. Trade partners such as Canada (especially with regard to dairy products), the European Union and the US (meat), are, hence, less prone to grant an attractive level of concessions in this area.

73 Another topical issue is the movement of natural persons, mainly in the area of services (so-called Mode 4). This is an important issue for several large developing countries, where services, increasingly IT services, are a vital part of their overall economic strategy. The most important case in point is India, which has a huge interest in being able to send professionals to provide services in partner countries. This seems not only to be a sensitive issue in several EFTA states, particularly Switzerland, but in future, after it regains its trade policy sovereignty, also in the UK as was clearly shown during Prime Minister May's visit to India in November 2016.[64]

74 As to technical cooperation and capacity building, EFTA normally offers less than, e.g., the EU. This is due to the fact that the scope of EFTA's FTA approach is narrower than that of the EU and development aid falls outside the institutional scope of EFTA.

75 On the side of offensive interests, the EFTA states, and here again Switzerland in particular, given its strong pharmaceutical industry, seek strong protection of IPRs. This, however, sometimes meets little enthusiasm on the part of developing countries. Failing to find a solution on IPRs seems to be one of the substantive issues delaying the conclusion of FTA negotiations between EFTA and India.

76 Generally, the four EFTA countries, even combined, seem not to have sufficient weight and therefore struggle to convince partners to undertake

64 https://www.bbc.com/news/uk-politics-37950198.

the desired regulatory change through FTAs, and hence to achieve sufficiently deep and comprehensive FTAs. This is especially the case in areas such as government procurement, IPRs as well as services and investment. By contrast, if such concessions have already been made to larger partners, such as the EU or the US, the EFTA states meet less resistance to being granted similar terms. However, when no such other agreements are in place, EFTA has sometimes had to lower its level of ambition to obtain a deal. This seems, hence, to be the downside of the first-mover advantage.

For the sake of completeness, the effect of Brexit should be briefly mentioned 77
as well. Of course, the re-emergence of the UK as an independent trade policy actor may also cause uncertainty for the four EFTA member states in the future. On the one hand, the United Kingdom is EFTA's third largest export market overall after the EU and the US and thus a vital partner for the EFTA states. On the other, as a competitor, the UK may well affect the global trade policy environment. Depending on what FTAs the UK can secure, EFTA economic operators may face possible new instances of discrimination in important markets.[65]

5.5.3. IS THE BENEFIT OF FREE TRADE OVERRATED?

There is a general idea that FTAs seem to have a positive effect on trade. 78
For instance, one study found that FTAs double bilateral trade within ten years.[66] Figures of EFTA's FTAs that entered into force between 2002 and 2015 suggest a growth rate of EFTA's exports of 7.7 per cent after entry into force, compared to 5.5 per cent prior to it.[67] However, it seems rather difficult to obtain reliable figures that clearly show an objective benefit. A comprehensive study undertaken on behalf of the Administrative Control Office of the Swiss Parliament[68] essentially found that, while data and therefore analysis is normally restricted to trade in goods, only limited direct effects on Swiss external trade can be shown. A closer look at some of the FTAs showed that sometimes the expectations and the results of

65 EFTA Background Note (n. 2 above) p. 12.

66 C. Baier and N. Bertrand, 'Do free trade agreements actually increase members' international trade?,' *Journal of International Economics*, 2017, 71, pp. 72–95.

67 EFTA Background Note (n. 2 above) p. 9.

68 Evaluation zu den Auswirkungen von Freihandelsabkommen, 26.10.2016, BBl (Swiss Federal Journal) 2017 7597.

a FTA did not necessarily match. Such a case is the FTA with Singapore where trade at some point even fell below pre-FTA rates. Unsurprisingly, however, the FTAs with larger partners, such as that between Switzerland and China, seem to yield good results, given the vast potential of a large market and Switzerland's first-mover advantage. Moreover, it seems that economic developments, globally and in partner countries, are more relevant for the development of Swiss exports. However, the benefit of having legally agreed rules for trade is perceived as an advantage per se.

Given the constraints described above and the questionable evidence of economic benefit, critics ask whether the benefits for the EFTA states of leading an independent external trade policy are not overrated.[69] They not only point to the lack of weight of the EFTA states in obtaining the same concessions from attractive free trade partners but they also point to the fact that trade autonomy in Europe outside the EU is a restricted one. On the one hand, the EU clearly is one of the standard setters with regard to shaping international trade law, both inside and outside the WTO. On the other, as a competitor, the EU will in the long run always manage to negotiate deeper and more comprehensive FTAs than EFTA. Furthermore, the EFTA countries also depend on the EU given their close geographical and economic links with the internal market. 79

The EFTA states' trade autonomy, therefore, seems to be much more a political wish than a reality based on hard economic facts. It should, however, not be underestimated either. Given the lack of (politically feasible) alternatives, such as joining the EU, it helps to create a level playing field and a reliable legal basis to access third-countries' markets. 80

---

69 See e.g. M. Oesch, 'Wird die handelspolitische Autonomie der EFTA-Staaten überschätzt?', conference paper, *25 Jahre EWR – Ein Integrationsszenarium auf dem Prüfstand*, University of Innsbruck, 4-5.4.2019.

CHAPTER 6

THE RELATIONS BETWEEN THE EFTA STATES AND THE EU/EEA

6.1. INTRODUCTION AND DEVELOPMENT OF PRINCIPLES

The relationship between EFTA and the EU has been, since its inception, the second policy objective of EFTA.[1] As shown earlier, real cooperation only materialised after the EEC had agreed to open accession negotiations with Denmark, Ireland, Norway and the UK in 1969, a decade after both blocs were founded. This chapter will trace the development of the EFTA states' increasingly comprehensive integration between Denmark's and the UK's move from EFTA to the EU in 1973 until the creation of the EEA and the sectoral (bilateral) agreements between Switzerland and the EU respectively. This is, largely, still the situation that exists today. 1

The Free Trade Agreements (FTAs) between the EEC and the remaining EFTA states led to a European free trade area but not yet, however, to anything close to what we know today to be internal market participation. As discussed earlier, this process was a lengthy one with a great deal of political reckoning on both sides and at times very difficult negotiations. It took another 20 years from the conclusion of the EEC-EFTA FTAs until the signing of the EEA Agreement. 2

In the process of coming to terms with having non-EEC/EC/EU member states participating in the EU's internal market, the EU had to develop some principles to, on the one hand, foster primarily economic integration in Europe while, on the other hand, maintaining and protecting the Community (or Union) of and amongst its member states. 3

These so-called 'Interlaken Principles' gained a wider publicity after a speech by the then European Commissioner for External Relations and 4

---

1 See Ch. 2.

Trade Policy, Willy de Clercq, at the ministerial meeting in Interlaken in 1987.[2] These were, however, developed earlier as a follow-up to the 1984 Luxembourg Declaration on extending 'Community-EFTA cooperation "with the aim of creating a dynamic European economic space of benefit to their countries"'.[3] Cooperation should be guided by the following 'four principles':

1. 'Community integration and the Community's independent powers of decision must under no circumstances be affected.
2. The elimination of technical barriers to trade and the simplification of administrative formalities at Community-EFTA frontiers are a logical extension of the Free Trade Agreements and should be pursued parallel to the progressive integration of the Community's internal market.
3. No specific field should be excluded *a priori* for cooperation. The Community must, for example, also step up coordination with EFTA countries in fields such as transport or environmental policy, which of their nature cannot be limited by frontiers and are also issues of great concern to ordinary people.
4. It will only be possible to progress towards achievement of a wider European market if the costs and benefits involved are shared equally. Measures taken in parallel must involve real reciprocity.'[4]

5 These principles were more or less literally repeated a year later in the Commission's paper on 'Relations between the European Community and the EFTA Countries: Implementation of the Luxembourg Declaration'.[5] The main change was that paragraph 4 of these principles was slightly sharpened:

4. 'It will only be possible to achieve a European economic space if the costs and benefits are shared fairly. Therefore, action taken between partners must involve real reciprocity.'[6]

6 Given the specificity of paragraphs 2 and 3 in the very context of the ongoing development of EC-EFTA relations and because these items were already being addressed in the period prior to the negotiation of

---

2 See Ch. 2.
3 COM(85) 206 final, p. 1.
4 COM(85) 206 final, pp. 2–3.
5 COM(86) 298 final.
6 COM(86) 298 final, p. 1.

the EEA Agreement, these principles were given a more general form that could be used in any of the future agreements on accessing the EU's internal market or even participating in internal market:

- the Community's (Union's) integration comes first;
- the autonomy of its decision-making must be preserved and
- there must be a balance of benefits and obligations.[7]

With further Western European non-EU association agreements (WEAAs)[8] being negotiated that would grant access to or even participation in the EU's internal market, the EU added further principles. These referred to the institutional set-up and the substantial coverage of such WEAAs. It is important to keep these in mind when the options for the UK to enter into an agreement with the EU after Brexit are weighed. 7

Although the EU does not always pay particular attention to such terminological differences, there is a clear distinction to be made between 'access to' the internal market and 'participating in' it. Put simply, participation in the EU's internal market grants partner countries treatment as if they were EU member states.[9] The legal basis generally is an association agreement according to Article 217 TFEU, and it typically covers the four freedoms as well as competition and other relevant policies. A level playing field is guaranteed by applying the internal market acquis. A *conditio sine qua non* is an institutional set-up of an at least partly 'quasi-supranational' character, as will be shown later in this chapter. By contrast, access to the EU's internal market only provides the EU's FTA partner countries with an improved market access under what is commonly known in the World Trade Organisation (WTO) as 'WTO+' terms, such as no or lower tariffs, as well as a reduction of non-tariff barriers to trade or the recognition of professional qualifications etc. Here the legal basis is normally Article 207 TFEU.[10] Enterprises from such 8

7 W. De Clercq, Speech at the EC-EFTA Ministerial Meeting, Interlaken, 20 May 1987, http://europa.eu/rapid/press-release_SPEECH-87-32_en.htm.

8 G. Baur, 'Privileged partnerships – The partner countries' (institutional) perspectives' in S. Gstöhl and D. Phinnemore (eds.), *The Proliferation of Privileged Partnerships between the European Union and its Neighbours*, Routledge, London and New York 2020 (2019), p. 28.

9 M. Emerson, 'Which Model for Brexit?', *CEPS Special Report 147*, Centre of European Policy Studies(CEPS), Brussels 2016, p. 3.

10 The newer, comprehensive trade and partnership agreements the EU has negotiated in recent years which go further than a mere FTA, however, also refer to Art. 217 TFEU;

FTA partner countries can only expect equivalent treatment compared to enterprises from within the internal market as far as there is no contradicting internal market legislation. They can, for instance, invest freely as 'all restrictions on the movement of capital between Member States and between Member States and third countries shall be prohibited'.[11] They have, however, no possibility, e.g., of obtaining financial services passports for the whole of the internal market or the right to cabotage[12] in carriage between states within the internal market. And, normally, in such FTAs there is no elaborate institutional framework.

9 As an example, Switzerland only participates in the internal market with regard to free movement of persons and air transport. However, Switzerland does not participate in the internal market with regard to free movement of goods (except for those which are covered by the Mutual Recognition Agreement (MRA)), nor in the internal market for capital or services, except for those covered by the Agreement on Free Movement of Persons (AFMP). In these areas it does, however, have access to the internal market according to FTA or WTO terms. Furthermore, Switzerland only has (partial) access where the EU grants such access, e.g., through equivalence decisions in the field of financial services.[13]

10 This is not the place to write extensively about either the EEA Agreement or the Bilateral Agreements between the EU and Switzerland. There is useful literature, mainly on the EEA Agreement.[14] However, in order to introduce EFTA's second main objective, i.e. improving relations between EFTA and the EU, the chapter will briefly describe the current set-up of agreements in pursuit of that objective.

---

see P. Van Elsuwege and M. Chamon, 'The meaning of association under EU law', European Parliament, Brussels 2019, p. 12.

11 Art. 63(1) TFEU.

12 Transport of goods or passengers – by road, rail, air or sea – between two places in the same country or common market by a transport operator from outside the country or common market. After rejecting the accession to the EEA, this problem arose, e.g., when Swiss lorry operators on their way to the UK intended to pick up goods in France.

13 More extensively on Switzerland, see 6.4 below.

14 See e.g. the recent comprehensive commentary on the EEA Agreement: F. Arnesen, H.H. Fredriksen, H.P. Graver, O. Mestad and Ch. Vedder (eds.), *Agreement on the European Economic Area – A Commentary*, Nomos, C.H. Beck, Hart, Universitetsforlaget, Baden-Baden, Munich, Oxford and Oslo 2018.

6.2. PREPARING THE 'EUROPEAN ECONOMIC SPACE'

With the accession of Denmark, Ireland and the UK to the (then) EEC, relations had also become closer between the EEC and the remaining EFTA countries (Austria, Finland, Iceland, Norway, Portugal, Sweden and Switzerland also on behalf of Liechtenstein). Each of these countries, in 1972 or 1973 respectively, concluded a standardised FTA with the EEC. In the period between 1978 and 1984, the EFTA countries realised the internal ambitions originally formulated in Vienna.[15] This was done by making an increased use of EFTA as a forum for discussions and consultations on the joint challenges related to trade and economics.[16] A further boost to the relations came in the 1980s when a series of agreements to facilitate trade across Europe was concluded between the EEC and EFTA. Some of these agreements that predate the EEA Agreement, or the EU-Switzerland Bilateral Agreements, are still in force. These were partly integrated into the new frameworks of the EEA or the Bilateral Agreements, partly they remained as standalone agreements between the EU and the EFTA states. 11

6.2.1. THE EEC-EFTA FTAs

The FTAs were signed – as individual, but standardised agreements – on 22 July 1972 by Austria, Iceland, Portugal, Sweden and Switzerland, on 14 May 1973 by Norway and on 5 October 1973 by Finland. They came into force on 1 January 1973 except for Portugal (1 March 1973), Norway (1 July 1973) and Finland (1 January 1974). At that time, agreements were also signed by the European Coal and Steel Community (ECSC) and each of the EFTA countries. With Austria, Finland and Sweden joining the (then) EC in 1995, the respective FTAs were no longer applicable. 12

The main objective of these EEC EFTA FTAs was the dismantling of tariff barriers. Hence, since 1 January 1984 all tariffs have been abolished, 13

15 Summit of Vienna in the spring of 1977, mentioned in L. Rye, 'EFTA's quest for free trade in Western Europe (1960–92)' in T. Grønningsæter (ed.), *EFTA Bulletin: The European Economic Area, Past, present and future*, EFTA, Brussels 2015, p. 9.

16 Ministerial meeting of the EFTA Council, Bergen, 2 and 3 June 1983, EFTA, 'W' Documents.

with exceptions, in trade between the Community and the individual EFTA countries.

14 A second objective of the EEC EFTA FTAs was the abolition of quantitative restrictions. These were abolished in bilateral trade at the date of entry into force of the agreements. Some EFTA countries have retained a small number of quantitative restrictions.

15 Apart from the agreement with Iceland where tariff concessions were granted for certain fish products, no liberalisation of primary agricultural trade was provided for in the FTAs.

16 Since the free trade zone is not a customs union, it was necessary to establish rules to define clearly which goods would be eligible for duty-free treatment (rules of origin). For the benefit of the reader, it is worth repeating[17] the basic function of rules of origin: i.e. in order to obtain the preferential originating status of a product, many FTAs require a certain proportion of domestic added value in order to be able to view the product as being manufactured in the country of origin. This is to prevent components of the goods from being delivered to a country and only being assembled in 'screwdriver factories' there, with the sole aim of obtaining their original status there. Depending on the FTA, the country of origin rules are summarised in different lists, which define the list conditions or list rules for each product. To take a simplified example: Country A and Country B are parties to a FTA. Country A is granted tariff-free access to the market of Country B for its lawnmowers, under the condition that their components are produced entirely or predominantly in the country itself. Without such rules, enterprises from Country C, not party to this FTA, could simply assemble their components produced in Country C in Country A into lawnmowers and export them free or nearly free of tariffs into Country B. Of course, in reality, this is much more complex, the more parties are involved and the more components are used, stemming either from countries that are parties to the FTA or not.

17 All the FTAs have an evolutive clause allowing for cooperation outside the trade area. These provisions have – prior to stepping up relations between the EC and EFTA in the early 1980s – been extensively used by all parties concerned and an interlinking network of cooperation

[17] See Ch. 3.

activities had been set up. This included a wide variety of subjects such as economic and monetary policy, the environment, workers' health and safety, consumer protection, transport, development aid, energy and industrial policy. Some of the EFTA states had also interconnected their data transmission networks with the Community's EURONET (Community data transmission network) and most also participated in the Community's Cooperation in Science and Technology etc. Most of these instances of cooperation and participation in Community (EU) policies have been substituted by those foreseen by the provisions of the EEA Agreement or, to some extent, the Bilateral Agreements between the EU and Switzerland.

It is interesting to note that based on these FTAs, there is no direct applicability (direct effect) of EU law or corresponding interpretation of the CJEU's case law in the EFTA states. This was made clear through jurisprudence in some of the EFTA states. In contrast to the EU's position that foresees direct effect of FTAs,[18] direct applicability of the FTA's provisions was mostly denied by the national courts of the EFTA states. Astonishingly, this was also the case in Switzerland and Austria, despite their monistic, international legal systems and their generally international law-friendly attitude. Sticking with Switzerland, the *Stanley Adams* case[19] was a very important example: The Swiss Federal Court held against someone who had 'blown a whistle' on his employer for illicit business practices that Article 23 FTA (competition and state aid) did not lay down concrete duties for private parties, but only outlined which practices were incompatible with the FTA provisions without expressly prohibiting these. Another case that clearly deviated from CJEU practice was the *OMO* case:[20] The CJEU allows the holder of an intellectual property right (e.g. a trademark) to block the placing of the product to which said right corresponds on the market by a competitor only for so long as the trademark owner has not placed the product on the relevant market themselves (here: the EU) for the first time. However, in its important decision in the *OMO* case, the Swiss Federal Tribunal refused to apply 18

18 Case C-104/81, *Hauptzollamt Mainz v C.A. Kupferberg & Cie KG a.A.*, ECLI:EU:C:1982:362.

19 Swiss Federal Court, BGE/ATF 104 IV 175, *S. Adams v. Staatsanwaltschaft des Kantons Basel-Stadt.*

20 Swiss Federal Court, BGE/ATF 105 II 49, a.k.a. ('*OMO*'), *Bosshard Partners Intertrading AG v. Sunlight AG.*

the same approach in the context of the FTA: Articles 13 (quantitative restrictions on imports) and 22 (principle of sincere co-operation) FTA were subject to autonomous interpretation and in its view, there was nothing that would allow for a corresponding application of the CJEU's jurisprudence, despite containing the same or similar wording. Consequently, the trademark owner could forbid parallel imports at all times. There were further cases confirming this view. As an answer to that jurisprudence, the CJEU developed its so-called 'Polydor doctrine' named after its famous landmark decision in the *Polydor* case.[21] That case concerned the importation into the United Kingdom of gramophone records from Portugal. The CJEU held that despite 'the similarity between the terms of Articles 14(2) and 23 of the FTA – here between the EEC and Portugal – on the one hand and those of Articles 30 and 36 of the EEC Treaty on the other' this was 'not a sufficient reason for applying the CJEU's case law to the FTA. It deemed such a distinction necessary because the scope of that case law had to be determined in the light of 'the Community's objectives and activities', i.e. merging 'national markets into a single market having the characteristics of a domestic market'.[22]

19 Although all four EFTA states are now linked to the EU by either the EEA Agreement or the Bilateral Agreements respectively, the FTAs are still partly in use. Mainly for Iceland and Norway the respective provisions on imports of fish and fisheries products into the EU are laid down in additional protocols to the respective FTAs. These protocols were regularly reopened when quotas for importation were raised as a trade-off for an increase in the payments into the Financial Mechanisms[23] following an EEA enlargement. For Switzerland, the EEC-Switzerland FTA still provides the legal basis for trade in goods. In addition, the agreement between the EU and Switzerland on mutual recognition in relation to conformity assessment (MRA), one of the Bilateral Agreements of the first package, also refers to the EEC-Switzerland FTA. Because of its customs union with Switzerland, Liechtenstein is also covered by this FTA. With regard to relations with the other EEA states (EU member states, Iceland and Norway) its provisions are, however,

---

21 Case C-270/80, *Polydor Limited and RSO Records Inc. v Harlequin Records Shops Limited and Simons Records Limited*, ECLI:EU:C:1982:43.

22 See *Polydor* (n. 21), para. 18.

23 See below paras. 57 to 60.

superseded by the EEA Agreement. The picture is thus more than a little complex.

6.2.2. OTHER PRE-EEA AGREEMENTS AND FORMS OF COOPERATION

6.2.2.1. Participation in European Standardisation Bodies

European standards are an indispensable tool for facilitating cross- 20
border trade – both within Europe's single market and also with the rest of the world. Internally, European standardisation is a key instrument for the consolidation of the single market and for strengthening the competitiveness of European companies, thereby creating the conditions for economic growth. They reduce unnecessary costs for both suppliers and purchasers of products and services – in both the public and private sectors. Standards can be used to improve safety and performance, raise energy efficiency levels, and protect consumers, workers and the environment. They complement European and national policies in these areas and make it easier for companies and other actors to respect relevant legislation. The objective of European standardisation is to agree on common specifications and/or procedures that respond to the needs of businesses and meet consumer expectations.

Members of standardisation bodies such as CEN/CENELEC or ETSI 21
are the national standardisation bodies of either EFTA states, EU Member states or EU candidate countries. Only these qualify for full membership. Other countries or organisations may be granted observer status.

6.2.2.2. Facilitation of Mutual Recognition of Conformity Assessment

Cross-border trade of goods generates costs for economic actors because 22
goods need to be checked for their suitability to the market they are destined for and whether they conform to the standards of that market. Establishing common standards alone will not suffice to do away with those costs which constitute technical barriers to trade (TBT). The importing country also needs to recognise the validity of conformity assessments carried out in the exporting country or market and or the respective institutions in charge. An instrument to achieve this is a mutual recognition agreement (MRA). An MRA is an international agreement

by which two or more countries agree to recognise one another's conformity assessments. MRAs have become increasingly common since the formation of the WTO in 1995. They have been forged within and among various trading blocs, including the European Union and EFTA.

23 MRAs are most commonly applied to goods, such as various quality control MRAs. However, the term is sometimes applied to agreements on the recognition of professional qualifications as well.

24 For the sake of completeness it should be mentioned that in 1984 EFTA and the EU (then EEC) decided to intensify their cooperation in this area in order to eliminate additional costs for conformity assessments. The mutual recognition of conformity assessments should have been a reality for all EFTA states with the entry into force of the EEA. However, because Switzerland did not accede to the EEA, the recognition of conformity assessments for Switzerland could only come into force as part of the first set of Bilateral Agreements.

25 Previously, the mutual recognition of conformity assessments among the EFTA states had been carried out under the terms of the Tampere Convention of 1988.[24] In the revised EFTA Convention, the recognition of conformity assessments between the four EFTA states was regulated in Annex I and entered into force on 1 June 2002. Thus, the Tampere Convention became obsolete and was repealed.[25]

6.2.2.3. Rules of Origin and Pan-Euro-Med Partnership

26 Rules of origin are another example of issues addressed well in advance of the EEA Agreement by EFTA and the EEC in order to facilitate trade amongst them. Currently they are governed by the so-called PEM Convention. This convention aims to have cumulation and harmonised rules of origin applied across the Euro-Mediterranean space. It establishes a single set of rules which can and should in the future be implemented to and applied in all bilateral or regional trade agreements among its signatories.[26]

---

24 Convention on the mutual recognition of test certificates and conformity assessments including annexes and the protocol on the application of the Convention to the Principality of Liechtenstein of 15.6.1988, BBl. (Swiss Federal Journal *German*) 1990, p. 484.

25 Withdrawal from the agreement declared by Switzerland on 22 November 2002, effective on 22 November 2003: AS (Swiss chronological law digest) 2003, p. 859.

26 https://www.wto.org/english/tratop_e/roi_e/roi_info_e.htm. See Ch. 3.

6.2.2.4. *Simplified Trade Formalities (EU-EFTA et al.)*

The Convention on the simplification of formalities in trade in goods from 20 May 1987[27] was concluded to simplify formalities in trade in goods between the Community and the EFTA countries. The main feature was to introduce the Single Administrative Document (SAD) to be used for any export and import procedure and for a common transit procedure applicable to trade between the contracting parties regardless of the kind and origin of the goods. 27

The SAD served to eliminate the 'between 35 and 40 separate documents, in as many as 360 copies, needed to conduct an operation of international trade in Western Europe. The new document saved an estimated 2 to 5 percent of the cost of an international transaction'.[28] 28

6.2.2.5. *Common Transit Procedure (EU-EFTA)*

The common transit procedure is used for the movement of goods between the EU member states, the EFTA countries (Iceland, Norway, Liechtenstein and Switzerland), Turkey (since 1 December 2012), the Republic of North Macedonia (since 1 July 2015) and Serbia (since 1 February 2016). It is laid down in the Convention on a common transit procedure of 13 August 1987.[29] It basically extends the Union transit procedure to the non-EU countries which are party to that convention. The Union transit procedure is used for customs transit operations between the EU member states (and Andorra and San Marino) and is, in general, applicable to the movement of non-Union goods for which customs duties and other charges at import are at stake, and of Union 29

---

27 Convention between the European Economic Community, the Republic of Austria, the Republic of Finland, the Republic of Iceland, the Kingdom of Norway, the Kingdom of Sweden and the Swiss Confederation on the simplification of formalities in trade in goods OJ L 134, 22.5.1987, pp. 2–77.

28 R. Griffiths, 'EFTA and European Integration 1973–1994, Vindication or Marginalisation?' in K. Bryn and G. Einarsson (eds.), *EFTA 1960–2010, elements of 50 Years of European History*, EFTA, Geneva 2010, p. 152; R. Senti, 'New protectionism in foreign trade. Forms and causes' in *EFTA Bulletin* 26, nr. 4 (1984), pp. 14–16; S-G. Lindström, 'A simplification of border formalities in Europe?' in *EFTA Bulletin* 27, nr. 2 (1986), pp. 8–9.

29 Convention between the European Economic Community, the Republic of Austria, the Republic of Finland, the Republic of Iceland, the Kingdom of Norway, the Kingdom of Sweden and the Swiss Confederation, on a common transit procedure, OJ L 226, 13.8.1987, pp. 2–117.

goods, which, between their point of departure and point of destination in the EU, have to pass through the territory of a third country.

6.2.2.6. Statistics

30 Statistics play a fundamental role in planning, developing and monitoring the economic, social and environmental aspects of the EU single market. In order to facilitate the integration of the EFTA National Statistical Institutes into the European Statistical System (ESS),[30] the EFTA Statistical Office (ESO) was established in 1991 as a liaison office between the EFTA National Statistical Institutes and Eurostat. Although ESO's tasks have somewhat expanded since then and today include activities in the field of statistical cooperation with partners beyond the EU and EFTA ('statistical capacity building'), its main objective was and still is to promote the full inclusion of the four EFTA states in the continuously evolving European Statistical System.

6.2.2.7. Lugano Convention

31 On 27 September 1968, the then EEC member states, concluded the Brussels Convention on Jurisdiction and the Enforcement of Judgments in Civil and Commercial Matters (Brussels Convention).[31] It was amended several times by conventions on the accession of the new member states to that convention. With the Treaty establishing the European Community, the competence with regard to civil justice matters became a EU competence.[32] Following this, the Brussels Convention was replaced by the Brussels I Regulation.[33] There had been further amendments. Denmark, however, has an opt-out from the Brussels I Regulation. It is linked to the other EU member states by an international agreement containing the substance of the Brussels I Regulation.[34]

---

[30] https://ec.europa.eu/eurostat/web/european-statistical-system/overview?locale=fr.

[31] At the time cooperation still had to be done through intergovernmental instruments according to Art. 293, fourth indent EEC.

[32] Art. 61(c) and Art. 67(1) TEC.

[33] Council Regulation (EC) No. 44/2001 of 22 December 2000 on jurisdiction and the recognition and enforcement of judgments in civil and commercial matter, OJ L 12, 16.01.2001, pp. 1–23.

[34] Agreement between the European Community and the Kingdom of Denmark on jurisdiction and the recognition and enforcement of judgments in civil and commercial matters, OJ L 299, 16.11.2005, pp. 61–70.

On 16 September 1988, member states and EFTA states concluded the Lugano Convention on Jurisdiction and the Enforcement of Judgments in Civil and Commercial Matters, which is a parallel convention to the 1968 Brussels Convention. The objective of the convention is to unify the rules on jurisdiction in civil and commercial matters and expand the applicability of the 'Brussels I' Regulation to the relations between the EU member states, on the one hand, and Norway, Iceland and Switzerland, on the other. All EU member states as well as the EFTA states Iceland, Norway and Switzerland are parties to the Lugano Convention. Liechtenstein never joined. The question, however, could be raised whether by not adhering to the Lugano Convention, Liechtenstein is violating the terms of the EEA Agreement. Indeed, many of the legal acts incorporated in the EEA imply that means of recognising and/or executing court decisions between EEA member states in the context of the matters regulated therein exist.[35] 32

The Lugano Convention had proven very useful and obviously served the parties well. However, several provisions of the parallel agreements have shown to be controversial and led to difficulties in the application of the law. In addition, recent developments, such as cross-border e-commerce, but also the desire to increase the efficiency of the recognition and enforcement procedures, have created pressure for a revision of the Lugano Convention. In 2007, the Lugano Convention was therefore revised to reflect most of the new features of the Brussels I Regulation. 33

The main innovations of the revised Lugano Convention in the area of jurisdictional norms concern: 34

- contractual jurisdiction and competence in consumer affairs, in particular with regard to e-commerce transactions;
- contractually autonomous definitions concerning *lis pendens* (in order to avoid concurrent proceedings before two courts in different countries) and the seat of legal persons; and
- minor adjustments to the rules on jurisdiction regarding employment and insurance matters, exclusive jurisdiction for real estate and intellectual property lawsuits and the coordination provisions for related proceedings.

35 G. Baur, 'Liechtenstein: eine Lücke von 160 km im Europäischen Rechtsraum' in Liechtenstein-Institut (ed.), *Beiträge zum liechtensteinischen Recht aus nationaler und internationaler Perspektive (FS Herbert Wille)*, LAG, Schaan 2014, pp. 33–37.

35 In the area of recognition and enforcement of decisions, the following significant adjustments have been made:

- material objections to the declaration of enforceability are only considered at the stage of appeal; and
- insignificant procedural errors in the transmission of the application can no longer, without more, prevent recognition and enforcement.

36 The most important change in practice results from the extension of the territorial scope of the Lugano area to the EU states which joined the EU in the context of the EU enlargement 2004, with the exception of Poland, which had already joined the Lugano Convention I.

37 The Lugano Convention II is open for accession to either:

- countries which become members of EFTA; or
- member states of the European Community acting on behalf of certain non-European territories that are part of the territory of that member state or for whose external relations that member state is responsible.[36]

38 While the first alternative above is essentially a standing invitation for Liechtenstein to finally join, no accession under the second alternative has taken place yet.

39 There is also a possibility for third countries being neither an EFTA state or an EU member state or dependent territory thereof: such a third country needs to – in particular – communicate to the depositary state, i.e. Switzerland, information on its:

- judicial system, including information on the appointment and independence of judges;
- internal law concerning civil procedure and enforcement of judgments; and
- private international law relating to civil procedure.[37]

40 That information will be transmitted to the other contracting parties prior to inviting the state concerned to accede. That third country will, however, only be invited to accede if there is unanimous agreement

---

36 Art. 70(1)(b) Lugano Convention (2007).

37 Art. 72(1) Lugano Convention (2007).

by the contracting parties, i.e. Denmark, the EU, Iceland, Norway and Switzerland. Even then, the convention will enter into force only in relations between the acceding third country and the contracting parties 'which have not made any objections to the accession before the first day of the third month following the deposit of the instrument of accession'.[38]

6.3. THE EEA AGREEMENT

6.3.1. ORIGINS OF THE EEA AGREEMENT

Since the establishment of EFTA in 1960, the European Community has been EFTA's most important trading partner. In 1972, individual EFTA countries signed FTAs with the then EEC with the aim of abolishing import duties on industrial products. This aim was more or less achieved by 1977. In the mid-1980s, the European Commission launched its ambitious project for a fully integrated internal market. The plan was set out in the Single European Act, signed in 1986. In 1984, the EFTA states and the EC adopted a declaration on the joint establishment of a dynamic European Economic Space (EES), listing possible ways of cooperation, specifically in the field of trade in goods. In contrast to the Luxembourg Process' focus on substance, the process that had started in 1989 with a view to establishing the EEA was defined by an additional focus on form.[39] 41

The EFTA states acknowledged the political determination of the EU to complete the internal market by 1 January 1993 and decided to proceed with EC after-relations in parallel with developments on the EU side. Between 1984 and 1989, the removal of obstacles to trade was undertaken on a case-by-case basis. However, it became difficult for the EFTA states and the EC to work on the basis of a situation where some areas were selected for cooperation while others were not. 42

In 1989, Jacques Delors, then President of the European Commission, therefore proposed a new and more structured form of partnership, which was to become the EEA Agreement (EEA). The EFTA states at that time, Austria, Finland, Iceland, Liechtenstein by way of its association with 43

38 Art. 72(2) Lugano Convention (2007).
39 Rye (n. 15 above) p. 14.

Switzerland, Norway, Sweden and Switzerland, welcomed the idea and formal negotiations began in June 1990. The Agreement on the European Economic Area was signed on 2 May 1992 in Oporto. After amendments to the agreement, caused by Switzerland having rejected its participation in a referendum, it entered into force on 1 January 1994.

44 Since its vote against EEA membership in December 1992, Switzerland has maintained and developed its relationship with the EU through bilateral agreements. After their accession to the EU on 1 January 1995, Austria, Finland and Sweden have participated in the EEA as EU member states. Liechtenstein became a full participant in the EEA on 1 May 1995. The EEA was expanded to include the 12 member states that joined the EU respectively in 2004 and 2007, and finally Croatia in 2014. It will, however, lose the UK upon its leaving the EU.

45 Now the European Economic Area unites the 27 EU member states and the three EEA EFTA states (Iceland, Liechtenstein and Norway) in an internal market governed by the same basic rules. These rules aim to enable goods, services, capital and persons to move freely about the EEA in an open and competitive environment, a concept referred to as the four freedoms. The objective of the EEA Agreement is to 'promote a continuous and balanced strengthening of trade and economic relations between the contracting parties (...) with the view to creating a homogeneous European economic area'.[40]

46 The EEA Agreement provides for equal conditions for businesses across the entire internal market, through competition and state aid rules. It also contains horizontal provisions relevant to the four freedoms, as well as cooperation outside the four freedoms in so-called flanking areas. The latter cover areas such as research and technological development, information services, education, training and youth, employment, enterprise and entrepreneurship, and civil protection. Cooperation is to be carried out through common activities of various types, such as EEA EFTA participation in EU programmes.

6.3.2. SCOPE: MOSTLY INTERNAL MARKET RULES

47 The aim of the EEA Agreement is to promote a continuous and balanced strengthening of trade and economic relations between the EEA states

[40] Art. 1 EEA.

with equal conditions of competition and respect of the same rules. Experience confirms that the EEA Agreement is functioning well and to the satisfaction of the EEA states. The EEA EFTA states have successfully adopted more than 12,000 legal acts of the acquis communautaire since the EEA Agreement came into force in 1994. All relevant Community legislation in the field of the internal market has been integrated into the agreement and implementation rates in the EEA EFTA states of this legislation are comparable to those of the EU member states. The internal market is governed by the same basic rules, enabling goods, services, capital and persons to move freely about the EEA.

Table 6.1. The four objectives of the EU and the EEA

The four objectives of the EU and the EEA			
Freedom, security and justice	**Internal Market**	**Economic and monetary union**	**Foreign policy**
Free movement of persons	Free movement of goods, services, capital and workers	Euro	Common foreign and security policy
External border controls	Sector policies and programmes	Stability and growth pact	Defence
Asylum and immigration	Cohesion	Treaty on stability cooperation and governance	Aid
Prevention and combating of crime	Custom union	European stability mechanism	Trade
			Enlargement

The Lisbon Treaty defines the four main objectives of the EU. The EEA covers one of these, the Internal Market, with the exception of the custom union.

Compared to the much wider scope of the EU, the EEA mostly focuses 48
on the internal market and those policies which relate to it. However, since the entry into force of the Lisbon Treaty there is no longer a strict pillar structure of EU policies, only 'objectives'. That, and the trend towards more encompassing legislation[41] may lead to 'cross-objective' legislation.

[41] See European Commission, *Communication from the Commission to the European Parliament, the Council, the European Economic and Social Committee and the Committee of the Regions, Commission Work Programme 2015*, COM(2014) 910 final, 16.12.2014, pp. 2–3.

For example, a directive or regulation may well have its legal basis in treaty provisions that refer to the internal market, but if it also contains provisions on criminal law sanctions this stems from the objective of freedom, security and justice which is not within the scope of the EEA Agreement. This may then lead to lengthy negotiations between the EEA EFTA states and the EU on adaptations or exemptions when incorporating such a legal act into the EEA Agreement.[42]

6.3.2.1. Four Freedoms

Free Movement of Goods

49 The internal market strives to ensure that goods can move freely across the borders of all the 30 countries in the EEA on the basis of equal conditions of competition. Buyers and sellers of goods do not have to pay customs duties when trading in most products. Prior to the internal market, there were many different national technical regulations and standards, which stipulated that products need to be manufactured and tested in specific ways or that the products had to have certain properties. Through mutual recognition or harmonisation of national technical standards, and through the mutual recognition of testing procedures, these technical barriers have been removed.

Free Movement of Persons

50 EEA EFTA and EU nationals have the right to enter the territory of any EEA member state in order to work. Students, pensioners and non-working persons also have the right to move and reside in another EEA state. There are also provisions regarding family members who may accompany these persons to another EEA state. The right to free movement is complemented and supported by a system for the coordination of social security schemes and the system to ensure the mutual recognition of diplomas. EEA states do, under certain circumstances, have the right to bar certain unwanted persons from entry into their territory or to expel them.[43]

---

[42] See para. 28.

[43] EFTA Court, E-15/12, *Jan Anfinn Wahl v the Icelandic State*, 22 June 2013.

Free Movement of Services

The ability to provide services in a member state of the EEA should not be restricted on the basis of nationality. The free movement of services is closely linked to the free movement of people and the right of establishment. Services also play an important role in many stages of the production of goods. Freeing the movement of services has taken time due to the many legal and non-legal barriers restraining their provision across national borders. It was, ultimately, the incorporation of the 'Services Directive'[44] into the EEA Agreement that liberated cross-border services from many of the national restrictions that had applied until then. 51

Free Movement of Capital

The free movement of capital is essential for the free movement of persons, services and goods. The ability to move capital without incurring unnecessary delays and transaction costs is a prerequisite to the smooth functioning of an internal market. The integration of financial markets has been an ongoing priority for developing the market and has gained considerable pace in recent years. 52

6.3.2.2. Horizontal Policies

In addition to the four freedoms, strict competition rules have been introduced to prevent companies from erecting barriers that ultimately reduce the benefits gained from the four freedoms in the EEA. Moreover, the EEA Agreement contains provisions governing the behaviour of state monopolies, to restrict the use of trade distorting state aid, and to open public procurement opportunities to the entire internal market. 53

The EEA Agreement also includes horizontal provisions. These are relevant to the four freedoms and constitute the legal basis for incorporating EU legislation on social policy (including health and safety at work, labour law and equal treatment of men and women), consumer protection, the environment, statistics and company law into the EEA Agreement. 54

---

44 Directive 2006/123/EC of the European Parliament and of the Council of 12 December 2006 on services in the internal market, OJ L 376, 27.12.2006, pp. 36–68.

6.3.2.3. *Cooperation Outside the Four Freedoms and Participation in Programmes*

55 In addition to providing for the free movement of goods, persons, services and capital, as well as the horizontal issues, the EEA Agreement also covers cooperation outside the four freedoms in so-called 'flanking' areas. In these areas, cooperation is to be strengthened and broadened, insofar as these matters are not regulated elsewhere in the agreement. Cooperation in the flanking areas is carried out through common activities of various types, ranging from dialogue between respective parties and common efforts to encouraging certain activities in the EEA through participation by the EEA EFTA states in EU programmes and the establishment of joint activities in specific areas.

56 The flanking areas currently are: research and technological development, information services, the environment, education, training and youth, social policy, consumer protection, tourism, culture, energy, employment, enterprise and entrepreneurship, civil protection and public health and statistics. This is not an exhaustive list as the contracting parties to the EEA Agreement may agree to add new areas as they see fit.

6.3.2.4. *Financial Mechanisms*

57 The EEA Financial Mechanism ('EEA Grants') is essentially the EEA EFTA states' cohesion fund. This is the financial contribution of Norway, Iceland and Liechtenstein towards reducing 'the economic and social disparities between their regions'.[45] The EEA Financial Mechanism nowadays benefits 15 EU (and therefore EEA) member states in Central and Southern Europe. The shares of the three EEA EFTA states are calculated according to their GDP. While Norway pays the lion's share of over 95 per cent, Iceland contributes 3 per cent and Liechtenstein 1.2 per cent. Given the country's population of roughly 40,000, the latter is the highest contribution per capita, however.

58 After the initial period, which lasted until 1999, the Financial Mechanisms were carried over each period of five years and increased with every accession round. The current EEA Financial Mechanism for the period from 2014 to 2021 amounts to EUR 1,548.1 million.

---

[45] Art. 115 EEA.

Since 2004 there has been a parallel Norwegian Financial Mechanism ('Norway Grants'), benefiting 13 countries, which amounts to doubling Norway's share in the EEA Financial Mechanism.[46] Both the EEA and the Norwegian Financial Mechanism are managed by the Financial Mechanism Office (FMO) in Brussels. The FMO is formally part of the EFTA Secretariat. Decisions regarding the FMO and the EEA Financial Mechanism are, however, taken by the Financial Mechanism Committee (FMC), which consists of representatives of the three EEA EFTA states. 59

There is a coordination with the respective cohesion policies of the EU; decisions are, however, taken independently. There is also an independent monitoring and auditing mechanism in place. Through the Financial Mechanism Iceland, Liechtenstein and Norway are also contributing to strengthening fundamental European values such as democracy, tolerance and the rule of law. 60

6.3.3. FURTHER POLICIES OUTSIDE THE SCOPE OF THE EEA AGREEMENT

6.3.3.1. Political Dialogue

The scope of the EEA Agreement does not encompass the more political parts of the EU's cooperation, such as the Common Foreign and Security Policy (CFSP). However, there is a so-called political dialogue on different levels. 61

The first level is the EEA Council where ministers regularly exchange views on politically relevant matters in a restricted setting before or after the regular Council meeting. Another level of political dialogues is that of EEA EFTA experts with the European External Action Service (EEAS) and Council experts in meetings parallel to those in the EU-Council formats. Such meetings are amongst others those on the Western Balkans (COWEB), the Council of Europe and the Organisation for Security and Co-operation in Europe (OSCE) (COSCE) or on the Middle Eastern Peace Process (COMEP). The aim is to exchange views among essentially like-minded partners beyond mere commercial links. The last level 62

46 https://eeagrants.org/sites/default/files/resources/FMO_10%2Bfacts%2Bleaflet_Update%2B2017_FIN.pdf.

is that of CFSP measures and declarations. In this context the EEA EFTA states are invited to – in the case of political declarations of the EU – align themselves and – in the case of CFSP measures, such as listing a certain political group in a civil war-torn country as 'terrorist' or issuing economic sanctions – support these. For the EEA EFTA states these measures are not binding. They will, however, in most cases align or support the EU's declarations or sanctions unless they have specific reasons not to do so, because, e.g., Norway is a facilitator in a specific conflict.

6.3.3.2. *Schengen and Dublin*

63 All four EFTA states participate in both the Schengen and the Dublin arrangements on free movement and police cooperation and immigration as well as asylum respectively. These sectoral association agreements are not part of the EEA Agreement, but of the Bilateral Agreements II between the EU and Switzerland. The four EFTA states participate in the respective Schengen joint committee meetings, however without voting rights. This is not the place to elaborate on the details, but it needs to be mentioned that the cooperation between the EU and the EFTA states has taken a variety of different forms.

6.3.4. WHAT DOES THE EEA NOT COVER?

64 The EEA Agreement does not cover the following EU policy areas: common agriculture and fisheries policies (although the agreement contains provisions on various aspects of trade in agricultural and fish products); a common foreign and security policy; justice and home affairs (even though all EFTA states participate in 'Schengen') and the monetary union (EMU).

6.3.5. LEGISLATION AND PROCEDURES

6.3.5.1. *Formal Structure*

65 The EEA Agreement is based on the primary legislation (Treaty of Rome, Single European Act) of the European Union and on the succeeding secondary legislation (EEA-relevant regulations, directives, decisions and

Table 6.2. Substantive scope of the EEA

Features of the EEA		**What the Internal Market is not for the EEA EFTA States**
The four freedoms: Goods • Competition, state aid, public procurement, IPR • Customs matters and trade facilitation • Industrial goods • Technical cooperation, Standardisation and Mutual Recognition Agreements Persons • Free movement of persons • Recognition of professional qualifications • Social security schemes **Horizontal policies:** • Company law • Consumer protection • Environment • Social policies • Statistics	Services • Electronic communication, audiovisual services and information society • Financial services • Postal services • Transport services Capital • Company law • Financial services **Flanking areas:** • Civil protection • Education, training and youth • Employment, enterprise and entrepreneurship • Energy • Information services • Public health • Research and technological development • Tourism, culture	• Area of freedom, security and justice (but Schengen Agreement and Dublin Regulation adopted by Iceland, Norway and Switzerland; Liechtenstein to join later) • Common Agricultural and Fisheries Policies (the EEA Agreement covers some aspects of agricultural and fisheries products) • Common external tariff (EU Customs Union) • Common Foreign and Security Policy • Common trade policy • Development policy • Economic and Monetary Union • Structural Funds and the Cohesion Fund • Tax Policy Strategy

Source: D. Rao.

certain non-binding instruments adopted by the EU institutions on an ongoing basis – referred to therein as a 'key community'). Hence, a large part of the EEA Agreement is identical to the relevant parts of the EEC Treaty governing the four freedoms.

The EEA Agreement is made up of 129 articles as well as 22 annexes 66
and 49 protocols. The annexes refer to the EU acts applicable in the EEA. The protocols include provisions on specific areas such as rules on the

origin of goods, transition periods for the EEA EFTA states in certain fields, and simplified customs procedures.

6.3.5.2. The Dynamic Aspects of the Agreement

67 One of the central features of the EEA Agreement is that its common rules are continuously updated by adding new EU legislation. This aspect is essential given the large output of EU legislation on the internal market. Each month, a number of EEA-relevant pieces of legislation are incorporated into the EEA Agreement by decision of the EEA Joint Committee.

6.3.5.3. Policy Shaping

68 The EEA EFTA states have the opportunity to influence the shaping of EEA relevant legislation, i.e. proposals at the proprietary or pre-pipeline stage by the EU. This opportunity is enshrined in the EEA Agreement as a right for representatives of the EEA EFTA states to participate in expert groups of the European Commission, and to submit EEA EFTA comments on upcoming legislation. While the EEA EFTA states use these opportunities to shape legislation actively, they have little influence on the final decision on the legislation on the EU side. They can neither sit nor vote in the European Parliament or the European Council (co-legislators on the EU side for most EEA relevant legislation) and hence have to incorporate into the EEA Agreement what has ultimately been decided, if not necessarily shaped, by others.

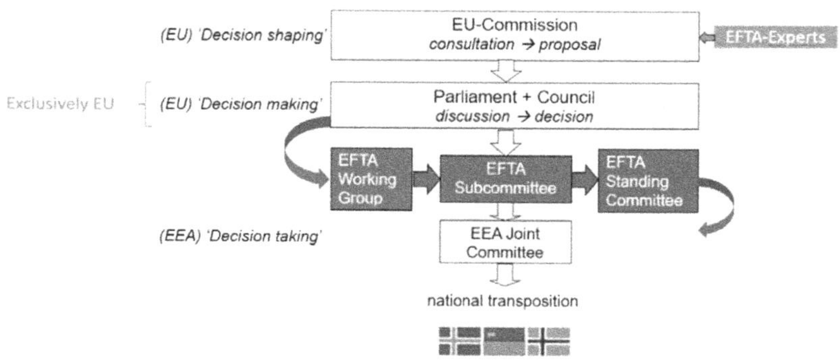

Figure 6.1. How EU law becomes EEA law

6.3.5.4. *Decision-Making*

Whenever an EEA-relevant legal act is amended or a new one adopted 69
by the EU, corresponding amendments should be made to the relevant annex of the EEA Agreement. This is essential in maintaining the principle of homogeneity of the EEA. Amendment of the EEA Agreement should ensure that the ensuing text is as close as possible to the adopted legislation on the EU side, with a view to permitting a simultaneous application in the EU and in the EFTA states. The EEA EFTA states can request a consultation on matters of concern. The EEA EFTA states can negotiate adaptations to EU legislation when this is called for by special circumstances and agreed on by both sides.

6.3.6. INSTITUTIONAL ASPECTS

6.3.6.1. *Main Principles*

Two-Pillar Structure

The Two-Pillar EEA Structure

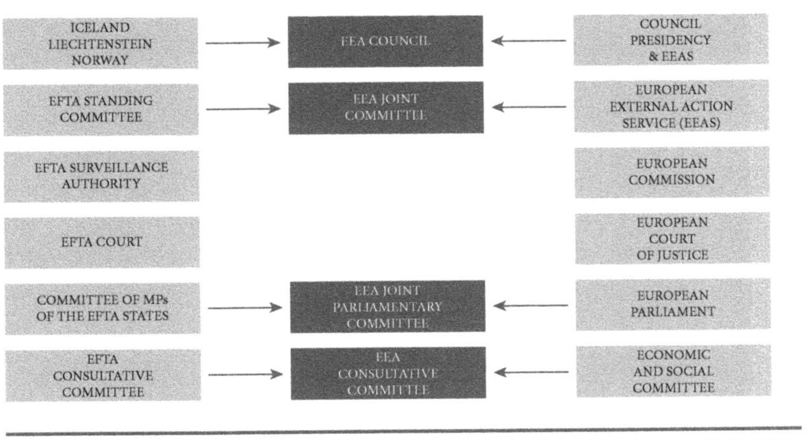

This diagram illustrates the management of the EEA Agreement. The left pillar shows the EFTA States and their institutions, while the right pillar shows the EU side. The joint EEA bodies are in the middle.

Figure 6.2. EEA two-pillar structure

70 The institutional arrangements under the EEA Agreement are laid down in a two-pillar structure with EEA EFTA institutions matching those

on the EU side. Substantive decisions relating to the EEA Agreement and its operation are a joint venture and are taken by joint bodies. The EEA EFTA states have not transferred any legislative competences to the EEA institutions. However, all decisions on the EEA EFTA side are therefore taken by unanimity. This provision reflects the fact that the EU member states do the same on their side, being represented by the EEAS in the joint meetings.

Homogeneity

71 The homogeneity principle is a – if not the – key principle of the EEA Agreement.[47] There are two major aspects of homogeneity: legislative and judicial homogeneity. Legislative homogeneity essentially deals with all aspects related to the incorporation of EU legal acts into the EEA Agreement. Here, the focus is on a substantially identical acquis in the EU's internal market and in the EEA. However, as 'homogeneous' does not mean 'the same', there is room for deviation according to differences, for instance, in the scope of the EEA Agreement compared to the EU's internal market legislation. The so-called Union Citizenship Directive[48] serves, again, as an example. As the scope of the EEA Agreement does not extend to certain aspects covered by that directive, such as EU citizenship or local voting rights, adaptions had to be made. Furthermore, there is a temporal element: 'as closely as possible', linking legislative homogeneity to a dynamic adaptation of the agreement. In order for the acquis to be homogeneous in both the EU and the three EEA EFTA states, the incorporation of legal acts should be done 'as closely as possible to the adoption by the EU of the corresponding new EU legislation with a view to permitting a simultaneous application'.[49] This has become more difficult in recent years for different reasons. Inter alia, there has been an increasing number of EU legal acts that contain

[47] G. Baur, 'Preliminary Rulings in the EEA – Bridging (Institutional) Homogeneity and Procedural Autonomy by Exchange of Information' in EFTA Court (ed.), *The EEA and the EFTA Court – Decentred Integration*, Hart Publishing, Oxford 2014, p. 170.

[48] Directive 2004/38/EC of the European Parliament and of the Council of 29 April 2004 on the right of citizens of the Union and their family members to move and reside freely within the territory of the Member States amending Regulation (EEC) No. 1612/68 and repealing Directives 64/221/EEC, 68/360/EEC, 72/194/EEC, 73/148/EEC, 75/34/EEC, 75/35/EEC, 90/364/EEC, 90/365/EEC and 93/96/EEC; OJ L 158 of 30.4.2004, pp. 77–123.

[49] Art. 102(1) EEA.

parts which are not covered by the scope of the EEA Agreement. Then the number of agencies has risen considerably, creating problems for the three EEA EFTA states as agencies are not foreseen in the EEA Agreement and a solution for the EEA EFTA states to participate needs to be found each time. Furthermore, the EU has shifted to making increasing use of regulations in its legislative activity. These 'shall as such be made part of the internal legal order of the Contracting Parties'.[50] Because they do not 'leave to the authorities of the Contracting Parties the choice of form and method of implementation',[51] EU member states, and afterwards in the EEA decision taking-process, the EEA EFTA states, are granted less time for incorporation and, in the case of Iceland and Norway, transformation into national law.

Judicial homogeneity means that interpretation by judicial bodies needs 72
to be aligned as closely as possible (see above), but, again, it does not mean there is no possibility to deviate from existing jurisprudence if the scope and aim of the EUs primary legislation and the EEA Agreement deviate accordingly. For example, while the EU's internal market is a customs union, the EEA is not.

6.3.6.2. *Joint Bodies*

The EEA Council is the top-level meeting where EEA EFTA ministers and 73
senior executives meet the EU Presidency's ministers, Commission and EEAS high-level officers. It provides political impetus for the development of the agreement and guidelines for the Joint Committee.

The EEA Joint Committee, convened about seven to eight times a year, is 74
the body responsible for the ongoing management of the EEA Agreement. It is a forum in which views are exchanged and decisions taken by consensus to incorporate EU legislation into the EEA Agreement. The Joint Committee is attended by the heads of mission of the EEA EFTA states as well as of the representatives of the EEAS and the European Commission. EU member states may sometimes participate as observers.

The EEA Joint Parliamentary Committee (EEA JPC) comprises members 75
of the national parliaments of the EEA EFTA states and members of

50 Art. 7(a) EEA.
51 Art. 7(b) EEA *e contrario*.

the European Parliament (MEPs). The committee contributes, through dialogue and debate, to a better understanding between the EU and the EFTA states of the fields covered by the agreement.

76 The EEA Consultative Committee comprises members of the EFTA consultative committee and the economic and social committee of the EU. The committee works to strengthen contacts between the social partners on both sides and to cooperate in an organised and regular manner to enhance awareness and provide input on the economic and social aspects of the EEA.

6.3.6.3. EEA EFTA Bodies (EFTA Pillar)

77 The Standing Committee of the EFTA states serves as a forum in which the EEA EFTA states consult one another and formally decide on a common position regarding Joint Committee Decisions (JCDs) before meeting with the EU in the EEA Joint Committee. It is made up of representatives of Iceland, Liechtenstein and Norway as well as observers from Switzerland and the EFTA Surveillance Authority. The committee substructure currently consists of five subcommittees. These subcommittees are Subcommittee I on the free movement of goods; Subcommittee II on the free movement of capital and services and company law; Subcommittee III on the free movement of persons; Subcommittee IV on flanking and horizontal policies, and Subcommittee V on legal and institutional matters. In practice, since 2003 subcommittees I to IV have met in the same meeting. The subcommittees coordinate positions of the EFTA states and finalise legal acts and JCDs before these are submitted to the Standing Committee. Under the subcommittees sit working groups which discuss legal acts and prepare JCDs.

78 Two other important bodies exist under the EEA EFTA pillar. The EFTA Surveillance Authority, based in Brussels, ensures that the EEA EFTA states fulfil their obligations under the EEA Agreement. In addition to general surveillance of compliance, the Surveillance Authority has powers in relation to competition, state aid and public procurement, reflecting the extended competences of the European Commission in these fields within the EU. The EFTA Court, based in Luxembourg, corresponds to the Court of Justice of the European Union in matters relating to the EEA EFTA states. The Court deals with infringement actions brought by the EFTA Surveillance Authority against an EFTA state with regard to the implementation, application or interpretation of EEA rules, and

with the settlement of disputes between two or more EFTA states. It also hears appeals concerning decisions taken by the EFTA Surveillance Authority and gives advisory opinions to courts in the EFTA states on the interpretation of EEA rules.

The ultimate control – judicial independence notwithstanding – regarding administration, personnel, finances, procedural rules etc. lies with the so-called ESA/Court Committee which is composed of the Head of Missions of the three EEA EFTA states. 79

6.3.6.4. *New Institutional Challenges: Agencies*

As discussed above, the scope and the substance of the EEA has grown over the last 25 years. Its main structure however, i.e. the main agreement, remained unchanged. Some of the tasks regarding new policies have been delegated to agencies. This concept, however, has not been introduced into the main text of EEA Agreement.[52] This created a certain challenge to the two-pillar structure. Depending on the specific case, in the EFTA pillar, the EFTA Surveillance Authority may take on the role that agencies exercise on behalf of the EU member states. There are cases where government organs of the EEA EFTA states participate directly in such agencies, albeit with no voting rights. 80

A special problem was created in the aftermath of the financial crisis of 2008. The EU built up a single financial supervisory structure to better supervise the financial services sector in the internal market and to anticipate future distortions of that market. To that end, several European financial supervisory authorities (ESAs) were set up. These have not only advisory functions, but they also have the competence to give national authorities or actors binding guidance if they fail to act as they are supposed to according to EU financial services law. It was, however, not possible for Iceland and Norway to accept this under their respective constitutions. Therefore, it was necessary to devise a complicated structure that would balance the two EEA EFTA states' constitutional barriers with the need for a centralised supervision of the internal market in financial services. The solution was found in the EFTA Surveillance Authority formally issuing any order directly affecting EEA EFTA authorities or actors, based on a draft decision prepared by the respective ESA. 81

[52] See para. 71 above.

In addition, the three EEA EFTA states join the ESAs as with EU agencies, with full participation rights but without voting rights.

6.3.7. FINANCIAL ISSUES

82 How much do the EEA/EFTA states pay for their participation in the EEA, i.e. the extended internal market? The major expenses stem from the EEA EFTA states' payments into (their own) Financial Mechanism, i.e. the three EEA EFTA states' cohesion fund, managed by themselves. Furthermore, considerable money is paid into the EEA EFTA states' participation in EU programmes. This is the only contribution to the EU budget. They, however, do so according to the same conditions as EU member states. Switzerland, by contrast, participates as a third country and therefore according to a different set of rules. Some money is also spent on the EEA EFTA states' own institutions, i.e. the EFTA Surveillance Authority and the EFTA Court. In addition, some costs are incurred for the translation of legal acts and other documents into Icelandic and Norwegian, which are – unlike German for Liechtenstein – not Union languages. This includes the publication in the EEA Annex, Icelandic and Norwegian versions of the Official Journal of the EU.

6.3.8. EXEMPTIONS, SAFEGUARD MEASURES ETC.

6.3.8.1. Exemptions

83 There are two main forms of deviating from the provisions of an EU legal act. First, an exemption, sometimes also referred to as 'derogation', is a flexibility built into the respective EU legal act. It is available to any party implementing it, either within the EU or the EEA.[53]

6.3.8.2. Adaptations[54]

84 Secondly, an adaptation may be needed. In most cases EU acts can be incorporated into the EEA Agreement without any adaptations. In some

[53] G. Baur, 'From EU law to EEA law: the decision-making process' in T. Grønningsaeter (ed.), *EFTA Bulletin 2015*, EFTA, Geneva 2015, p. 23.

[54] Ibid., pp. 23–24.

cases, however, adaptations of a technical or substantive nature may be needed owing to the particular features of the EEA Agreement or the particular situation of an EEA EFTA state. An adaption is technical if it is needed to reflect the institutional set-up of the EEA Agreement or other two-pillar related issues in the respective EU act to be incorporated. For instance, when the so-called Union Citizenship Directive had to be incorporated into the EEA Agreement, the following adaptation was technically needed: 'The words "Union citizen(s)" shall be replaced by the words 'national(s) of EC Member States and EFTA States.'[55] A substantive adaption, however, may be needed when an EU act is considered partially outside the scope of the EEA Agreement or if the deficit in the EEA EFTA states' participation in deciding on the substance of the legal act in question needs to be compensated. An example for a substantial adaptation in the same Union Citizenship Directive would be: 'The concept of "Union Citizenship" is not included in the Agreement' or 'Immigration policy is not part of the Agreement' as both are not covered by the EEA Agreement.[56]

Specific situations in the EEA EFTA states that are not taken into account in an EU act may also require specific adaptations, mostly of a substantive nature. This could be the case inter alia where geography, topography, climate, infrastructure, the economic or demographic situation and other similar circumstances are concerned. Such adaptations are, however, less likely to be agreed to, if similar wishes were already discussed and refused in comparable cases within the EU, e.g. if Norway asks for an adaptation that had previously been denied to Sweden in a similar situation. 85

In order to avoid recurring general adaptations, Protocol 1 EEA sets out how EU acts incorporated into the EEA Agreement's annexes are to be applied under the EEA Agreement. 86

6.3.8.3. *Safeguard Measures*

There are several scenarios which may lead to safeguard measures. These depend on what effect these are supposed to have and who is the intended target. 87

---

55 Art. 1(1)(3)(c) of the Decision of the EEA Joint Committee No. 158/2007 of 7 December 2007 amending Annex V (Free movement of workers) and Annex VIII (Right of establishment) to the EEA Agreement, OJ L 124, 8.5.2008, p. 20.

56 8th and 9th preambles respectively to JCD No. 158/2007 (see n. 48 above).

88 The general safeguard rules according to Article 112 EEA et seq. are of an essentially defensive character. They are applied to protect the member state concerned against a disproportionate effect of the market freedoms. Such measures apply to all. When the transitional period regarding Liechtenstein's restrictions on the right to residence elapsed in 1999, and prior to finalising negotiations on a new regime allowing that country further restriction of that freedom, Liechtenstein activated safeguard measures according to Article 112 EEA.

89 The same is true for safeguard measures regarding the free movement of capital according to Article 43 and 44 EEA. These constitute a *lex specialis* to Article 112 EEA et seq. This article was used to justify the restrictions of free movement of capital in Iceland after the financial crisis in 2008.

90 Sectoral safeguard measures, on the other hand, mainly with regard to the free movement of goods, have the character of compensatory measures. These have their origins in WTO rules transposed into the context of the internal market and are usually aimed at one or several market participant(s) allegedly infringing trade rules. In such cases the general provisions on safeguard measures may also be applied complementarily and *mutatis mutandis*. An example of these was the safeguard measures on imports of steel taken by the EU in 2002.[57] Then again, the EU Commission exempted the EEA EFTA states from the EU's safeguard measures regarding steel products in 2018 because of their participation in the EEA, whereas Switzerland was not similarly exempted.[58]

---

57 Commission Regulation (EC) No. 1337/2002 of 24 July 2002 amending Regulation (EC) No. 76/2002 introducing prior Community surveillance of imports of certain iron and steel products covered by the ECSC and EC Treaties originating in certain third countries, OJ No. L 195 of 24.7.2002, 1, and based on Council regulation (EC) No. 3285/94 of 22 December 1994 on the common rules for imports and repealing Regulation (EC) No. 518/94, OJ L 349 of 31.12.94, 53, as last amended by Regulation (EC) No. 2474/2000, OJ L 286, 11.11.2000, 1, as well as Council regulation (EC) No. 519/94 of 7 March 1994 on common rules for imports from certain third countries and repealing Regulations (EEC) Nos. 1765/82, 1766/82 and 3420/83, OJ L 67, 10.3.1994, 89.

58 European Commission, 'Trade: Commission imposes provisional safeguard measures concerning imports of a number of steel products', Press Release IP/18/4563, 18 July 2018.

6.3.8.4. *Special Solution for Liechtenstein on 'Parallel Marketability' of Goods*[59]

As the outcomes of the referendums on membership of the EEA were different in Switzerland and Liechtenstein, a potential conflict resulted from the fact that Liechtenstein would belong to two different economic areas, namely the EEA and the Swiss customs territory. On the part of the EU, participating in the EEA meant the free movement of goods. This, in turn, could only work if harmonisation of, e.g., product standards and product liability was fully implemented or catered for by the *Cassis de Dijon* principle in the non-harmonised area. In Liechtenstein, Swiss product standards are applied on the basis of the customs treaty (CT). However, because of its membership of the EEA and after expiry of the transitional periods, the product standards of the EU will apply. 91

The first question that arose was whether Liechtenstein could maintain the CT with Switzerland at all. The other EEA member states and Switzerland, however, agreed to Liechtenstein's participation in both areas.[60] Based on the reasons mentioned above, a solution had to be found which allowed Liechtenstein to be a member of both economic areas. In view of Liechtenstein's special situation,[61] all parties agreed on the principle of parallel marketability of goods.[62] This means that – within the harmonised area – goods that comply with Swiss and EU technical regulations (and, where applicable, standards) can be freely circulated in Liechtenstein. Goods that comply exclusively with EU regulations may be placed on the market in Liechtenstein but cannot be imported into Switzerland, and those that comply exclusively with Swiss regulations (and, where applicable, standards) may also be placed on the market in Liechtenstein, but not be exported to the EEA. Two regimes of free movements of goods are hereby created: one within the customs area and the other on the basis of free movement of goods within the EEA. Both regimes are independent in their legislation and content. For this 92

59 G. Baur, 'Die „parallele Verkehrsfähigkeit" und analoge Verfahren des Europarechts' in F. Baur and G. Baur (eds.), *Aktuelle Rechtsfragen 1996*, Schulthess, Zürich 1996.

60 e.g. Art. 1 of the Decision of the EEA Council No. 1/95 of 10 March 1995 on the entry into force of the Agreement on the European Economic Area for the Principality of Liechtenstein, OJ L 86, 20.4.1995, pp. 58–84.

61 Declaration by the EEA Council on free movement of persons, especially para. 2, in Decision of the EEA Council No. 1/95 (n. 53 above).

62 Annex 2 to the Decision of the EEA Council No. 1/95 (n. 53 above).

to function well, however, some measures had to be taken and a market surveillance system put in place. Its main purpose is to prevent goods that are not supposed to enter the 'other' economic zone from doing so.

93 The problem of Liechtenstein's participation in two (competing) agreements was solved in a satisfactory manner thanks to the goodwill of the (other) EEA states and Switzerland. It has been working smoothly since the accession of Liechtenstein to the EEA.

6.3.8.5. *Special Solution for Liechtenstein on Freedom of Residence*

94 Evidently, despite all principles, the EU is also willing and able to tolerate individual arrangements and even agree to particular functions of the EEA Agreement. This is confirmed not only by the construction of parallel marketability, but also by the exemption from a fundamental principle of the European Union, namely the free movement of persons. Nevertheless, the Union agreed to allowing Liechtenstein a certain restriction of free movement of persons, i.e. regarding the right to residence.

95 By virtue of Protocol 15 EEA on transitional periods with regard to the free movement of persons, Liechtenstein was entitled to maintain national provisions until 1 January 1998. Over several steps and in the context of the negotiations on the accession of the new EU member states to the EEA, Liechtenstein managed to negotiate a more durable formula. Essentially, Liechtenstein may maintain a system which subjects the right to residence to prior approval. However, a certain quota has to be distributed in an equitable manner, i.e. also giving a chance to people who are not particularly wealthy. Further, the quota has to gradually rise.[63] The particular solution for Liechtenstein on residence no longer lapses after a particular period but is subject to a review every five years.

---

[63] 'The number of residence permits available annually for nationals of Iceland, Norway or an EU Member State exercising an economic activity in Liechtenstein shall be determined in such a way that the yearly net increase from the previous year in the number of economically active nationals of those countries resident in Liechtenstein is not less than 1,75% of their number on 1 January 1998. Residence permits to persons naturalised in the course of a year shall be deducted from the basis on which the increase for the next year is calculated. Residence permits granted in excess of the minimum number shall not be counted against the increase due the following year.', Art. 1(II)(1) of the Decision of the EEA Joint Committee No. 191/1999 of 17 December 1999 amending Annexes VIII (Right of establishment) and V (Free movement of workers) to the EEA Agreement, OJ L 74, 15.3.2001, pp. 29–31; see also EFTA Court, E-2/19, *D and E*, 13 November 2019.

It will be brought forward unless a decision of the EEA Joint Committee decides otherwise.[64]

6.4. THE SECTORAL AGREEMENTS BETWEEN SWITZERLAND AND THE EU

6.4.1. INTRODUCTION

96 As mentioned in Chapter 2.4, Switzerland, being an EFTA state like Iceland, Liechtenstein and Norway, has a set of sectoral agreements with the EU that differs in many ways from the EEA Agreement. Compared with the latter, two main differences need to be highlighted: first, the absence of a comprehensive approach. Secondly, there is no overarching institutional framework that would allow for a dynamic development of the legislation or give the parties legal certainty. Hence, the aim of guaranteeing homogeneity among the two parties cannot be achieved.

97 The system of Switzerland-EU bilateral agreements comprises about 20 main agreements and 100 other bilateral agreements. The system of bilateral agreements between Switzerland and the EU, and the relevant provisions of these agreements, are summarised in the following sections.

6.4.2. IN THE BEGINNING: FTA AND INSURANCE

98 The first element of this network of agreements was the 1972 FTA, which regulates, in particular, the reduction or elimination of customs duties in bilateral trade in industrial products and processed agricultural products.

99 The 1989 Insurance Agreement[65] guarantees freedom of establishment on a reciprocal basis: Swiss insurers may establish or acquire branches and

64 P. Schafhauser, 'Personenverkehr in Liechtenstein: Unde venit – status quo – quo vadit? Ein Abriss der Entwicklung des Personenverkehrs' in G. Baur (ed.), *Europäer – Botschafter – Mensch, Liber Amicorum Prince Nikolaus von Liechtenstein*, Liechtenstein Verlag, Schaan 2007, pp. 209–211.

65 Agreement of 10 October 1989 between the Swiss Confederation and the European Economic Community concerning direct insurance other than life assurance, OJ L 205, 27.7.1991, pp. 3–44.

agencies within the EU in the field of non-life insurance which, directly cover different types of damage (household insurance, vehicles, travel, liability, etc.). The same is true for EU insurers in Switzerland.

6.4.3. FIRST SET OF SECTORAL AGREEMENTS (BILATERAL AGREEMENTS I)

100 Following the rejection of Switzerland's participation in the Agreement on the European Economic Area (EEA) by its people and the cantons, on 6 December 1992, Switzerland led, as early as 1994, negotiations with the EU, which resulted in seven agreements (Bilateral Agreements I) on:

- free movement of persons;
- technical barriers to trade (MRA);
- public procurement;
- agriculture;
- land transport;
- air transport (civil aviation); and
- research.

101 These agreements were signed in 1999 and entered into force in 2002 after their approval by the people by a large majority.[66] At the time, the conclusion of Bilateral Agreements I was an important element of the reform efforts of the 1990s, which went hand-in-hand with a relatively high unemployment rate (by Swiss standards). Many Swiss companies were suffering from their unfavourable position regarding market access compared to their competitors based in the EU. Thus, the issue of securing market access by removing regulatory differences and trade barriers was of great importance.

102 With the exception of the Agreement on Research, the Bilateral Agreements I aimed at improving market access, most of the time through approximation or alignment of the applicable rules: with the Agreement on the Free Movement of Persons (AFMP),[67] Swiss and EU nationals were

---

[66] Message concerning the approval of sectoral agreements between Switzerland and the European Community of 23 June 1999, FF (Swiss Federal Journal *French*) 1999 5440.

[67] Agreement of 21 June 1999 between the Swiss Confederation on the one hand, and the European Community and its Member States, on the other, on the free movement of persons, OJ L 114, 30.4.2002, pp. 6–22.

granted the right to choose freely their place of work and domicile in the territory of both parties. To do this, they must have a valid employment contract, be self-employed or, if they are not gainfully employed, have sufficient financial means and extended health insurance. In addition, the AFMP coordinates social security systems and regulates the mutual recognition of professional qualifications in the field of regulated professions. The AFMP has considerably facilitated the recruitment of labour for Swiss companies. Free movement of persons remains, however, strongly contested by many in Switzerland.

The Agreement on the Elimination of Technical Barriers to Trade (also 103
known as the MRA, Mutual Recognition Agreement)[68] regulates the recognition, compliance and examinations of many industrial products traded between Switzerland and the EU. This is done on the basis of harmonisation of the law and equivalence of product requirements. Thus, placing products on the market is facilitated reciprocally in almost 20 sectors, in particular for machinery, motor vehicles, medical devices, electrical equipment and telecommunications equipment. The latter, e.g., helps integrate Switzerland into the EU's telecommunications market.

The Agreement on Government Procurement[69] expands the scope of the 104
WTO Agreement on Government Procurement. Swiss and European companies thus benefit from enhanced market access.

The Agricultural Agreement[70] facilitates trade in agricultural products 105
between Switzerland and the EU. This involves the reduction or removal of tariffs and import quotas and non-tariff barriers (mutual recognition of product and marketing requirements and the abolition of border controls, for example in the veterinary field) in certain areas of production.

The Land Transport Agreement[71] liberalises the road and rail transport 106
market for the transport of goods and people between Switzerland and

---

68 Agreement of 21 June 1999 between the Swiss Confederation and the European Community on mutual recognition in conformity assessment, OJ L 114, 30.4.2002, pp. 369–429.

69 Agreement of 21 June 1999 between the Swiss Confederation and the European Community on certain aspects of public procurement, OJ L 114, 30.4.2002, pp. 430–467.

70 Agreement of 21 June 1999 between the Swiss Confederation and the European Community concerning trade in agricultural products, OJ L 114, 30.4.2002, pp. 132–368.

71 Agreement of 21 June 1999 between the Swiss Confederation and the European Community on the carriage of goods and passengers by rail and by road, OJ L 114, 30.4.2002, pp. 91–131.

the EU. The agreement also ensured the recognition at European level of the Swiss policy of redirecting the transfer of freight from road to rail.

107 The Agreement on Air Transport[72] regulates access to the reciprocal market for airlines and thus allows for the integration of Switzerland into the liberalised European air transport market. Thanks to the reciprocal granting of traffic rights and the prohibition of all discrimination, Swiss companies are placed on an equal footing with their European competitors. This agreement exceptionally contains an institutional set-up whereby surveillance is – partly – executed by the European Commission and the competence for dispute resolution lies with the CJEU.

108 The Research Agreement laid the groundwork for Switzerland's participation in some of the research cooperation projects within the EU. The 2004 and 2007 specific agreements have enabled Switzerland to participate fully in the designated programmes. An agreement on a partial association of Switzerland with the eighth generation of 2014–20 research framework programmes ('Horizon 2020') was signed on 5 December 2014.[73] With the deadlock regarding the conclusion of an institutional framework agreement (IFA), the outlook for further Swiss participation looked rather bleak at the time of writing.

6.4.4. SECOND SET OF SECTORAL AGREEMENTS (BILATERAL AGREEMENTS II)

109 The second set of agreements concluded subsequently, the Bilateral Agreements II, took into account other economic interests, and expanded the cooperation between Switzerland and the EU to new areas beyond the existing framework. The agreements of the second package are:

- Schengen/Dublin;
- taxation of savings;

---

[72] Agreement of 21 June 1999 between the Swiss Confederation and the European Community on Air Transport, OJ L 114, 30.4.2002, pp. 73–90.

[73] Agreement on Scientific and Technological Cooperation between the European Union and the European Atomic Energy Community and the Swiss Confederation associating the Swiss Confederation with the Horizon 2020 framework program for research and innovation and the research and training program of the European Atomic Energy Community complementing the Horizon 2020 framework program and regulating the participation of the Swiss Confederation ITER activities carried out by Fusion for Energy, OJ L 370, 30.12.2014, p. 3.

- fight against fraud;
- processed agricultural products;
- the environment;
- statistics;
- MEDIA programme;
- education programmes; and
- pensions.

The Schengen Association Agreement[74] facilitates travel between Switzerland and the EU through the removal of identity controls at the internal borders of the Schengen Area. In addition, it sets common rules for entry into the Schengen Area, introduces a homogeneous policy for short-term visas and improves international cooperation in the areas of justice and the police in the fight against crime. The Dublin Association Agreement[75] ensures that an asylum application is examined by only one state in the Dublin Area. The Dublin criteria make it possible to determine competences in this field in a clear way; this makes it possible to prevent asylum seekers from making several requests or being sent back from one country to another.[76] 110

The Agreement on the Taxation of Savings[77] allows for the imposition of cross-border payments of interest to natural persons domiciled in 111

74 Agreement of 26 October 2004 between the Swiss Confederation, the European Union and the European Community on the Association of the Swiss Confederation in the Implementation, Application and Development of the Schengen acquis, OJ L 53, 27.2.2008, pp. 52–79.

75 Agreement of 26 October 2004 between the Swiss Confederation and the European Community on the criteria and mechanisms for determining the State responsible for examining an asylum application lodged in a Member State or in Switzerland, OJ L 53, 27.2.2008, pp. 5–17.

76 Since the signing of these agreements on 26 October 2004, 168 developments of the Schengen acquis and four developments of the Dublin/Eurodac acquis have been notified to Switzerland (status as at March 2015). Depending on the content of the legal act, the Federal Council or the Parliament is competent for its incorporation. In the latter case, there is the possibility of resorting to the option of a referendum. Parliament's approval is or has been necessary for the incorporation of 26 legal developments, including the introduction of the Schengen Information System (SIS), the amendment of the Schengen Borders Code or participation in the Agency for the Protection of Human Rights as well as in FRONTEX (European Border and Coast Guard Agency).

77 Agreement of 26 October 2004 between the Swiss Confederation and the European Community providing for measures equivalent to those provided for in Council Directive 2003/48/EC on the taxation of savings income in the form of interest payments, OJ L 385, 29.12.2004, pp. 30–49.

the EU: Swiss paying agents (e.g. banks) levy a withholding tax on interest credited in Switzerland and which has been collected by EU taxpayers (in a similar way to Swiss withholding tax).

112 The Anti-Fraud Agreement[78] enhances cooperation between Switzerland and the EU in the fight against smuggling and other crimes in the area of indirect taxes (e.g. customs duties, value added tax, taxes on consumption), subsidies and public procurement.

113 The Agreement on Processed Agricultural Products[79] substantially revises Protocol No. 2 of the 1972 EU-Switzerland FTA,[80] which regulates trade in processed agricultural products (e.g. chocolate, coffee, beverages, biscuits, pasta, pastries, soups, sauces, etc.). The industrial component of these products is mutually exempted from customs duties. Protocol 2 allows Switzerland to continue to compensate domestic producers for price differences between Switzerland and the EU for certain processed agricultural raw materials.

114 The Environment Agreement[81] regulates the modalities of Switzerland's participation in the European Environment Agency, which is one of the most important instruments of European environmental cooperation.

115 The Agreement on Statistical Cooperation[82] lays the groundwork for harmonising the collection of statistical data in Switzerland and the EU. It guarantees access to a vast database, which is an important support for political and economic decision-making.

---

78 Cooperation Agreement of 26 October 2004 between the Swiss Confederation, of the one part, and the European Community and its Member States, of the other part, to combat fraud and any other illegal activity affecting their financial interests, OJ L 46, 17.2.2009, pp. 8–35. This agreement has not yet entered into force. However, Switzerland has been applying the agreement early since 2009 to EU member states that have also ratified the agreement and made a declaration on its early implementation. Thus, the agreement is already applied by Switzerland, the EU and several member states.

79 Agreement of 26 October 2004 between the Swiss Confederation and the European Community amending the Agreement between the Swiss Confederation and the European Economic Community of 22 July 1972 as regards the provisions applicable to processed agricultural products, OJ L 23, 26.1.2005, pp. 19–48.

80 Protocol No. 2 of 22 July 1972 concerning certain processed agricultural products, OJ L 300, 31.12.1972, pp. 191–282.

81 Agreement of 26 October 2004 between the Swiss Confederation and the European Community concerning the participation of Switzerland in the European Environment Agency and in the European Network and information for the environment (EIONET), OJ L 90, 28.3.2006, pp. 37–47.

82 Agreement of 26 October 2004 between the Swiss Confederation and the European Community on statistical cooperation, OJ L 90, 28.3.2006, pp. 2–20.

Until it ended in 2013, the MEDIA Agreement[83] enabled Switzerland to participate in the EU film support programme 'MEDIA 2007–2013'. The aim of this programme was to encourage the development, distribution and marketing of European film production. Since the beginning of 2014, the MEDIA programme has been integrated into the EU Culture Promotion Programme 'Creative Europe'. There is currently no agreement providing for the participation of Switzerland in this programme. 116

The Pensions Agreement[84] avoids double taxation of former EU officials domiciled in Switzerland. 117

6.4.5. FURTHER AGREEMENTS

In addition, other agreements have been concluded between Switzerland and the EU: the 2004 Agreement[85] between Switzerland and Europol, the EU's criminal prosecution authority, improves police cooperation in preventing and combating international crime and terrorism. 118

The 2008 Agreement[86] between Switzerland and Eurojust, the EU's judicial cooperation unit, strengthens international cooperation in the fight against serious crime. 119

The 1990 Agreement on the Transport of Goods regulated customs controls and formalities in the exchange of goods between Switzerland and the EU. It simplified the clearance of goods and coordinated cooperation at customs posts. In 2009, it was replaced by the new Agreement on Customs Facilitation and Security.[87] This complements the previous agreement by regulating security cooperation in the area of trade in goods. It prevents Switzerland from being subject to the corresponding EU 120

---

83 Agreement of 11 October 2007 between the Swiss Confederation and the European Community in the audiovisual field, establishing the terms and conditions for the participation of the Swiss Confederation in the Community program MEDIA 2007, OJ L 303, 21.11.2007, pp. 11–23.

84 Agreement of 26 October 2004 between the Swiss Federal Council and the Commission of the European Communities to avoid the double taxation of Retired officials of the institutions and agencies of the European Communities residing in Switzerland, SR/RS 0.672.926.81.

85 Agreement of 24 September 2004 between the Swiss Confederation and the European Police Office, SR/RS 0.362.2.

86 Agreement between Switzerland and Eurojust of 27 November 2008, SR/RS 0351.6.

87 Agreement of 25 June 2009 between the Swiss Confederation and the European Community on the facilitation of checks and formalities in the transport of goods and on customs security measures, OJ L 199, 31.7.2009, pp. 24–42.

measures, which the EU has taken autonomously and which complicates the importation of goods from third countries, such as the prior declaration requirement for the imports.

121 The 2010 Education Agreement enabled Switzerland to participate fully in the 2007–13 EU programmes in education, vocational training and youth. The agreement gave Swiss women and men full access to all the mobility and cooperation projects provided for by these programmes. There is currently no agreement for Switzerland's participation in the new 2014–20 training programme (Erasmus +).

122 The 2013 Competition Cooperation Agreement[88] allows for effective cooperation between the two parties' competition authorities in combating cross-border restrictions on competition. Due to the close economic relations between Switzerland and the EU, effective enforcement of national competition rules is proving increasingly difficult in the absence of such cooperation.

123 The Satellite Navigation Agreement[89] of 2013 allows Switzerland to participate in the European Galileo and EGNOS programmes. Galileo is a global satellite positioning system that aims to eliminate dependence on the American GPS system. EGNOS is a regional navigation system that improves the accuracy and reliability of global satellite signals.

124 The Participation Agreement to EASO[90] of 2014 provides for the participation of Switzerland in the European Asylum Support Office (EASO). The main objective of EASO is to support states that are parties to the Dublin Agreement and whose asylum and reception systems are under particular pressure.

125 The Arrangement for Armed Collaboration with the European Defence Agency (EDA)[91] of 2012 enables Switzerland to identify developments

[88] Agreement of 17 May 2013 between the Swiss Confederation and the European Union concerning cooperation on the application of their competition laws, OJ L 347, 3.12.2014, pp. 3–9.

[89] Cooperation agreement of 18 December 2013 between the Confederation Switzerland, on the one hand, and the European Union and its Member States, on the other, on European satellite navigation programs, OJ L 15, 20.1.2014, pp. 3–17.

[90] Arrangement of 10 June 2014 between the Swiss Confederation and the European Union on the modalities of its participation in the European Asylum Support Office, OJ L 65, 11.3.2016, pp. 22–37.

[91] Framework for cooperation between the European Defence Agency and the Federal Department of Defence, Civil Protection and Sports of the Swiss Confederation non-binding, for text see https://register.consilium.europa.eu/doc/srv?l=EN&f=ST%20 17172%202011%20INIT.

in armaments policy early enough and to gain access to cooperation projects in Europe, mainly in the areas of research and development and the acquisition and maintenance of armaments.

6.4.6. 'AUTONOMOUS ADAPTATION'

Given the only partial participation of Switzerland in the internal market 126
there are areas of Swiss law which are not subject to formal adaptation to EU law. It is, however, in the economic interest of Switzerland to legislate as closely as possible to EU law in order to create as few difficulties as possible for the exporting industry. Out of that need the Swiss concept of autonomous adaptation ('*autonomer Nachvollzug*', '*reprise autonome*')[92] was born. The most recent example of such an autonomous adaptation is the unilateral introduction of the 'Cassis de Dijon principle' by which Switzerland unilaterally allows products corresponding to EU standards to access its market.[93] When European law is adopted without the existence of a legal obligation in this regard, there is, of course, a wide variety of ways to do this. One speaks of 'autonomous adaptation' when the European model is adopted more or less unchanged. European influence can, however, also be exerted in a more general inspiration that does not differ fundamentally from the influence of other preparatory work, e.g. on a bill.[94] Of course, if the adjustment is based not on economic incentives but on pressure, there can no longer be any talk of an 'autonomous' process. This is, for example, the case when compatibility with European law is a prerequisite for access to the EU's internal market.[95]

---

92 See more extensively e.g.: F. Maiani, 'Legal Europeanization as Legal Transformation: Some Insights from Swiss "Outer Europe"', in F. Maiani, R. Petrov, and E. Mouliarova (eds.), *European Integration Without EU Membership: Models, Experiences, Perspectives, EUI MWP, 2009/10*, pp. 4–9, retrieved from Cadmus, European University Institute Research Repository, at: http://hdl.handle.net/1814/11294, 21.1.2020; M. Oesch, *Switzerland and the European Union*, Dike/Nomos, Zurich/St. Gallen 2018, pp. 139–53.

93 An introduction can be found in M. Oesch (n. 90), pp. 149–51.

94 For terminology that alternates between 'autonomous adaptation' and 'inspiration', see the Swiss Federal Council *Europe Report 2006*, BBl. (Federal Gazette) 2006, 6815, pp. 6831–33 (German). As a criterion for choosing the form of adaptation ibid., p. 6831: 'The so-called autonomous adaptation is sought wherever economic interests (competitiveness) require or justify it.' (Translation by the author).

95 A. Heinemann, 'Rechtliche Transplantate zwischen Europäischer Union und der Schweiz', in L. Fahrländer, et al., *Europäisierung der schweizerischen Rechtsordnung*, Dike, Zürich 2013, p. 20.

6.4.7. PROBLEM OF LACKING INSTITUTIONAL FRAMEWORK

127 Since 2006, when it became clear that Switzerland would neither join the EU in the near future nor attempt a second referendum on the EEA,[96] the EU has increasingly expressed its dissatisfaction with the Bilateral Agreements it once entered into with Switzerland. It bears repeating that the EU only accepted the piecemeal approach at the time, assuming Switzerland might either try again to join the EEA or then join the EU altogether. None of this happened. Upon the EU's insistence, Switzerland had agreed to negotiate with the EU an institutional framework agreement in order to bring the relationship between the EU and Switzerland closer to the standards mentioned above.

128 Such an agreement would establish a common framework for five of the several Bilateral Agreements, namely those on the free movement of persons, including the right of establishment and the posting of workers, land transport, civil aviation, TBT/MRA and agriculture. Several other agreements, most notably the EU-Switzerland FTA, are not included. There would be a dispute settlement mechanism whereby the parties, if they failed to arrive at a consensus in the Joint Committee, could choose to bring the dispute before an arbitration panel. This panel is bound to refer questions of interpretation of EU law to the CJEU. The decisions of the CJEU are binding upon the arbitration panel and, hence, the parties.

129 Upon finalising the negotiations of the IFA in November 2018,[97] the Swiss government did not sign but organised a consultation of the major parties and stakeholders. In its feedback, the three most contested elements were:

- including the Swiss so-called 'flanking measures', adding national measures to the rules on posting of workers as per the AFMP, as Swiss trade unions fear this would facilitate more 'social dumping';

---

96 With the ratification of the second round of bilateral treaties, the Swiss Federal Council downgraded its characterisation of a full EU membership of Switzerland from a 'strategic goal' to an 'option' in 2006, Swiss Federal Council, 'Rapport Europe 2006', 06.064, 28.06.2006, FF 2006 6461, p. 6620 (French).

97 Swiss Federal Department of Foreign Affairs, 'Accord facilitant les relations bilatérales entre l'Union européenne et la Confédération suisse dans les parties du marché intérieur auxquelles la Suisse participe', 23 November 2018, https://www.eda.admin.ch/dam/dea/fr/documents/abkommen/Acccord-inst-Projet-de-texte_fr.pdf.

- incorporating rules on state aid, as cantons fear their cantonal banks would lose their privilege to extend state guarantees for savings; and
- eventually incorporating the Union Citizenship Directive[98] as this is seen by some to further open Switzerland up to foreign immigration.

Hence, the Swiss government requested 'clarifications' on these points as the EU had – as with the discussions about the Withdrawal Agreement between the EU and the UK – refused to reopen or renegotiate the agreement. It seems that currently there is a deadlock. 130

6.5. OUTLOOK

6.5.1. FURTHER DEVELOPMENT OF EU PRINCIPLES

Further to the general principles ('Interlaken Principles') that the EU had established for participation in the EU's internal market and before that, the enhanced EFTA-EC cooperation, the EU established certain refined conditions for other association agreements.[99] Taking the EEA Agreement as the benchmark,[100] the EU has repeatedly made clear that it expects the following four institutional horizontal conditions as well as the homogeneity principle to be included in any framework agreement in order to ensure 'legal certainty for authorities, operators and individual citizens'.[101] 131

The first condition is that there has to be a 'dynamic' approach to the relationship, i.e. the adoption of new legislation occurs at regular intervals, which in turn leads to a huge increase in the number of Joint Committee meetings. Due to their frequency and the need to act at a much quicker pace than in classical agreements and because these decisions have a direct impact on national legislation, conflicts may arise with the democratic process in some of the states, especially if the national constitutional requirement includes referendums. This can cause 132

98 See n. 46 above.

99 See generally G. Baur, 'Privileged partnerships – The partner countries' (institutional) perspectives' in S. Gstöhl and D. Phinnemore (eds.), *The Proliferation of Privileged Partnerships between the European Union and its Neighbours*, Routledge, London and New York 2020 (2019).

100 Ibid., pp. 28–29.

101 Council of the EU, 'Council Conclusions on EU Relations with EFTA Countries', 3060th General Affairs Council meeting, Brussels, 14 December 2010, para. 42.

delays in decision-making. Secondly, independent surveillance and, thirdly, judicial enforcement should ensure that the associated country or countries effectively abide by the rules. These institutions should also be international.[102] Hence, a national supervisory body and a national legal institution for enforcement will not suffice. Fourthly, dispute settlement is the tool to settle disputes between the contracting parties to an agreement, but it does not give individuals and economic operators access to supranational justice. Finally, if non-members participate in the internal market, there needs to be a 'homogeneous interpretation of the agreements'.[103] This is closely linked to the first horizontal condition, namely the dynamic adaptation of the agreement. The homogeneity principle does not, however, only encompass the incorporated acquis, but also the future acquis to be incorporated. Furthermore, it also applies to the jurisprudence of the CJEU.

133 Next to the aforementioned institutional conditions, the EU also requires a new partner to an association agreement in the Western European context, granting participation in the EU's internal market, the commitment to the entire set of the four freedoms, essentially as covered by the scope of the EEA Agreement.[104]

6.5.2. PRE-EEA AGREEMENTS: STILL OF VALUE

134 By 1976, EEC policy towards the EFTA countries was essentially restricted to the management and improvement of the industrial free trade regime and it did not want any institutional constraints. The policy towards the EFTA countries was thus to be informal and pragmatic, and to exclude explicit recourse to the FTA evolutionary clauses.[105] In 1978, however, the Commission started to see the need to improve relations, 'to perfect the agreements, something that in turn would demand an

---

[102] Council of the EU, 'Council Conclusions on EU Relations with EFTA Countries', Brussels, 20 December 2012, p. 6.

[103] Ibid.

[104] CJEU, Case C-547/10 P, *Swiss Confederation v European Commission*, ECLI:EU:C:2013:139, nr. 78.

[105] Document de travail. Poursuite et développement des relations entre la Communauté et les pays de l'AELE, sans date, BAC 48/1984, No. 102, HAEC, mentioned in L. Rye, 'Slow train coming. EFTA's quest for free trade in Western Europe (1960–92)' in T. Grønningsaeter (ed.), *EFTA Bulletin 2015*, EFTA, Geneva 2015, p. 10.

improvement of consultation procedures'.[106] An important reason for this was the economic crisis of the time. Another was that it was becoming increasingly difficult to differentiate between domestic and external affairs, mainly with regard to policies on employment, industrial restructuring and state aid 'where domestic policies had inevitable and often immediate consequences for relations with other countries'.[107] While the relationship between EFTA and the EC remained informal and pragmatic, closer cooperation slowly came about and new areas of cooperation, such as rules of origin, trade in agricultural products, processed agricultural products, TBT, the Community trade mark, public contracts, state aid and environment were examined. With the Luxembourg Declaration in 1984, extended cooperation between the EFTA countries and the EC beyond the boundaries of the FTAs was publicly agreed. The parties agreed to pursue more precisely their efforts in the following areas: harmonisation of standards, elimination of technical barriers, simplification of border facilities and rules of origin, elimination of unfair trading practices, state aid and access to government procurement. The aim was to create what at this point was being referred to as 'a dynamic economic space'. In so doing, the parties should proceed as before, by means of 'continued pragmatic and flexible cooperation'.[108]

Within EFTA, the Luxembourg Process led to a growing awareness of the need to intensify preparatory work, to harmonise positions and quite generally to make better use of the EFTA Secretariat. However, the piecemeal approach did not match the hopes EFTA had placed in this revived form of cooperation with the EC, certainly not with regard to a certain parallelism between the development of mutual relations and the development of the (then) EC's internal market. 135

But these first steps that were taken in this period, producing concrete agreements in areas such as public procurement, state aid, technical regulations and the simplification of the rules of origin etc. laid the basis for what was to come later. And most importantly, these agreements, partly amended and transferred into the EEA Agreement or the Bilateral Agreements between the EU and Switzerland, are still used in the EFTA-EU cooperation. 136

---

106 Ibid.

107 Ibid.

108 Rye (n. 93 above) p. 11.

6.5.3. EEA: BENCHMARK

137 The EEA Agreement is, until now, the only association agreement that provides for an 'economically integrated entity with a single market, based on common rules between its members'.[109] It is also the only association agreement that is multilateral, covering two groups of countries. They meet in the joint bodies with each group having one voice. The EU member states coordinate their positions in their institutions (Working Groups, the Committee of Permanent Representatives [COREPER], Council). In the joint bodies of the EEA, the EU is then represented by the European External Action Service (EEAS). Such 'discipline' for the purpose of decision-making in the EEA Agreement had to be introduced on the EFTA side as well. Hence, the EEA EFTA states must 'speak with one voice'.[110] The process is, however, of an intergovernmental rather than a supranational nature. This requirement that the EEA EFTA states speak with one voice is the precondition for the functioning of the two-pillar structure. From this also follows that membership of the EEA can only be through membership of either the EU or EFTA.

138 The 'benchmark' of the EEA Agreement involves a sophisticated institutional arrangement to achieve the dynamic incorporation of new EU law through so-called Joint Committee Decisions (JCDs) which serve as the legal basis on which EU legal acts are transposed into EEA law. The dynamic element is the regular and – compared to 'old style' international agreements – much better structured and more intense calendar of meetings that allows for amending the agreement as closely as possible to reflect the adoption of corresponding EU legislation 'with a view to permitting a simultaneous application'.[111] This has worked rather well over the last 25 years.

6.5.4. EU-SWITZERLAND 'BILATERAL AGREEMENTS': PROVISIONAL PIECEMEAL APPROACH, OR IS IT?

139 The EU–Switzerland relationship lacks a comprehensive institutional framework. This leads to an overall different treatment by the EU compared with Switzerland's fellow EFTA members – Iceland, Liechtenstein and

---

109 *Swiss Confederation v European Commission* (n. 104 above) para. 78.
110 Art. 93(2) EEA.
111 Art. 102(1) EEA.

Norway. For example, the latter are, through membership of the EEA, exempt from EU safeguard measures regarding steel products, whereas Switzerland is not.[112] Switzerland is in the process of rearranging its relationship with the EU. In late 2018 the EU and Switzerland concluded negotiations on a draft institutional framework agreement covering existing and future bilateral market access agreements.[113]

With regard to Switzerland, however, it is only the Schengen and Dublin Agreements with the EU as well as the Agreement on Customs Facilitation and Security that contain provisions on their own development.[114] These adaptations are discussed in the respective joint committees. From the Swiss point of view, this has the advantage that changes cannot be imposed by the EU. Furthermore, Switzerland is – for now – in a position where it can delay, and *de facto* block, unwanted amendments. A prominent example is the so-called Union Citizenship Directive, which Switzerland – despite the EU's insistence – has refused to incorporate into the AFMP. 140

For the foreseeable future it can be assumed that little will change with regard to the current EFTA states' respective forms of relationship with the EU. 141

---

112 European Commission, 'Trade: Commission Imposes Provisional Safeguard Measures Concerning Imports of a Number of Steel Products', Press Release IP/18/4563, 18 July 2018.

113 See n. 97 above.

114 M. Oesch, *Switzerland and the European Union*, Dike and Nomos, Zürich/St. Gallen/Baden-Baden 2018, pp. 42–43.

CHAPTER 7
CONCLUSION
EFTA Membership for the UK Post-Brexit?

7.1. INTRODUCTION

In this final chapter of the present book, the discussion turns to the potential benefits of (renewed) EFTA membership for the UK post Brexit. The issue has to be seen against the background of the fact that, rather soon after the referendum on Brexit, it started to dawn on many that the UK will, by leaving the EU, also leave the EU's FTA network. Furthermore, it will need a new basis for its trade relationships with its closest partners in Europe, including in particular the EU member states as well as the EFTA states of Iceland, Liechtenstein, Norway and Switzerland. 1

The idea that the UK could or should (re-)join EFTA, was not only promoted by certain political groups in the discussion after the referendum of 23 June 2016.[1] In 2017, there was also a report of the House of Commons International Trade Committee,[2] which stated the following: 2

> 'We recommend that the Government now evaluate the implications of the UK's rejoining the European Free Trade Association (EFTA), which would offer an opportunity for a smoother transition as the UK exits the EU in 2019. We were impressed by the potential benefits of EFTA membership, given there is close alignment between the UK's economy and those of EFTA members, albeit the UK would be considerably the largest member were it to join. The prospect of UK membership of EFTA from 2019 onwards could clearly be to Britain's

1 e.g. 'EFTA 4 UK', https://efta4uk.co.uk.

2 House of Commons International Trade Committee, 'UK trade options beyond 2019', First Report of Session 2016–17, HC 817, 7 March 2017, https://publications.parliament.uk/pa/cm201617/cmselect/cmintrade/817/817.pdf.

advantage and we, therefore, recommend that the Secretary of State publish a White Paper on EFTA membership before summer 2017, so that negotiations can commence before the end of the year.'[3]

3 However, this recommendation was not taken up by the UK government.

4 Since the General Election of December 2019, the UK is set to leave the EU on 31 January 2020. After that, there is a rather short time frame until 31 December 2020 in which to negotiate the new relationship with the EU and also FTAs to replace the EU's FTA network which the UK will leave by that date. Extensions may be possible, but the revised Withdrawal Agreement Bill (WAB) now also contains a clause 'prohibiting any UK Minister from agreeing to an extension of the transition or implementation period in the Joint Committee (new clause 33)'.[4] That, of course, limits the UK government's leeway and makes the issue of time an even more important one.[5] Even 'no deal', in the event of a stalemate between the negotiating parties, may be possible again. Nevertheless, given this short time frame, the question remains: could (re-)joining EFTA benefit the UK and if so, in which way?

5 Just for the sake of completeness it needs to be said that with leaving the EU, the UK will also leave the EEA.[6]

6 This chapter aims to answer this question by highlighting some of the most important elements of EFTA that may prove relevant from a UK perspective post-Brexit. In this context, it will be shown that

---

3 Ibid., p. 4.

4 European Union (Withdrawal Agreement) Act 2020, clause 33 introducing a new Art. 15A after section 15 of the European Union (Withdrawal) Act 2018; see https://commonslibrary.parliament.uk/brexit/legislation/the-new-eu-withdrawal-agreement-bill-whats-changed/.

5 See below, para. 28.

6 This follows – inter alia – from the two-pillar structure of the EEA Agreement and Art. 126 EEA, which states that the EEA Agreement applies to the territory of the EU and the three EEA EFTA states (see e.g. C.A.P. Hillion, 'Brexit means Br(EEA)xit – The UK withdrawal from the EU and its implications for the EEA', *Common Market Law Review*, 2018, (2018) 55(1), pp. 135–56). While this question is not unchallenged in academic writing (see e.g. U.G. Schroeter and H. Nemeczek, 'The (Uncertain) Impact of Brexit on the United Kingdom's Membership in the European Economic Area', EULR 2016, pp. 921–958), politically there is agreement on the matter. All parties – the EEA EFTA states, EU27 and the UK government – agreed that the EEA Agreement will not apply to the UK after its withdrawal from the EU. Hence, a parallel Withdrawal Agreement (EEA) was drafted.

EFTA membership concerns not only the legal relationship among the EFTA countries themselves but also has implications and creates opportunities for the relationship with other countries, both EU member states and other third countries.

The chapter begins by listing a number of important benefits of EFTA membership internally, among the EFTA members (7.2. below). Thereafter, it turns to the role that EFTA can play as a platform for legal relationships with other countries, here notably the EU and its member states, but also FTAs with the wider world. This issue has to be seen against the broader background of the UK's future relationship with the EU after the transitional period of the Withdrawal Agreement, which is currently uncertain (7.3. below). A short conclusion will round this chapter off. 7

7.2. BENEFITS OF EFTA IN THE INTERNAL RELATIONS AMONG ITS MEMBERS

7.2.1. SUBSTANCE OF EFTA LAW

When considering EFTA membership of the UK, the question needs to be asked whether the internal, substantive rules of the EFTA Convention would be attractive or rather stand in the way of the UK's aims with regard to its post-Brexit trade policy. As will be shown, the former seems to be the case. 8

EFTA, as a link between its member states, is still essentially a free trade zone, i.e. it deals with abolishing or at least minimising tariffs in trade between them. Furthermore, EFTA states grant each other at least WTO+ conditions in most areas covered. In order to give each other rights that are analogous to those resulting from their respective relations with the EU, internal market elements have been incorporated into the EFTA Convention with its revision in 2001. These are, in the first instance, the classical 'four freedoms' (freedom of movement of goods, persons, services and capital) and related areas and substantially correspond to respective EU law. However, there is a big functional difference with regard to whether they are derived EU law. They are not identical to the EU's internal market rules or those of the EEA and they do not directly depend on these. More precisely this is to say that these elements exist in the context of the EFTA Convention because the 9

EFTA states so wish and not because they have to as a consequence of an association agreement with the EU.

7.2.2. THE INSTITUTIONAL FRAMEWORK

10 A similar question as in the previous chapter can be asked with regard to the institutional framework provided by the EFTA Convention. This was an important point in the Leave campaign and, subsequently, of the UK government's position on the future relationship between the UK and the EU.[7] As shown in Chapter 4, the institutional framework is very light touch. Essentially, it is an intergovernmental organisation and the EFTA states did not surrender any sovereign rights to a supranational or other body.

11 The Council, where the EFTA states are represented, is the supreme organ. This is where all decision-making happens; decisions are taken by consensus. It has put in place several committees with specific tasks, however, under its control. Taking strategic decisions or the signing of new FTAs, everything is down to the Council, i.e. the member states.

12 The administration of the EFTA Convention is the responsibility of the EFTA Secretariat. This includes the main EFTA activities, such as the relationship between the EFTA states and their support for the negotiation of FTAs, and also the bulk of the management of the EEA Agreement. The EFTA Secretariat, from a legal point of view, only provides services to the EFTA states, comparable, e.g., to the Council Secretariat for the EU. It does not act, e.g., as 'guardians of the treaties', such as the EU Commission.

13 There is no supervision as is the case in the EEA Agreement, nor is there a court, whether that of the EU or of the EEA EFTA states, which could create a jurisprudence binding upon the EFTA states.

14 Since its revision, the EFTA Convention has contained a chapter on dispute settlement. It provides for an arbitration procedure which may result in annulment of the contested measures or compensation etc.[8]

7 HM Government, 'The future relationship between the United Kingdom and the European Union', Cm 9593, July 2018, p. 1.

8 Art. 48 EFTA Convention and Annex T; see Ch. 4.

Its terms are effective only between the EFTA states. Claims made by persons or companies are to be asserted before the national courts. This, again, is a logical consequence of the fundamentally intergovernmental nature of EFTA.

7.2.3. FUTURE RELATIONS BETWEEN THE UK AND THE EFTA STATES

Just for the sake of completeness, it should be mentioned that there are 15
already provisions in place for the future relations between the UK and the EFTA states post Brexit. These were partly put in place in case the UK were to leave the EU without an agreement, an option that can currently still not be excluded. Then, there is a set of draft agreements between the UK and Switzerland which simply carry over the agreements between the EU and Switzerland when the UK leaves the EU. Finally, there is a draft Withdrawal Agreement (EEA) that will take the UK out of the EEA Agreement and which, given the reduced scope, reproduces parts of the Withdrawal Agreement (EU), essentially on free movement of persons. The new relationship between the UK and Iceland, Liechtenstein as well as Norway will to some extent depend on the future agreement the UK may conclude with the EU. All of this would, however, not stand in the way should the UK wish to join EFTA and have its relationship with Iceland, Liechtenstein, Norway and Switzerland governed by the terms of the EFTA Convention.

7.3. BENEFITS IN THE LEGAL RELATIONS WITH NON-MEMBERS, IN PARTICULAR THE EU AND ITS MEMBER STATES

7.3.1. THE LARGER CONTEXT: THE FUTURE EU-UK RELATIONS

7.3.1.1. The EU Framework for Economic Relations with Third States

Essentially, there are two options and respective legal bases in the 16
treaties for relations the EU concludes with third countries: either EU association agreements according to Article 217 TFEU or other types of trade agreements according to Article 207 TFEU. The former provide

for '(...) special, privileged links with a non-member country which must, at least to a certain extent, take part in the Community system (...)'.[9] This is not the case with the latter. Hence, there is a

> 'basic distinction between what [Eekhout] terms the market integration and trade liberalization paradigms. That distinction divides the different models, with Norway, Switzerland and Ukraine broadly on the market integration side, and Turkey, Canada and the WTO on the trade liberalization side. This is a divide which, if not unbridgeable, is deeper than is often assumed. The reasons and causes are of an economic, political, and particularly also of a legal and institutional nature (lawyers would in fact say "constitutional").'[10]

17 Association agreements may well differ in their details one from another. However, they are all concluded under specific principles. These become more important the closer a relationship moves to participation in the EU's internal market and, hence, its regulatory set-up. This is quite logical as this touches a sphere where the EU's internal decision-making is involved. This is not the case if the economic relationship between the EU and a third country is restricted to a mere FTA, thus without any involvement of EU regulatory competence.

18 There are, firstly, basic principles applicable to any form of association, the so called 'Interlaken Principles'. Added to these, there is the requirement for a certain institutional set-up.[11] As to the material scope, suffice to say that the EU generally insists on subscribing to the undivided four freedoms – the free movement of goods, persons, services and capital – and the competition policies that accompany these freedoms in order to allow for *full participation* in the internal market.[12] Therefore, the EU has already made it quite clear that it is not willing to repeat the Swiss experience with a sectoral approach. Finally, there is another principle that should not be forgotten: geography matters!

---

9 Case 12/86, *Meryem Demirel v Stadt Schwäbisch Gmünd*, ECLI:EU:C:1987:400, n. 9.

10 P. Eekhout, 'Future trade relations between the EU and the UK: Options after Brexit', European Union, 2018, p. 6.

11 See Ch. 6; G. Baur, 'Privileged partnerships – The partner countries' (institutional) perspectives' in S. Gstöhl and D. Phinnemore (eds.), *The Proliferation of Privileged Partnerships between the European Union and its Neighbours*, Routledge, London & New York 2020 (2019), p. 28.

12 Revised text of the Political Declaration setting out the framework for the future relationship between the European Union and the United Kingdom as agreed at negotiators' level on 17 October 2019, to replace the one published in OJ C 66I of 19.2.2019, TF50 (2019) 65, nr. 4.

The geographical closeness to the EU's internal market will to some extent determine the kind of agreement it is likely to conclude, and its content. The ambitiousness of an agreement will most likely increase with proximity. Hence, it can be expected that the UK will be treated differently on both accounts, rights and obligations, than e.g. Canada which is not as close to the EU's internal market, but rather is oriented towards the US market.[13]

At the other end of the spectrum there is the option of essentially a free trade agreement (FTA) according to Article 207 TFEU. Such agreements concluded according to the EU's common commercial policy may cover 'trade in goods and services, and the commercial aspects of intellectual property, foreign direct investment, the achievement of uniformity in measures of liberalisation, export policy and measures to protect trade such as those to be taken in the event of dumping or subsidies'.[14] 19

The significant difference between these two approaches is that a FTA according to Article 207 TFEU does not seek to create internal market conditions through legal harmonisation. It would therefore seek to facilitate market access which would be feasible without legal harmonisation. This means: no adoption of EU law and no contractually agreed and monitored equivalence of rules. An example for such a 'bare-bones FTA'[15] would be the EU-Switzerland FTA from 1972[16] which is still in force.[17] In procedural terms, association agreements are mixed agreements that require ratification by member states as well. Only a simple FTA would definitely be ratified by the EU alone. 20

Let's take product standards as a practical example: currently, under the internal market paradigm, e.g. Norwegian or Swiss and EU law are either harmonised or recognised as equivalent. Goods produced under either law will lead to reciprocal marketing authorisation without diverging product specifications and without further controls. By contrast, under 21

13 Ibid., nr. 3: 'These arise from their geography (…)'.

14 Art. 207(1) TFEU.

15 https://www.businessinsider.com/eu-uk-will-only-be-given-bare-bones-trade-deal-after-brexit-2019-11?r=US&IR=T.

16 [Free Trade] Agreement between the European Economic Community and the Swiss Confederation OJ L 300, 31.12.1972, p. 189–280 (English special edition: ibid. pp. 191–282).

17 The parallel FTAs between the (then) EEC and Iceland or Norway respectively, have been replaced by the EEA Agreement but for some provisions not covered by the latter, notably on trade in fish.

the trade facilitation paradigm, even the recent CETA does not foresee harmonisation of product regulations, but only the possibility for mutual conformity assessment bodies to be mutually recognised. Thus, testing agencies of one contracting party could check products according to the regulations of the other party, but the export products must continue to comply with the national regulations of the importing country. The FTA will therefore have no impact on the product regulations of the parties. The parties will continue to determine their product regulations independently. This further requires that products that are to be marketed in both markets must undergo two different conformance tests and, correspondingly, meet the product requirements of both parties. This requires the production of two different product series. Swiss experiences with an MRA that does not cover all types of goods indicate that this creates an increase of costs of 0.5 to 1 per cent of the product value.[18]

7.3.1.2. A Future EU-UK Agreement: Political Path Dependency

22 In the revised Political Declaration, 'The Parties note that the overarching institutional framework could take the form of an Association Agreement.'[19] It is, however, 'almost impossible to arrive at a precise definition'.[20] The quote from the revised Political Declaration itself, therefore, does not give a clear indication as to what kind of agreement the EU and the UK might ultimately conclude.

23 In order to venture into assessing possible future UK-EU arrangements, comparing the already existing partnerships may provide valuable insight. Assuming path dependence,[21] any new agreement that the EU negotiates will most likely follow known models.[22] It seems, at this point in time,

---

[18] Based on figures of 2011, Swiss exports of around CHF 32 billion were (positively) affected by the MRA; i.e. approx. a quarter of all industrial products exported to the EU could be exported to the EU thanks to the MRA without double conformity testing or without adaptation to other regulations. The additional costs due to additional conformity assessments are estimated to be be-tween 0.5% to 1% of the product value. Based on the above figures this corresponds to CHF 160 to 320 million (Reply of the Swiss Federal Council to the postulate of senator Karin Keller-Sutter, nr. 13.4022, June 2015 (German or French)).

[19] Revised text of the Political Declaration (n. 12), nr. 120.

[20] Ibid., p. 9.

[21] See e.g. P.A. Hall, and R.C.R. Taylor, 'Political Science and the Three New Institutional- isms', *Political Studies*, 1996, 44 (5), p. 954.

[22] In this vein, see also P. Van Elsuwege and M. Chamon, 'The meaning of association under EU law', European Parliament, Brussels 2019, p. 31.

rather unlikely that negotiations will lead to a 'bespoke agreement',[23] at least not in the sense that something absolutely different from existing agreements will result. It is much more realistic to assume that a future UK-EU agreement will follow the scope, structure, general content and the institutional set-up of one or other agreements in force or currently being negotiated.[24] This is also suggested by the EU's chief negotiator's comparison of the UK negotiating 'red lines' with available models.[25]

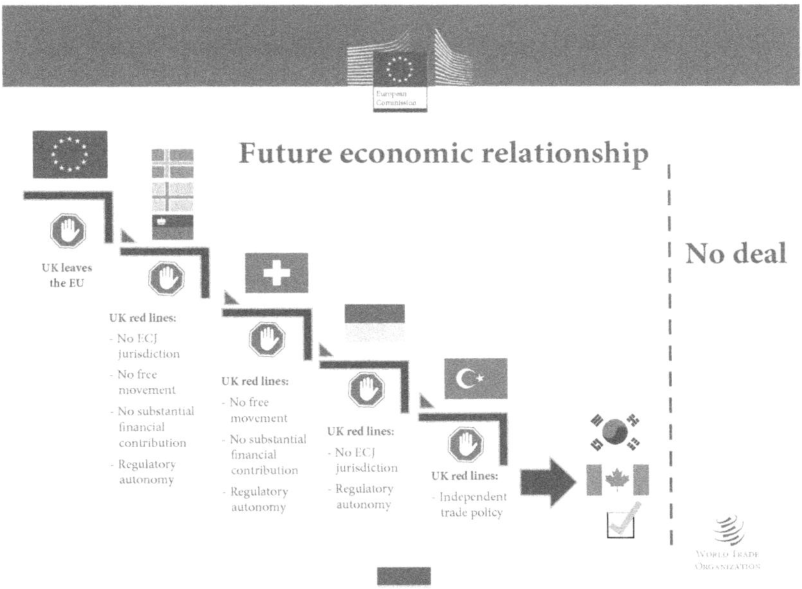

Figure 7.1. Future relationship
Source: European Commission Task Force 50.

Of the elaborate types at the top of Figure 7.1., only the EEA would be 24
available as the EU has already ruled out considering entering into a 'Swiss

23 The Guardian, 'Cabinet Agrees to Demand Bespoke Deal after First Proper Discussion on Brexit Outcome – As It Happened', 19.12.2017.

24 M. Emerson, 'Which Model for Brexit?', CEPS Special Report 147, Brussels, Centre of European Policy Studies, p. 1.

25 European Commission, Slide Presented by Michel Barnier, European Commission Chief Negotiator, to the Heads of State and Government at the European Council (Article 50) on 15 December 2017, TF50 (2017) 21 – Commission to EU27, Brussels, 19 December, https://ec.europa.eu/commission/sites/beta-political/files/slide_presented_by_barnier_at_euco_15-12-2017.pdf.

type' (set of) agreement(s).[26] For obvious reasons – the agreement under negotiation aims at integrating very small states with limited resources into the EU's internal market – this chapter will not elaborate further on the relationship between the EU and the AMS states (Andorra, Monaco and San Marino) which are currently negotiating their association with the EU as well. Neither will the Georgia/Moldova/Ukraine type be of any appeal to replace the UK's current EU membership, given its general aim to rather bring these countries' economies, which only recently freed themselves from that of the Soviet Union, up to a certain level. And the Ankara Agreement with a partial customs union would be of no use to the UK per se. Hence, it could only be a third type next to the EEA and the EU-Swiss Bilateral Agreements which would, however, need to respect the EU's principles. Indeed, beyond an association agreement there is only a FTA available. The additional points of interest, like security cooperation or foreign policy coordination, need not formally be included in that agreement. These issues might as well be negotiated and concluded in separate agreements as these are not related to either the internal market or the commercial policy in general.

7.3.1.3. The UK's Aims

25 Of course, there is an element of speculation; it can, however, be said with a fair amount of certainty that the UK is aiming at negotiating a Comprehensive Free Trade Agreement (CFTA). This has been – more or less consistently – the UK government's position throughout the Brexit process.[27] The EU seems to be open to such an approach, having made it clear, however, that there could not be mixing of types of agreements, such as picking more advantageous elements from an internal market context like 'passporting' rights for financial services. Negotiating a CFTA – although called an 'ambitious FTA' – now seems to be the common 'landing zone' according to the revised Political Declaration.[28]

---

[26] See European Council, 'Guidelines following the United Kingdom's notification under Article 50 TEU', EUCO XT 20004/17, 29.4.2017, nr. 20.

[27] See e.g. HM Government White Paper 'The Future Relationship Between the United Kingdom and the European Union', p. 7, https://assets.publishing.service.gov.uk/government/uploads/system/uploads/attachment_data/file/786626/The_Future_Relationship_between_the_United_Kingdom_and_the_European_Union_120319.pdf.

[28] Revised text of the Political Declaration (n. 12 above), nr. 3; European Commission press release: Brexit: European Commission recommends the European Council

As shown above, this does not necessarily contradict the statement according to which the 'institutional framework could take the form of an Association Agreement'.[29]

The UK government says it wants to leave 'the Single Market and the Customs Union, ending free movement and the jurisdiction of the European Court of Justice in this country, leaving the Common Agricultural Policy and the Common Fisheries Policy, and ending the days of sending vast sums of money to the EU every year',[30] extracting itself from market integration and in particular its institutional consequences.[31] Nonetheless, the UK government wants 'a deep and comprehensive economic partnership between the UK and the EU'.[32] Overall, the UK government proposes an association agreement in substance with the institutional set-up of a basic FTA. It argues that the EU has already set precedents 26

> 'which all have some form of institutional architecture. For instance, the EU-Canada Comprehensive Economic and Trade Agreement (CETA) and the EU-Ukraine Association Agreement include an overarching institutional structure. (...) The EU and Switzerland are also currently in negotiations over a new institutional framework agreement.'[33]

This, however, overlooks the basic distinction between the trade liberalisation paradigm and the market integration paradigm. It is rather unlikely that the EU could agree to such an agreement blurring all distinctions which are not mere legal theory but entail quite distinct consequences.

The wording, whether 'deep', 'ambitious' or otherwise distinguished, suggests a form of FTA, and therefore seems to be 'on the face of things coming within the trade liberalization paradigm'. Nonetheless, it 'maintains elements of the market integration paradigm – or would even come mainly within that paradigm'.[34] Therefore, such a 'third type association agreement' would, however, also have to follow certain principles the 27

(Article 50) to endorse the agreement reached on the revised Protocol on Ireland / Northern Ireland and revised Political Declaration, 17.10.2019.

29 See para. 22.

30 HM Government White Paper (n. 27 above) p. 1.

31 Ibid., p. 84.

32 Ibid., p. 13.

33 HM Government White Paper (n. 27 above) p. 85.

34 Eekhout (n. 10 above) p. 21.

EU has developed over the past decades and, in particular, would have to include 'a common institutional framework for the governance of post-Brexit relations between the EU and the UK'.[35]

7.3.1.4. *The Problem of Time*

28 After the UK formally left the EU on 31 January 2020, there is a time frame of 11 months left in which to negotiate a new agreement between the EU and the UK. If we look at the time 'normal' FTAs have taken to be negotiated, be it those concluded by EFTA or those concluded by the EU, this time frame already seems rather challenging. Let's take the FTA between the EFTA states and Canada, a 'first-generation' agreement: negotiations started in 1999 and were concluded in 2007, signed in 2008 and entered into force on 1 July 2009. The parallel but more comprehensive ('ambitious') CETA between the EU and Canada took even longer: negotiations started in 2009, after a framework for such an agreement had already been agreed in 2004. Negotiations were concluded in 2014 and the agreement signed in 2016. On the EU's part it has, until now, only been ratified by the European Parliament and has been provisionally and partly applied since 2017. It saw different political challenges during that period. The ratification by all parliaments of the EU member states is still outstanding.

29 The above example shows, first, that FTAs quite generally take a certain time to negotiate. Secondly, if it is an agreement with the EU that involves ratification by member states it takes even longer.

7.3.2. EFTA AS A USEFUL PLATFORM FOR AN ASSOCIATION AGREEMENT

30 Whichever form of an association agreement will be chosen, the EU made it quite clear, that

> 'the Parties indicate that should a dispute raise a question of interpretation of provisions or concepts of Union law, which may also be indicated by either Party, the arbitration panel should refer the question to the Court of Justice of the European Union (CJEU) as the sole arbiter of Union law, for

---

35 Van Elsuwege and Chamon (n. 22 above) p. 31.

> a binding ruling as regards the interpretation of Union law. Conversely, there should be no reference to the CJEU where a dispute does not raise such a question.'[36]

That eventuality may quite easily occur, even in the case of an association agreement with the least possible link to the internal market. That is obvious given the broad scope of the possible future agreement and Union law determining many of the fields of potential cooperation. 31

However, any form of potential competence of the CJEU bears the risk of political opposition in the UK as it was one of the major arguments of the Leave campaign to free the UK from the CJEU's jurisprudence.[37] A similar discussion has been taking place in Switzerland where one of the strongly contested points in the draft Institutional Framework Agreement (IFA) between the EU and Switzerland is exactly this: 32

> 'Lorsque le différend soulève une question concernant l'interprétation ou l'application d'une disposition visée dans le deuxième paragraphe de l'article 4 du présent accord, et si son interprétation est pertinente pour régler le différend et nécessaire pour lui permettre de statuer, le tribunal arbitral saisit la Cour de justice de l'Union européenne. L'arrêt de la Cour de justice de l'Union européenne lie le tribunal arbitral.'[38]

Were the UK to choose to join EFTA with the aim of entering into an association agreement with the EU, it would have access to EFTA's institutions that serve the EEA Agreement. Both the EFTA Surveillance Authority and the EFTA Court are such institutions. In the view represented here, participating in both institutions does not require membership of the EEA. EFTA provides for a platform for several kinds of association agreements of its members with the EU. 33

---

36 Revised text of the Political Declaration (n. 12 above) nr. 131.

37 N. Skoutaris, 'Taking back control? Brexit and the Court of Justice' in A. Kent, N. Skoutaris and J. Trinidad, *The Future of International Courts*, London, Routledge 2019, pp. 161–174.

38 Art. 10(3) draft Institutional Framework Agreement between the EU and Switzerland: 'When the dispute raises a question concerning the interpretation or application of a provision referred to in the second paragraph of Article 4 [principle of uniform interpretation] of this Agreement, and if its interpretation is relevant to the resolution of the dispute and necessary to enable it to rule, the arbitral tribunal appeals to the Court of Justice of the European Union. The judgment of the Court of Justice of the European Union binds the arbitral tribunal.' (Translation by the author).

Given the institutional set-up required by the EU,[39] there is most likely no opposition to be expected from their side either. The EU has already stated as much in its conclusions with regard to its wish to improve the institutional set-up with Switzerland and the respective negotiation mandate:

> 'All in all, this institutional framework should present a level of legal certainty and independence equivalent to the mechanisms created under the EEA Agreement',[40] and in particular 'an independent surveillance and judicial enforcement mechanism and a dispute settlement mechanism.'[41]

35 If this is true for Switzerland there is no reason why the UK, were it an EFTA state, should not also join the EFTA Surveillance Authority and the EFTA Court.[42] That would allow the UK to maintain formal independence from EU institutions, albeit that homogeneity requires close alignment.

7.3.3. EFTA AS A PLATFORM FOR TRADE FACILITATION AND OTHER AGREEMENTS WITH THE EU NOT DIRECTLY SUBJECT TO MARKET INTEGRATION

36 As mentioned in Chapter 6, the EU (then EEC) and the EFTA states, prior to starting negotiations on the EEA Agreement, concluded several agreements to prepare for a European Economic Space. These agreements are partially still in force, particularly with regard to Switzerland which is not a member of the EEA. These agreements can, in principle, be said to be subject to the trade facilitation paradigm. They would thus be open to the UK should it decide to (re-)join EFTA, however not with the aim of any link to the internal market through an association agreement. The most important ones are the following.

7.3.3.1. Participation in European Standardisation Bodies

37 In order to be able to offer goods cross-border and qualify under respective mutual recognition agreements, these goods must meet certain norms or standards. Developing such standards is done by recognised

39 See para. 18.

40 European Council, Conclusions on EU relations with EFTA countries, 3213th Transport, Telecommunications and Energy Council meeting, 20.12.2012, nr. 33.

41 Council of the European Union, Press statement: Negotiating mandate for an EU-Switzerland institutional framework agreement, 9525/14, 6.5.2014, 4th para.

42 In that vein also Eekhout (n. 10 above) p. 18.

European standardisation bodies. The most important ones are CEN[43] (general standards), CENELEC[44] (electro-technical standards) and ETSI[45] (telecommunications standards). Currently, only the national standardisation bodies of EFTA states, EU member states or EU candidate countries qualify for full membership. This would mean that the British Institute for Standardisation (BIS) would be relegated to a status of observer. Were the UK a member of EFTA, the status of the BIS would, however, not change.

7.3.3.2. *Rules of Origin*

In today's goods production with extensive value chains, only very few goods consist of components from one country alone. In order for a product to be recognised as originating from the free trade partner, it is necessary to determine the proportion of the elements originating from the exporting country. In addition, cumulation, i.e. the degree of parts not stemming from that free trade partner, must also be regulated. There may be privileged third parties whose contribution to products of the exporting country can be added and (still) have a positive impact on the tariff agreed between the free trade partners. This is of course irrelevant inside a customs union. However, for the wider European free trade zone including a series of countries from the southern rim of the Mediterranean, this is now regulated by the Pan-Euro-Med (PEM) Convention.[46] Members are the EFTA states, the EU, Turkey as well as the countries which signed the Barcelona Declaration, the Western Balkans and the Faroe Islands. Upon exiting the EU, the UK would – in principle – become a third country, also with regard to that convention. It could, however, re-join provided that the UK has a FTA in force, providing for preferential rules of origin, with at least one of the contracting parties.[47] 38

7.3.3.3. *Simplified Trade Formalities*

The main contents of the respective convention[48] are as follows: the convention lays down measures to simplify the formalities relating to 39

43 European Committee for Standardisation.
44 European Committee for Electrotechnical Standardisation.
45 European Telecommunications Standards Institute.
46 Regional Convention on pan-Euro-Mediterranean preferential rules of origin (PEM Convention), OJ L 54, 26.2.2013, pp. 4–158.
47 Art. 5(1) PEM Convention (n. 46 above).
48 Convention between the European Economic Community, the Republic of Austria, the Republic of Finland, the Republic of Iceland, the Kingdom of Norway, the

the movement of goods between the EU and the EFTA states, but also between the EFTA states themselves. In particular, a standard form is introduced. In addition to the standard form, additional administrative documents may only be required if the information in the single form is not sufficient to carry out the procedure, e.g. the declaration for the determination of the customs value, or if these other documents are provided for in international agreements, e.g. regarding veterinary and phytosanitary products. The convention also contains a provision on administrative assistance between the customs administrations of the EFTA states and the EU member states. Upon leaving the EU, the UK will, again, be a third country. As such, it may apply to become a contracting party to this convention if invited to do so by the depositary following a decision of the joint committee.[49] On 30 January 2019, the UK deposited its instrument of accession. This will, however, only enter into force

> 'from the date on which those Conventions will no longer apply to and in the United Kingdom as a Member of the European Union or, should the European Union and the United Kingdom agree on transitional arrangements whereby the Conventions would apply to and in the United Kingdom, as from the date on which such transitional arrangements cease to apply'.[50]

7.3.3.4. Common Transit Procedure

40 The common transit procedure between the EU and the EFTA states[51] makes it possible, in simplified terms, to transport goods without being subject to successive national customs procedures. Customs supervision

Kingdom of Sweden and the Swiss Confederation on the simplification of formalities in trade in goods OJ L 134, 22.5.1987, pp. 2–77; see Ch. 6.2.2.4. For the EEA EFTA states, see also Protocol 10 to the EEA agreement on simplification of inspections and formalities in respect of carriage of goods which with regard to Switzerland is to be adapted in parallel with the Convention.

49 Art.11a(1) Convention on the simplification of formalities in trade in goods (footnote 48).

50 European Commission – DG Taxud, Note for the attention of the Trade Contact Group on the Accession of the United Kingdom of Great Britain and Northern Ireland to the Convention on a common transit procedure and to the Convention on simplification of formalities in trade in goods, ARES(2019)686599, 4.2.2019.

51 Convention between the European Economic Community, the Republic of Austria, the Republic of Finland, the Republic of Iceland, the Kingdom of Norway, the Kingdom of Sweden and the Swiss Confederation, on a common transit procedure, OJ L 226, 13.8.1987, pp. 2–117; see Ch. 6.2.2.5.

shall be carried out without interruption from the place of departure to the place of destination. That convention also allows for third countries to accede.[52] The UK has deposited its instrument of accession with regard to the convention on the simplification of formalities in trade in goods on the same date as for the simplified customs formalities.

7.3.3.5. Statistics

The area of statistics is also very important, e.g. for analysing the flow of goods, but also for the calculation of contributions in different contexts. It is important for this to be done in a harmonised way. Statistical work in Europe is also based on close cooperation between EFTA and the EU. The EFTA Statistical Office (ESO) was created in 1991 as a liaison office between the Statistical Office of the European Union (Eurostat) and the EFTA national statistical institutes (NSIs). ESO's main objective is to sustain the integration of the EFTA states into the evolving European Statistical System (ESS), thereby providing harmonised and comparable statistics supporting the general cooperation process between EFTA and the EU.[53] Today, the participation of Iceland, Liechtenstein and Norway is covered by the EEA Agreement[54] and that of Switzerland by the respective Bilateral Agreement.[55] The legal basis on which they operate, however, is EU law that is being incorporated by both the EEA EFTA states and Switzerland into their respective Agreements with the EU.[56] Should the UK wish to participate in the European Statistical System, it would, therefore, have to negotiate a respective agreement with the EU. 41

52 Art. 15a of the Convention on a common transit procedure (n. 51 above).

53 EFTA Bulletin 1–2011, 'EFTA/EU Statistical Cooperation Handbook', EFTA, Geneva 2011, p. 7.

54 Annex XXI to the EEA Agreement.

55 Agreement between the European Community and the Swiss Confederation on cooperation in the field of statistics, OJ L 90, 28.3.2006, pp. 2–20.

56 See e.g. Regulation (EC) No. 223/2009 of the European Parliament and of the Council of 11 March 2009 on European statistics and repealing Regulation (EC, Euratom) No. 1101/2008 of the European Parliament and of the Council on the transmission of data subject to statistical confidentiality to the Statistical Office of the European Communities, Council Regulation (EC) No. 322/97 on Community Statistics, and Council Decision 89/382/EEC, Euratom establishing a Committee on the Statistical Programmes of the European Communities, OJ L 87, 31.3.2009, pp. 164–173.

7.3.3.6. *Recognition and Enforcement of Civil Judgments*

42 The recognition and enforcement of civil judgments is of great importance in economic life and trade relations.[57] In the relationship between the EU and the EFTA states, this is done on the terms of the Lugano Convention.[58]

43 The UK, and London in particular, as a venue for court proceedings and arbitration in international trade and finance matters stands to lose a great deal should they be excluded from the mechanisms of recognition and enforcement of civil judgments in Europe. Upon exiting the EU, the respective EU Regulation[59] will cease to apply and the UK will *a priori* not be party to the Lugano Convention through the EU anymore.

44 The Lugano Convention would be open for accession to the UK when it ceases to be a member state of the EU if the UK were an EFTA state. Of course, the UK could also apply for membership as a mere third country. In this case a reporting procedure applies and accession is subject to unanimous agreement of the contracting parties.

7.3.3.7. *Relations (FTAs) with Third Countries and Organisations Other than the EU*

45 Given the UK government's aim to deliver an independent trade policy,[60] one of the obvious interests the UK could have in (re-)joining EFTA would be to join an existing parallel network of FTAs. This could to some extent replace the network the UK will be leaving once it leaves that of the EU, subject of course to also leaving the EU Customs Union.

46 The EFTA states are trying to minimise the disadvantages with regard to their market access in third countries in comparison to the EU by developing their own free trade network in parallel to the EU. It has, over the years, grown considerably and covers many countries or groups of countries in parallel to the EU's FTAs. As there is no common trade

[57] See Ch. 6.

[58] Convention on jurisdiction and the recognition and enforcement of judgments in civil and commercial matters, OJ L 339, 21.12.2007, pp. 3–41.

[59] Council Regulation (EC) No. 44/2001 of 22 December 2000 on jurisdiction and the recognition and enforcement of judgments in civil and commercial matter, OJ L 12, 16.1.2001, pp. 1–23.

[60] HM Government White Paper (n. 27 above) p. 48.

policy and because the EFTA states negotiate in common out of their own volition, there is also some flexibility. EFTA states may, but need not act jointly. For example, Switzerland negotiated a FTA with Japan on its own, while until now only Iceland and Switzerland have concluded a FTA with China. Then there is the flexibility within a set of agreements: for instance, in the EFTA-Korea FTA, the chapter on investments was not included in the main agreement, but negotiated as an independent instrument, only between Korea and the EFTA states of Iceland, Liechtenstein and Switzerland, because Norway did not want to participate in this chapter.[61]

There has been a discussion on whether the UK could comply with Article 56(3) of the EFTA Convention in case it wanted to remain within the EU Customs Union. According to Article 56(3) EFTA, a new EFTA member state 'shall apply to become a party to the free trade agreements between the Member States on the one hand and third states, unions of states or international organisations on the other'. From this some conclude that a country acceding to EFTA could not comply with this obligation if it is a member of a customs union with the EU.[62] 47

It is arguable, however, that Article 56 EFTA is more flexible than is suggested: paragraphs 1 and 2, which deal with accession to the EFTA, do not define any clear criteria in this respect. In practice, conditions for membership are decided by the currently four EFTA states on predominantly political grounds. In this respect they enjoy, unlike in the more legally structured case of the EU, a vast discretion. Indeed, there are examples where a large amount of flexibility was shown, as in the case of Finland which – formally – only became an 'associate EFTA member' in order to accommodate its particularly sensitive relations with the then Soviet Union during the Cold War era. Similarly, paragraph 3 on FTAs offers flexibility. Even its wording ('shall apply to become') indicates the possibility that an acceding country may ultimately, for whatever reason, not accede to EFTA's FTAs. It could, for instance, also happen that a third country refuses to negotiate the inclusion of a new EFTA member into an existing FTA. This interpretation is confirmed by the fact that 'EFTA membership does not preclude from entering into a 48

61 For more details, see Ch. 5.

62 See G. Baur, '"Norway+" or "Common Market 2.0": The problems are not where they seem to be', https://www.efta-studies.org/blog/norway-or-common-market-2-0-the-problems-are-not-where-they-seem-to-be.

customs arrangement with the EU'.[63] Hence, if the current EFTA states agree and waive the 'obligation' of Article 56(3) EFTA, having a customs arrangement with the EU need not stand in the way of the UK's EFTA membership.

49 Finally, it needs to mentioned that, while the UK certainly 'weighs' thrice the economic power of the current EFTA states together, the general foreign trade interests of the UK and the current EFTA states seem to be match quite well.[64]

7.4. CONCLUSION

50 Many of the above points may be seen by some as tipping the balance in favour of the UK (re-)joining EFTA while others will certainly remain unconvinced. Some might find EFTA a useful basis for the UK's future relations with the EU in some regard and to join in a manner to safeguard its sovereignty in a group of, however, small, but strong and 'like-minded' economies. In addition, it might give them access to an existing free trade network, one of the largest in the world. Some might say – and they are undoubtedly right as well – that the UK will also and without any doubt be able to do this all on its own. Its economy still equals to three times that of the four current EFTA states together.[65] We have seen before that few agreements or bodies are only open to either EU or EFTA states or their respective national bodies. However, in most cases also third countries, as the UK will be post Brexit, can join even though maybe under more cumbersome procedures and conditions.

51 One aspect, however, gained little attention in the context of EFTA: time. As the UK formally left the EU on 31 January 2020, there is a window for negotiations on a new agreement between the UK and the EU until the end of 2020, less than one year. Of course, this period may be extended as negotiations will most likely take longer than that year. If we look at the available figures of negotiations either the EU or EFTA undertook in terms of concluding association agreements or FTAs, a time frame of several years seems to be a fair assumption, not to speak of the time until an agreement will be fully operational.

---

63 https://www.efta.int/About-EFTA/Frequently-asked-questions-EFTA-EEA-EFTA-membership-and-Brexit-328676.

64 Information from the EFTA Secretariat.

65 Ibid.

We can look at some examples, like Canada or Ukraine. But one should not forget the problem created by the fact that a closely integrated economy is being put on a much lower level of integration. This will – different from any other example of trade negotiations – create the wish on the part of the UK to keep as many of the advantages it had under its membership status whilst on the part of the EU there will be a strong will to exclude the UK from any benefit linked to the UKs former status. Furthermore, we have to bear in mind that in the event of an association agreement being negotiated, this will be a mixed agreement.[66] Hence, all EU member states will have to agree. And the risks deriving therefrom could be seen in both the negotiations of the Ukraine Association Agreement with the Dutch parliament blocking ratification and CETA being held up by the parliament of the Belgian region of Wallonia. 52

For as long as there is no clarity about the result of such negotiations, investments will be held back and economic actors will seek to hedge their risk with regard to an unfavourable outcome. The longer this takes, the longer such effects might occur. Switzerland is currently experiencing the first signs of such a development: because there is no movement with regard to the draft Institutional framework Agreement,[67] published but not signed by Switzerland in November 2018, the EU embarked on a policy of 'erosion' of the current bilateral agreements in force. For example, the Swiss Stock Exchange lost its equivalence recognition at the end of June 2019. Furthermore, the MRA between Switzerland and the EU is likely not to be adapted when the new Medical Devices Regulation (MDR)[68] and In Vitro Diagnostic Medical Devices Regulation (IVDR)[69] will enter into force, which will require an adjustment of the MRA.[70] It does not seem far-fetched to assume similar effects on the UK economy given the likelihood of longer delays in concluding whatever agreement is negotiated with the EU. Furthermore, it can be expected that third 53

66 Van Elsuwege and Chamon (n. 23 above) pp. 18–19.

67 See Ch. 6.

68 Regulation (EU) 2017/745 of the European Parliament and of the Council of 5 April 2017 on medical devices, amending Directive 2001/83/EC, Regulation (EC) No 178/2002 and Regulation (EC) No 1223/2009 and repealing Council Directives 90/385/EEC and 93/42/EEC, OJ L 117, 5.5.2017, p. 1.

69 Regulation (EU) 2017/746 of the European Parliament and of the Council of 5 April 2017 on in vitro diagnostic medical devices and repealing Directive 98/79/EC and Commission Decision 2010/227/EU, OJ L 117 5.5.2017, p. 176.

70 See https://www.bag.admin.ch/bag/en/home/medizin-und-forschung/heilmittel/aktuelle-rechtsetzungsprojekte/revision-med-prod-verord-mepv.html.

countries with which the UK would like to conclude FTAs might wish to know the result of negotiations between the UK and the EU to finalise a FTA with the UK. This can also be concluded from the 'US trade objectives' which expressly refer to the future relationship between the UK and the EU.[71]

54 Here, the opportunity of (re-)joining EFTA might be helpful in some ways: this could at least smoothen some of the effects that are to be expected once Brexit happens, and in the event that replacement at treaty level is not yet in place.

55 EFTA is an international organisation that has so far been disputed neither in the most critical – regarding a close relationship with the EU – of the EFTA states, Switzerland, nor in the other three member states. This might, on the one hand, be due to its inconspicuous role in relation to general politics as it primarily deals with trade issues. It is also regarded as an alternative to the EU, especially in Switzerland's Eurosceptic climate, at least as an instrument for gaining market access to global markets in parallel to the EU.

56 On the other hand, EFTA is not a supranational organisation; there is no supervisory authority and no court. This is, again, due to the desired intergovernmental character which takes into account the narrow understanding of sovereignty by Iceland, Norway and Switzerland, compared to that of other European countries.

57 Finally let us look into the future in the context of Brexit: we have shown that EFTA serves its member states as a platform for their respective relations with the EU. If we look at the UK government's 'red lines' with respect to its negotiations with the EU about a future relationship (no participation in the internal market, no participation in the EU Customs Union, taking back control of movement of persons, and no jurisdiction of the Court of Justice of the European Union), these lines are not crossed in the relationships between the EFTA states. However, from what has been said earlier it seems to be equally clear that the UK does not need EFTA to pursue its post-Brexit Agenda. In some cases, re-joining EFTA might merely facilitate joining certain agreements or bodies. But the longer negotiations of a new relationship with the

71 See e.g. Office of the United States Trade Representative, 'United States-United Kingdom Negotiations, Summary of Specific Negotiating Objectives', February 2019, p. 8, https://ustr.gov/sites/default/files/Summary_of_U.S.-UK_Negotiating_Objectives.pdf.

EU take, and in some cases also adhering to some agreements currently not open to third countries, the time element might prove crucial. Joining EFTA could then not be an advantage but become a necessity.

Also, joining EFTA's FTA-network might prove a great time saver, given how difficult and time-consuming negotiating FTAs often proves to be. At least from a legal perspective, re-joining EFTA, as suggested by a committee of the House of Commons,[72] might then not be such a bad idea after all. 58

[72] See n. 2 above.

CONVENTION ESTABLISHING THE EUROPEAN FREE TRADE ASSOCIATION

The Republic of Iceland, the Principality of Liechtenstein, the Kingdom of Norway and the Swiss Confederation (hereinafter referred to as the "Member States");

Having regard to the conclusion on 4 January 1960, between the Republic of Austria, the Kingdom of Denmark, the Kingdom of Norway, the Portuguese Republic, the Kingdom of Sweden, the Swiss Confederation and the United Kingdom of Great Britain and Northern Ireland, of the Convention establishing the European Free Trade Association (hereinafter referred to as the "Convention");

Having regard to the association with the Republic of Finland and its subsequent accession on 1 January 1986, and to the accessions by the Republic of Iceland on 1 March 1970 and by the Principality of Liechtenstein on 1 September 1991;

Having regard to the successive withdrawals from the Convention by the Kingdom of Denmark and the United Kingdom on 1 January 1973; the Republic of Portugal on 1 January 1986; the Republic of Austria, the Republic of Finland and the Kingdom of Sweden on 1 January 1995;

Having regard to the free trade agreements between the Member States on the one hand and third parties on the other;

Reaffirming the high priority they attach to the privileged relationship between the Member States and to the facilitation of continuity in their respective good relations with the European Union, which are based on proximity, long-standing common values and European identity;

Resolved to deepen the co-operation instituted within the European Free Trade Association, further facilitating the free movement of goods, aiming at the progressive attainment of free movement of persons and the progressive liberalisation of trade in services and investment, further opening up the public procurement markets in the EFTA States, and providing for the appropriate protection of intellectual property rights, under fair conditions of competition;

Building on their respective rights and obligations under the Agreement establishing the World Trade Organization and other multilateral and bilateral instruments of co-operation;

Recognising the need for mutually supportive trade and environmental policies in order to achieve the objective of sustainable development;

Affirming their commitment to the observance of recognised core labour standards, noting their endeavours to promote such standards in the appropriate multilateral fora and expressing their belief that economic growth and development fostered by increased trade and further trade liberalisation contribute to the promotion of these standards;

Have agreed as follows:

CHAPTER I: OBJECTIVES

Article 1

The Association

An international organisation to be known as the European Free Trade Association, hereinafter referred to as "the Association", is hereby established.

Article 2

Objectives

The objectives of the Association shall be

(a) to promote a continued and balanced strengthening of trade and economic relations between the Member States with fair conditions of competition, and the respect of equivalent rules, within the area of the Association;
(b) the free trade in goods;
(c) to progressively liberalise the free movement of persons;
(d) the progressive liberalisation of trade in services and of investment;
(e) to provide fair conditions of competition affecting trade between the Member States;

(f) to open the public procurement markets of the Member States;
(g) to provide appropriate protection of intellectual property rights, in accordance with the highest international standards.

CHAPTER II: FREE MOVEMENT OF GOODS[1]

Article 3

Customs duties on imports and exports, and charges having equivalent effect

Customs duties on imports and exports, and any charges having equivalent effect, shall be prohibited between the Member States. This shall also apply to customs duties of a fiscal nature.

Article 4

Internal taxation

1. No Member State shall impose, directly or indirectly, on the products of other Member States any internal taxation of any kind in excess of that imposed directly or indirectly on similar domestic products.
2. Furthermore, no Member State shall impose on the products of other Member States any internal taxation of such a nature as to afford indirect protection to other products.
3. Where products are exported to the territory of any Member State, any repayment of internal taxation shall not exceed the internal taxation imposed on them whether directly or indirectly.

ARTICLE 5[2]

Rules of origin and administrative cooperation

1. With respect to the rights and obligations of the Member States concerning rules of origin and administrative cooperation between the customs authorities of the Member States, the Regional Convention

---

1 As a result of the customs union established by the Treaty of 29 March 1923 between Switzerland and the Principality of Liechtenstein, Switzerland shall represent the Principality of Liechtenstein in matters covered thereby. (Footnote added by Council Decision No 2/2012 of 21 June 2012, e.i.f 1 July 2013).

2 Amended by Council Decision No 2/2012 of 21 June 2012, e.i.f 1 July 2013.

on Pan-Euro-Mediterranean Preferential Rules of Origin (hereinafter referred to as the "Pan-Euro-Med Convention") shall apply to and is hereby incorporated into and made part of this Agreement, mutatis mutandis, without prejudice to Article 15.

2. For basic agricultural products referred to in Annex V and processed agricultural products referred to in Annex W, Article 3 of Appendix I to the Pan-Euro-Med Convention shall allow only for bilateral cumulation between the Member States.
3. If a Member State withdraws from the Pan-Euro-Med Convention, the Member States shall immediately enter into negotiations on new rules of origin applicable to this Convention. Until such rules enter into force, the rules of origin contained in the Pan-Euro-Med Convention shall apply to and remain incorporated into and part of this Convention, mutatis mutandis, allowing only for cumulation between the Member States.

Article 6

Mutual assistance in customs matters

1. Member States shall assist each other in customs matters in general in accordance with the provisions of Annex B in order to ensure that their customs legislation is correctly applied.
2. Annex B shall apply to all products whether or not covered by the provisions of this Convention.

Article 7

Quantitative restrictions on imports and exports, and measures having equivalent effect

Quantitative restrictions on imports and exports, and all measures having equivalent effect, shall be prohibited between the Member States.

Article 8[3]

Agricultural goods

In view of the special considerations affecting agriculture, Articles 2, 3, 4 and 7 as well as Chapter IV on state aid, Chapter VI on competition and

---

3 Amended by Council Decision No 2/2012 of 21 June 2012, e.i.f 1 July 2013.

Chapter XII on public procurement shall not apply to agricultural goods classified under chapters 1–24 of the Harmonized Commodity Description and Coding System (HS) or specified in Annex X, except as provided for in:

(a) Annex V, in relation to basic agricultural products, or
(b) Annex W, in relation to processed agricultural products.

Article 9[4]

Article 10

Fish and other marine products

The provisions of this Convention shall apply in relation to fish and other marine products.

Article 11

Seeds and Organic Agriculture

1. Specific rules on seeds are set out in Annex E.
2. Specific rules on organic agriculture are set out in Annex F.

Article 12

Sanitary and phytosanitary measures

The rights and obligations of the Member States in respect of sanitary and phytosanitary measures shall be governed by Annex G.

Article 13

Exceptions

The provisions of Article 7 shall not preclude prohibitions or restrictions on imports, exports or goods in transit justified on grounds of public morality; public policy or public security; the protection of health and life of humans, animals or plants and of the environment; the protection of national treasures possessing artistic, historic or archaeological value; or

4 Repealed by Council Decision No 2/2012 of 21 June 2012, e.i.f 1 July 2013.

the protection of industrial and commercial property. Such prohibitions or restrictions shall not, however, constitute a means of arbitrary discrimination or a disguised restriction on trade between the Member States.

CHAPTER III: TECHNICAL BARRIERS TO TRADE

Article 14

Notification of draft technical regulations

1. Member States shall notify to the Council at the earliest practicable stage all draft technical regulations or amendments thereto.
2. The provisions on the notification procedure are set out in Annex H.

Article 15

Mutual recognition of conformity assessment

Without prejudice to Article 7, Switzerland, on the one hand, and Iceland, Liechtenstein and Norway, on the other, grant mutual acceptance of reports, certificates, authorisations, conformity marks and manufacturer's declarations of conformity in accordance with Annex I.

CHAPTER IV: STATE AID

Article 16

State aid

1. The rights and obligations of the Member States relating to State aid shall be based on Article XVI of the GATT 1994 and the WTO Agreement on Subsidies and Countervailing Measures, which are incorporated and made part of the Convention, except as otherwise provided for in Annex Q.
2. Member States shall not apply countervailing measures as provided for under Part V of the WTO Agreement on Subsidies and Countervailing Measures in relation to any other Member State in accordance with Article 36.

3. The Member States shall review the scope of application of this Chapter with a view to extending the disciplines with respect to State aid to the field of services, taking into account international developments in the sector. The reviews shall take place at yearly intervals.

CHAPTER V: PUBLIC UNDERTAKINGS AND MONOPOLIES

Article 17

Public undertakings and monopolies

1. Member States shall ensure that public undertakings refrain from applying
   (a) measures the effect of which is to afford protection to domestic production which would be inconsistent with this Convention if achieved by means of a duty or charge with equivalent effect, quantitative restriction or government aid, or
   (b) trade discrimination on grounds of nationality in so far as it frustrates the benefits expected from the removal or absence of duties and quantitative restrictions on trade between Member States.
2. For the purposes of this Article, "public undertakings" means central, regional, or local government authorities, public enterprises and any other organisation by means of which a Member State, by law or in practice, controls or appreciably influences imports from, or exports to, the territory of a Member State.
3. The provisions of paragraph 1 of Article 18 shall also apply to the activities of public undertakings, and undertakings for which the Member States grant special or exclusive rights, in so far as the application of these provisions does not obstruct the performance, in law or in fact, of the particular public tasks assigned to them.
4. Paragraph 3 shall apply to Annex Q. The Member States shall review the scope of application of this Chapter with a view to extending the disciplines to other services, taking into account international developments in the sector. The reviews shall take place at yearly intervals.

5. Member States shall ensure that new practices of the kind described in paragraph 1 of this Article are not introduced.
6. Where Member States do not have the necessary legal powers to control the activities of regional or local government authorities or enterprises under their control in these matters, they shall nevertheless endeavour to ensure that those authorities or enterprises comply with the provisions of this Article.

CHAPTER VI: RULES OF COMPETITION

ARTICLE 18

Competition

1. Member States recognise that the following practices are incompatible with this Convention in so far as they frustrate the benefits arising from this Convention:
   (a) agreements between enterprises, decisions by associations of enterprises and concerted practices between enterprises which have as their object or result the prevention, restriction or distortion of competition;
   (b) abuse by one or more undertakings of a dominant position in the territories of the Member States as a whole or in a substantial part thereof.
2. Should a Member State consider that a given practice is incompatible with this Article, it may ask for consultations in accordance with the procedures set out in Article 47 and take appropriate measures under the conditions set out in paragraph 2 of Article 40 to deal with the difficulties resulting from the practice in question.

CHAPTER VII: PROTECTION OF INTELLECTUAL PROPERTY

ARTICLE 19

1. Member States shall grant and ensure adequate and effective protection of intellectual property rights, and provide for measures

for the enforcement of such rights against infringement thereof, counterfeiting and piracy, in accordance with the provisions of this Article, Annex J and the international agreements referred to therein.

2. Member States shall accord to each other's nationals treatment no less favourable than that they accord to their own nationals. Exemptions from this obligation must be in accordance with the substantive provisions of Article 3 of the TRIPS Agreement.
3. Member States shall grant to each other's nationals treatment no less favourable than that accorded to nationals of any other State. Exemptions from this obligation must be in accordance with the substantive provisions of the TRIPS Agreement, in particular Articles 4 and 5 thereof.
4. Member States agree, upon request of any Member State, to review the provisions on the protection of intellectual property rights contained in the present Article and in Annex J, with a view to further improve levels of protection and to avoid or remedy trade distortions caused by actual levels of protection of intellectual property rights.

CHAPTER VIII: FREE MOVEMENT OF PERSONS

Article 20

Movement of persons

1. Freedom of movement of persons shall be secured among Member States in accordance with the provisions set out in Annex K and in the Protocol to Annex K on the free movement of persons between Liechtenstein and Switzerland.
2. The objective of this Article for the benefit of the nationals of the Member States shall be:
   (a) to accord a right of entry, residence, access to work as employed persons, establishment on a self-employed basis and the right to stay in the territory of the Member States;
   (b) to facilitate the provision of services in the territory of the Member States, and in particular to liberalise the provision of services of brief duration;

(c) to accord a right of entry into, and residence in, the territory of the Member States to persons without an economic activity in the host State;
(d) to accord the same living, employment and working conditions as those accorded to nationals.

Article 21

Coordination of social security systems

In order to provide freedom of movement of persons, the Member States shall make provision, in accordance with Appendix 2 of Annex K and with the Protocol to Annex K on the free movement of persons between Liechtenstein and Switzerland, for the coordination of social security systems with the aim in particular of:

(a) securing equality of treatment;
(b) determining the legislation applicable;
(c) aggregating, for the purpose of acquiring and retaining the right to benefit and of calculating the amount of benefit, of all periods taken into consideration by the national legislation of the States concerned;
(d) paying benefits to persons resident in the territories of the Member States;
(e) fostering mutual administrative assistance and cooperation between authorities and institutions.

Article 22

Mutual recognition of professional qualifications

In order to make it easier for nationals of the Member States to take up and pursue activities as workers and self-employed persons, the Member States shall take the necessary measures, as contained in Appendix 3 to Annex K and in the Protocol to Annex K on the free movement of persons between Liechtenstein and Switzerland, concerning the mutual recognition of diplomas, certificates and other evidence of formal qualifications, and the coordination of the provisions laid down by law, regulation or administrative action in the Member States concerning the taking up and pursuit of activities by workers and self-employed persons.

CHAPTER IX: INVESTMENT

Section I: Establishment

Article 23

Principles and scope

1. Within the framework of, and subject to, the provisions of this Convention, there shall be no restrictions on the right of establishment of companies or firms, formed in accordance with the law of a Member State and having their registered office, central administration or principal place of business in the territory of the Member States. This shall also apply to the setting up of agencies, branches or subsidiaries by companies or firms of any Member State established in the territory of any other Member State.

   The right of establishment shall include the right to set up, acquire and manage undertakings, in particular companies or firms within the meaning of paragraph 2, under the conditions laid down for its own undertakings by the law of the Member State where such establishment is effected, subject to the provisions set out hereafter.
2. For the purposes of this Chapter:
   (a) "subsidiary" of a company shall mean a company which is effectively controlled by the first company;
   (b) "companies or firms" shall mean companies or firms constituted under civil or commercial law, including cooperative societies, and other legal persons governed by public or private law, save for those which are non-profit-making; in order to be considered as a company or firm of a Member State, the company or firm shall have a real and continuous link with the economy in that Member State.
3. Annexes L to O contain specific provisions and exemptions regarding the right of establishment. The Member States shall endeavour to eliminate gradually remaining discriminations, which they may maintain in accordance with Annexes L to O. The Member States agree to review the present provision, including its Annexes, within two years after the entry into force of the Agreement amending the Convention establishing the European Free Trade Association of 21 June 2001 with a view to reducing, and ultimately eliminating, the remaining restrictions.

4. From the date of entry into force of the Agreement amending the Convention establishing the European Free Trade Association of 21 June 2001, neither Member State shall adopt new, or more, discriminatory measures as regards the establishment and operation of companies or firms of another Member State, in comparison with the treatment accorded to its own companies or firms.
5. In sectors covered by an exemption as contained in Annexes L to O, each Member State shall accord to companies or firms of another Member State treatment no less favourable than that accorded to companies or firms of third parties other than the European Community. As regards any new agreements concluded between any Member State and the European Community, the Member States further undertake to extend to each other, on the basis of reciprocity, the benefits of such agreements, subject to a decision by the Council.
6. The right of establishment in the field of road, rail and air transport shall be governed by the provisions of Article 35 and Annexes P and Q, subject to the specific provisions and exemptions set out in Annexes L and M.
7. The right of establishment of natural persons shall be governed by the provisions of Article 20, Annexes K and the Protocol to Annex K on movement of persons between Liechtenstein and Switzerland.

ARTICLE 24

National treatment

1. Within the scope of application of this Chapter, and without prejudice to any special provisions contained herein:
   (a) Member States shall grant treatment no less favourable than that accorded to their own companies or firms;
   (b) each Member State may regulate the establishment and operation of companies or firms on its territory, in so far as these regulations do not discriminate against companies or firms of the other Member States in comparison to its own companies or firms.
2. The provisions of this Article do not preclude the application by a Member State of particular rules concerning the establishment and operation in its territory of branches and agencies of companies of another Member State not incorporated in the territory of the first Member State, which are justified by legal or technical differences between such branches and agencies as compared to branches and

agencies of companies incorporated in its territory. The difference in treatment shall not go beyond what is strictly necessary as a result of such legal or technical differences.

Article 25

Financial market regulation

1. In respect of financial services, this Chapter does not prejudice the right of the Member States to adopt measures necessary for prudential grounds in order to ensure the protection of investors, depositors, policy holders, or persons to whom a fiduciary duty is owed, or to ensure the integrity and stability of the financial system. These measures shall not discriminate against companies or firms of the other Member States in comparison to its own companies or firms.
2. Nothing in this Chapter shall be construed to require a Member State to disclose information relating to the affairs and accounts of individual customers or any confidential or proprietary information in the possession of public entities.

Article 26

Recognition

1. A Member State may enter into an agreement or arrangement with a particular State providing for the recognition of standards, criteria for authorization, licensing or certification of service suppliers, in which case it shall offer adequate opportunity for any other Member State to negotiate its accession to such an agreement or arrangement or to negotiate comparable ones with it.
2. Where a Member State accords recognition as provided for in paragraph 1 autonomously, it shall afford adequate opportunity for any other Member State to demonstrate that experience, licences or certifications obtained or requirements met in that other Member State's territory should be recognised.
3. A Member State shall not accord recognition in a manner which would constitute a means of discrimination between countries in the application of its standards or criteria for the authorisation, licensing or certification of service suppliers, or a disguised restriction to establishment in the services sector.

Article 27

Exceptions

1. The provisions of this Chapter shall not apply, so far as any given Member State is concerned, to activities which in that Member State are connected, even occasionally, with the exercise of official authority.
2. The provisions of this Chapter and measures taken in pursuance thereof shall not prejudice the applicability of provisions laid down by law, regulation or administrative action providing for special treatment for foreign companies or firms on grounds of public policy, public security, public health or the environment.
3. Subject to the requirement that such measures are not applied in a manner which would constitute a means of arbitrary or unjustifiable discrimination between States where like conditions prevail, or a disguised restriction on trade in services, nothing in this Convention shall be construed to prevent the adoption or enforcement by any Member State of measures:
   (a) inconsistent with Article 24, provided that the difference in treatment is aimed at ensuring the equitable or effective[4[sic]] imposition or collection of direct taxes in respect of services or service suppliers of other Member States;

[4[sic]] Measures that are aimed at ensuring the equitable or effective imposition or collection of direct taxes include measures taken by a Member under its taxation system which:

(i) apply to non-resident service suppliers in recognition of the fact that the tax obligation of non-residents is determined with respect to taxable items sourced or located in the Member State's territory; or
(ii) apply to non-residents in order to ensure the imposition or collection of taxes in the Member State's territory; or
(iii) apply to non-residents or residents in order to prevent the avoidance or evasion of taxes, including compliance measures; or
(iv) apply to consumers of services supplied in or from the territory of another Member State in order to ensure the imposition or collection of taxes of such consumers derived from sources in the Member State's territory; or
(v) distinguish service suppliers subject to tax on worldwide taxable items from other service suppliers, in recognition of the difference in the nature of the tax base between them; or
(vi) determine, allocate or apportion income, profit, gain, loss, deduction or credit of resident persons or branches, or between related persons or branches of the same person, in order to safeguard the Member State's tax base.

Tax terms or concepts in paragraph 3(a) of Article 27 and in this footnote are determined according to tax definitions and concepts, or equivalent or similar definitions and concepts, under the domestic law of the Member State taking the measure.

(b) inconsistent with paragraph 5 of Article 23, provided that the difference in treatment is the result of an agreement on the avoidance of double taxation or provisions on the avoidance of double taxation in any other international agreement or arrangement by which the Member State is bound.

Section II: Capital Movement

Article 28

1. Within the framework of this Chapter, there shall be no restrictions between the Member States on the movement of capital relating to the establishment in another Member State's territory of a company or firm of that Member State.
2. The movement of capital not relating to establishment between the Member States shall be ensured in accordance with the international agreements to which they are parties.
3. The Member States agree to review the present provision within two years after the entry into force of the Agreement amending the Convention establishing the European Free Trade Association of 21 June 2001 in order to broaden the scope of, and ultimately eliminate the remaining restrictions to, the movement of capital.

CHAPTER X: TRADE IN SERVICES

Article 29

Principles and scope

1. Within the framework of, and subject to, the provisions of this Convention, there shall be no restrictions on the right to supply services within the territory of the Member States in respect of natural persons, companies or firms of Member States who are established in a Member State other than that of the natural person, company or firm for whom the services are intended.
2. For the purposes of this Chapter, services shall be considered to be "services" within the meaning of this Convention where they are normally supplied for remuneration
   (a) from the territory of one Member State into the territory of another Member State;

(b) in the territory of a Member State to the service consumer of another Member State in accordance with paragraph 7 below;
(c) by service supplier of a Member State, through presence of natural persons of that Member State in the territory of another Member State in accordance with paragraph 7 below.

3. Annexes L to O contain specific provisions and exemptions regarding the right to supply services. The Member States shall endeavour to eliminate gradually remaining discriminations, which they may maintain in accordance with Annexes L to O. The Member States agree to review the present provision, including its Annexes, within two years after the entry into force of the Agreement amending the Convention establishing the European Free Trade Association of 21 June 2001 with a view to reducing, and ultimately eliminating, the remaining restrictions.
4. From the date of entry into force of the Agreement amending the Convention establishing the European Free Trade Association of 21 June 2001, neither Member State shall adopt new, or more, discriminatory measures as regards services or service suppliers of another Member State, in comparison with the treatment accorded to its own like services or service suppliers.
5. In sectors covered by an exemption as contained in Annexes L to O, each Member State shall accord to services or service suppliers of another Member State treatment no less favourable than that accorded to like services or service suppliers of third parties other than the European Community. As regards any new agreements concluded between any Member State and the European Community, the Member States further undertake to extend to each other, on the basis of reciprocity, the benefits of such agreements, subject to a decision by the Council.
6. The right to supply services in the field of road, rail and air transport shall be governed by the provisions of Article 35 and Annexes P and Q, subject to the specific provisions and exemptions set out in Annex M.
7. The supply or consumption of services by natural persons as provided for in paragraphs 2(b) and (c) shall be governed by the relevant provisions of Article 20, Annex K and the Protocol to Annex K on movement of persons between Liechtenstein and Switzerland, in accordance with the principles set out hereinafter.

Article 30

National treatment

Within the scope of application of this Chapter, and without prejudice to any special provisions contained herein:

(a) Member States shall grant treatment no less favourable than that accorded to their own natural persons, companies or firms providing services;
(b) each Member State may regulate services activities within its territory in so far as these regulations do not discriminate against natural persons, companies or firms of the other Member States in comparison to its own natural persons, companies or firms.

Article 31

Financial market regulation

1. In respect of financial services, this Chapter does not prejudice the right of the Member States to adopt measures necessary for prudential grounds in order to ensure the protection of investors, depositors, policy holders, or persons to whom a fiduciary duty is owed, or to ensure the integrity and stability of the financial system. These measures shall not discriminate against natural persons, companies or firms of the other Member States in comparison to its own natural persons, companies or firms.
2. Nothing in this Chapter shall be construed to require a Member State to disclose information relating to the affairs and accounts of individual customers or any confidential or proprietary information in the possession of public entities.

Article 32

Recognition

1. The mutual recognition between the Member States of diplomas, certificates and other evidence of formal qualifications, and the

coordination of the provisions laid down by law, regulation or administrative action in the Member States concerning the taking up and pursuit of activities by natural persons, shall be governed by the relevant provisions of Article 22, Annex K and Appendix 3 thereto and the Protocol to Annex K on movement of persons between Liechtenstein and Switzerland.

2. A Member State may enter into an agreement or arrangement with a particular State providing for the recognition of standards, criteria for authorization, licensing or certification of service suppliers, in which case it shall offer adequate opportunity for any other Member State to negotiate its accession to such an agreement or arrangement or to negotiate comparable ones with it.
3. Where a Member State accords recognition as provided for in paragraph 2 autonomously, it shall afford adequate opportunity for any other Member State to demonstrate that experience, licences or certifications obtained or requirements met in that other Member State's territory should be recognised.
4. A Member State shall not accord recognition in a manner which would constitute a means of discrimination between countries in the application of its standards or criteria for the authorisation, licensing or certification of service suppliers, or a disguised restriction to trade in services.

Article 33

Exceptions

1. The provisions of this Chapter shall not apply, so far as any given Member State is concerned, to activities which in that Member State are connected, even occasionally, with the exercise of official authority.
2. The provisions of this Chapter and measures taken in pursuance thereof shall not prejudice the applicability of provisions laid down by law, regulation or administrative action providing for special treatment of foreign service suppliers on grounds of public policy, public security, public health or the environment.
3. Subject to the requirement that such measures are not applied in a manner which would constitute a means of arbitrary or unjustifiable discrimination between States where like conditions prevail, or a

disguised restriction on trade in services, nothing in this Convention shall be construed to prevent the adoption or enforcement by any Member State of measures:

(a) inconsistent with Article 30, provided that the difference in treatment is aimed at ensuring the equitable or effective[5[sic]] imposition or collection of direct taxes in respect of services or service suppliers of other Member States;

(b) inconsistent with paragraph 5 of Article 29, provided that the difference in treatment is the result of an agreement on the avoidance of double taxation or provisions on the avoidance of double taxation in any other international agreement or arrangement by which the Member State is bound.

Article 34

Public procurement

Nothing in this Chapter shall be construed to impose any obligations with respect to public procurement.

5[sic] Measures that are aimed at ensuring the equitable or effective imposition or collection of direct taxes include measures taken by a Member under its taxation system which:

(i) apply to non-resident service suppliers in recognition of the fact that the tax obligation of non-residents is determined with respect to taxable items sourced or located in the Member State's territory; or

(ii) apply to non-residents in order to ensure the imposition or collection of taxes in the Member State's territory; or

(iii) apply to non-residents or residents in order to prevent the avoidance or evasion of taxes, including compliance measures; or

(iv) apply to consumers of services supplied in or from the territory of another Member State in order to ensure the imposition or collection of taxes of such consumers derived from sources in the Member State's territory; or

(v) distinguish service suppliers subject to tax on worldwide taxable items from other service suppliers, in recognition of the difference in the nature of the tax base between them; or

(vi) determine, allocate or apportion income, profit, gain, loss, deduction or credit of resident persons or branches, or between related persons or branches of the same person, in order to safeguard the Member State's tax base.

Tax terms or concepts in paragraph 3(a) of Article 27 and in this footnote are determined according to tax definitions and concepts, or equivalent or similar definitions and concepts, under the domestic law of the Member State taking the measure.

Article 35

Transport

The Member States shall liberalise the access to each other's transport markets for the carriage of passengers and goods by road, rail and air in accordance with the provisions set out in Annex P and Annex Q respectively.

CHAPTER XI: DUMPING

Article 36

Anti-dumping measures, countervailing duties and measures against illicit commercial practices attributable to third countries shall not be applied in relations between the Member States.

CHAPTER XII: PUBLIC PROCUREMENT

Article 37

1. The Member States reaffirm their rights and obligations under the WTO Agreement on Government Procurement (GPA). Under this Convention, the Member States broaden the scope of their commitments under the WTO Government Procurement Agreement with an aim to pursue liberalisation in public procurement markets in accordance with Annex R.
2. To this effect, the Member States shall secure non-discriminative, transparent and reciprocal access to their respective public procurement markets and shall ensure open and effective competition based on equal treatment.

CHAPTER XIII: CURRENT PAYMENTS

Article 38

Current payments connected with the movement of goods, persons, services or capital as defined in Article 28 between Member States within the framework of the provisions of this Convention shall be free of all restrictions.

CHAPTER XIV: EXCEPTIONS AND SAFEGUARDS

Article 39

Security exceptions

Nothing in this Convention shall prevent a Member State from taking any measures:

(a) which it considers necessary to prevent the disclosure of information contrary to its essential security interests;
(b) which relate to the production of, or trade in, arms, munitions and war materials or other products or services indispensable for defence purposes or to research, development or production indispensable for defence purposes, provided that such measures do not impair the conditions of competition in respect of products or services not intended for specifically military purposes;
(c) which it considers essential to its own security in the event of serious internal disturbances affecting the maintenance of law and order, in time of war or serious international tension constituting threat of war or in order to carry out obligations it has accepted for the purpose of maintaining peace and international security.

Safeguard measures

Article 40

1. If serious economic, societal or environmental difficulties of a sectorial or regional nature liable to persist are arising, a Member State may unilaterally take appropriate measures under the conditions and procedures set out in Article 41.
2. Such safeguard measures shall be restricted with regard to their scope and duration to what is strictly necessary in order to remedy the situation. Priority shall be given to such measures as will least disturb the functioning of this Convention.
3. The safeguard measures shall apply with regard to all Member States.

4. This Article is without prejudice to the application of specific safeguard provisions set out in the Annexes to this Convention or of special safeguard measures in accordance with Article 5 of the WTO Agreement on Agriculture.

Article 41

1. A Member State which is considering taking safeguard measures under Article 40, shall, without delay, notify the other Member States through the Council and shall provide all relevant information.
2. The Member States shall immediately enter into consultations in the Council with a view to finding a commonly acceptable solution.
3. The Member State concerned may not take safeguard measures until one month has elapsed after the date of notification under paragraph 1, unless the consultation procedure under paragraph 2 has been concluded before the expiration of the stated time limit. When exceptional circumstances requiring immediate action exclude prior examination, the Member State concerned may apply forthwith the protective measures strictly necessary to remedy the situation.
4. The Member State concerned shall, without delay, notify the measures taken to the Council and shall provide all relevant information.
5. The safeguard measures taken shall be the subject of consultations in the Council every three months from the date of their adoption with a view to their abolition before the date of expiry envisaged, or to the limitation of their scope of application.

   Each Member State may at any time request the Council to review such measures.

CHAPTER XV: ECONOMIC AND MONETARY POLICY CO-OPERATION

Article 42

The Member States shall exchange views and information concerning the implementation of this Convention and the impact of the integration on economic activities and on the conduct of economic and monetary policies.

Furthermore, they may discuss macro-economic situations, policies and prospects. This exchange of views and information shall take place on a non-binding basis.

CHAPTER XVI: INSTITUTIONAL PROVISIONS

Article 43

The Council

1. It shall be the responsibility of the Council
   (a) to exercise such powers and functions as are conferred upon it by this Convention;
   (b) to decide on amendments to this Convention in accordance with the provisions herein;
   (c) to supervise the application of this Convention and keep its operation under review;
   (d) to consider whether further action should be taken by Member States in order to promote the attainment of the objectives of the Association;
   (e) to facilitate the establishment of closer links with other States and unions of States;
   (f) to seek to establish such relationships with other international organisations as may facilitate the attainment of the objectives of the Association;
   (g) to negotiate trade and co-operation agreements between the Member States and any other State, union of States or international organisation;
   (h) to endeavour to resolve disputes that may arise regarding the interpretation or application of this Convention; and
   (i) to consider any other matter that may affect the operation of this Convention.
2. Each Member State shall be represented in the Council and shall have one vote.
3. The Council may decide to set up such organs, committees and other bodies, as it considers necessary to assist it in accomplishing its tasks. These organs, committees and other bodies are listed in Annex S.

4. In exercising its responsibility under this Article, the Council may take decisions, which shall be binding on all Member States, and may make recommendations to Member States.
5. Decisions and recommendations of the Council shall be made by unanimous vote, except in so far as this Convention provides otherwise. Decisions or recommendations shall be regarded as unanimous unless any Member State casts a negative vote. Decisions and recommendations which are to be made by majority vote, require the affirmative vote of three Member States.
6. If the number of the Member States changes, the Council may decide to amend the number of votes required for decisions and recommendations which are to be made by majority vote.

Article 44

Administrative arrangements of the Association

The Council shall take decisions for the following purposes:

(a) to lay down the Rules of Procedure of the Council and of any other bodies of the Association, which may include provision that procedural questions may be decided by majority vote;
(b) to make arrangements for the secretariat services required by the Association;
(c) to establish the financial arrangements necessary for the administrative expenses of the Association, the procedure for establishing a budget and the apportionment of those expenses between the Member States.

Article 45

Legal capacity, privileges and immunities

1. The legal capacity, privileges and immunities to be recognised and granted by the Member States in connection with the Association shall be laid down in a Protocol to this Convention.
2. The Council, acting on behalf of the Association, may conclude with the Government of the State in whose territory the headquarters will be situated an agreement relating to the legal capacity and the privileges and immunities to be recognised and granted in connection with the Association.

CHAPTER XVII: CONSULTATIONS AND DISPUTE SETTLEMENT

Article 46

Scope

The provisions of this Chapter shall apply to any matter arising from this Convention, unless otherwise specified in this Convention.

Article 47

Consultations

1. The Member States shall at all times endeavour to agree on the interpretation and application of this Convention, and shall make every attempt through cooperation and consultations to arrive at a mutually satisfactory resolution of any matter that might affect its operation.
2. Any Member State may bring any matter, which concerns the interpretation or application of this Convention before the Council. The Council shall be provided with all information, which might be of use in making possible an in-depth examination of the situation, with a view to finding an acceptable solution. To this end, the Council shall examine all possibilities to maintain the good functioning of the Convention.
3. A meeting of the Council shall be held within 30 days from the receipt of the request for consultations.

Article 48

Arbitration

1. In case a Member State considers that a measure applied by another Member State violates the Convention and the matter has not been resolved within 45 days after consultations have been held pursuant to Article 47, such matter may be referred to arbitration by one or more Member States parties to the dispute by means of a written notification addressed to the Member State complained against. A copy of this notification shall be communicated to all Member States

so that each may determine whether it has a substantial interest in the matter. Where more than one Member State requests the submission to an arbitration tribunal of a dispute with the same Member State relating to the same question a single arbitration tribunal should be established to consider such disputes whenever feasible.

2. A Member State which is not a party to the dispute, on delivery of a written notice to the disputing Member States, shall be entitled to make written submissions to the arbitration tribunal, receive written submissions of the disputing Member States, attend all hearings and make oral submissions.
3. The award of the arbitration tribunal shall be final and binding upon the Member States parties to the dispute and shall be complied with promptly.
4. The establishment and functioning of the arbitration tribunal and the implementation of arbitral awards are governed by the rules set out in Annex T.

CHAPTER XVIII: GENERAL PROVISIONS

Article 49

Obligations under other international agreements

1. Nothing in this Convention shall be regarded as exempting any Member State from obligations which it has undertaken by virtue of agreements with third States or multilateral agreements to which they are parties.
2. This Convention shall be without prejudice to the rules applicable to Member States governed by the Agreement on the European Economic Area, the Nordic cooperation and the regional union between Switzerland and Liechtenstein

Article 50

Rights and obligations of the Member States

The Member States shall take all appropriate measures, whether general or particular, to ensure fulfilment of the obligations arising out of this Convention. They shall abstain from any measure which could jeopardize the attainment of the objectives of this Convention.

Article 51

Transparency

1. The Member States shall publish their laws, or otherwise make publicly available their laws, regulations, procedures and administrative rulings and judicial decisions of general application as well as the international agreements which may affect the operation of this Convention.
2. The Member States shall promptly respond to specific questions and provide, upon request, information to each other on matters referred to in paragraph 1.

Article 52

Confidentiality

The representatives, delegates and experts of the Member States, as well as officials and other servants acting under this Convention shall be required, even after their duties have ceased, not to disclose information of the kind covered by the obligation of professional secrecy, in particular information about undertakings, their business relations or their cost components.

Article 53

Annexes

1. The Annexes, Appendices and Protocols to this Convention shall form an integral part of it.
2. The Annexes to this Convention are the following:

Annex A	on Rules of Origin
Annex B	on mutual administrative assistance in customs matters
Annex C	List of agricultural goods and goods processed from agricultural raw materials referred to in paragraph 1 of Article 8
Annex D	List of tariff concessions to agricultural products
Annex E	Seeds
Annex F	Organic agriculture
Annex G	Sanitary and phytosanitary measures

(continued)

continued

Annex H	Procedure for the provision of information in the field of technical regulations and of rules on Information Society services
Annex I	Mutual recognition in relation to conformity assessment
Annex J	Intellectual property rights
Annex K	Movement of persons
Annex L	Reservations by Iceland on investment and services
Annex M	Reservations by Liechtenstein on investment and services
Annex N	Reservations by Norway on investment and services
Annex O	Reservations by Switzerland on investment and services
Annex P	Land transport
Annex Q	Air transport
Annex R	Public procurement
Annex S	Organs, committees and other bodies set up by the Council
Annex T	Arbitration
Annex U	Territorial application

The Council may decide to amend the provisions to this paragraph.

3. The Council may decide to amend Annexes A, C, H, S and T, as well as the Appendices to Annexes E, F, K, P, Q and R, unless otherwise provided in the Annexes.
4[7]. The Committee established under Annex I may decide to amend Article 3 of that Annex as well as the Appendix thereto. It shall inform the Council of its decision-making.

Article 54

Ratification

1. This Convention shall be ratified by the signatory States. The instruments of ratification shall be deposited with the Government of Sweden, which shall notify all other signatory States.
2. The Government of Norway shall act as Depositary as of 17 November 1995.
3. The Council may decide to amend the provisions of this Article.

7 As amended by Decision of the Council No. 2 of 2009 (16 June 2009).

Article 55

Entry into force

This Convention shall enter into force on the deposit of instruments of ratification by all signatory States.

Article 56

Accession and association

1. Any State may accede to this Convention, provided that the Council decides to approve its accession, on such terms and conditions as may be set out in that decision. The instrument of accession shall be deposited with the Depositary, which shall notify all other Member States. This Convention shall enter into force in relation to an acceding State on the date indicated in that decision.
2. The Council may negotiate an agreement between the Member States and any other State, union of States or international organisation, creating an association embodying such reciprocal rights and obligations, common actions and special procedures as may be appropriate. Such an agreement shall be submitted to the Member States for acceptance and shall enter into force provided that it is accepted by all Member States. Instruments of acceptance shall be deposited with the Depositary, which shall notify all other Member States.
3. Any State acceding to this Convention shall apply to become a party to the free trade agreements between the Member States on the one hand and third states, unions of states or international organisations on the other.

Article 57

Withdrawal

1. Any Member State may withdraw from this Convention provided that it gives twelve months' notice in writing to the Depositary, which shall notify all other Member States.
2. Before the withdrawal takes effect, the Member States shall agree on appropriate arrangements and equitable cost-sharing relating to the withdrawal.

Article 58

Territorial application

This Convention shall apply to the territories of the Member States except as provided for in Annex U.

Article 59

Amendment

Except as otherwise provided for in this Convention, an amendment to the provisions of this Convention shall be subject to a decision of the Council which shall be submitted to the Member States for acceptance in accordance with their internal legal requirements. It shall enter into force, unless otherwise provided, on the first day of the second month following the deposit of the instruments of acceptance by all Member States with the Depositary, which shall notify all other Member States.

IN WITNESS WHEREOF the undersigned, duly authorised thereto, have signed the present Convention.

DONE at Stockholm this 4th day of January, 1960, in a single copy in the English and French languages, both texts being equally authentic, which shall be deposited with the Government of Sweden, by which certified copies shall be transmitted to all other signatory and acceding States.

AMENDED at Vaduz this 21st day of June, 2001, in a single authentic copy in the English language, which shall be deposited with the Government of Norway.

ANNEX K
FREE MOVEMENT OF PERSONS
(CHAPTER VIII)

I. BASIC PROVISIONS

Article 1

Objectives

The objectives of this Annex, for the benefit of nationals of the Member States, are:

(a) to accord a right of entry, residence, access to work as employed persons, establishment on a self-employed basis and the right to stay in the territory of the Member States;
(b) to facilitate the provision of services in the territory of the Member States, and in particular to liberalise the provision of services of brief duration;
(c) to accord a right of entry into, and residence in, the territory of the Member States to persons without an economic activity in the host State;
(d) to accord the same living, employment and working conditions as those accorded to nationals of the host State.

Article 2

Non-discrimination

Nationals of one Member State who are lawfully resident in the territory of another Member State shall not, in application of and in accordance with the provisions of Appendices 1, 2 and 3 to this Annex, be the subject of any discrimination on grounds of nationality.

Article 3

Right of entry

The right of entry of nationals of one Member State into the territory of another Member State shall be guaranteed in accordance with the provisions laid down in Appendix 1.

Article 4

Right of residence and access to an economic activity

The right of residence and access to an economic activity shall be guaranteed unless otherwise provided in Article 10 and in accordance with the provisions of Appendix 1.

Article 5

Persons providing services

1. Without prejudice to other specific agreements between the Member States specifically concerning the provision of services (including the Government Procurement Agreement in so far as it covers the provision of services), persons providing services, including companies in accordance with the provisions of Appendix 1, shall have the right to provide a service in the territory of another Member State for a period not exceeding 90 days' of actual work in a calendar year.
2. Providers of services shall have the right of entry into, and residence in, the territory of the other Member State:
   (a) where they have the right to provide a service under paragraph 1 or by virtue of the provisions of an agreement mentioned in paragraph 1; or
   (b) if the conditions specified in (a) are not fulfilled, where they have received authorisation to provide a service from the competent authorities of the Member State concerned.
3. Nationals of a Member State entering the territory of another Member State solely to receive services shall have the right of entry and residence.

4. The rights referred to in this Article shall be guaranteed in accordance with the provisions laid down in Appendices 1, 2 and 3. The quantitative limits of Article 10 may not be relied upon as against persons referred to in this Article.

Article 6

Right of residence for persons not pursuing an economic activity

The right of residence in the territory of a Member State shall be guaranteed to persons not pursuing an economic activity in accordance with the provisions of Appendix 1 relating to non-active people.

Article 7

Other rights

The Member States shall make provision, in accordance with Appendix 1, for the following rights in relation to the free movement of persons:

(a) the right to equal treatment with nationals in respect of access to, and the pursuit of, an economic activity, and living, employment and working conditions;
(b) the right to occupational and geographical mobility which enables nationals of the other Member States to move freely within the territory of the host State and to pursue the occupation of their choice;
(c) the right to stay in the territory of a Member State after the end of an economic activity;
(d) the right of residence for members of the family, irrespective of their nationality;
(e) the right of family members to pursue an economic activity, irrespective of their nationality;
(f) the right to acquire immovable property in so far as this is linked to the exercise of rights conferred by this Annex;
(g) during the transitional period, the right, after the end of an economic activity or period of residence in the territory of a Member State, to return there for the purposes of pursuing an economic activity and the right to have a temporary residence permit converted into a permanent one.

Article 8

Coordination of social security systems

The Member States shall make provision, in accordance with Appendix 2, for the coordination of social security systems with the aim in particular of:

(a) securing equality of treatment;
(b) determining the legislation applicable;
(c) aggregating, for the purpose of acquiring and retaining the right to benefits, and of calculating such benefits, all periods taken into consideration by the national legislation of the States concerned;
(d) paying benefits to persons residing in the territory of the Member States;
(e) fostering mutual administrative assistance and co-operation between authorities and institutions.

Article 9

Mutual recognition of professional qualifications
(diplomas, certificates and other evidence of formal qualifications)

In order to make it easier for nationals of the Member States to gain access to and pursue activities as employed and self-employed persons and to provide services, the Member States shall take the necessary measures, in accordance with Appendix 3, concerning the mutual recognition of diplomas, certificates and other evidence of formal qualifications, and with the coordination of the laws, regulations and administrative provisions of the Member States on access to and pursuit of activities as employed and self-employed persons and the provision of services.

II. GENERAL AND FINAL PROVISIONS

Article 10

Transitional provisions and development of this Annex

1. For 51[1] years after the entry into force of the Agreement between the European Community and its Member States, of the one part,

[1] *The transitional period should expire at the same time as the corresponding period in the bilateral agreement between Switzerland and the European Community.*

and the Swiss Confederation of the other, on the free movement of persons (hereinafter the "Swiss-EC Agreement on the free movement of persons"), Switzerland may maintain quantitative limits in respect of access to an economic activity for the following two categories of residence: residence for a period of more than four months and less than one year and residence for a period equal to, or exceeding, one year. There shall be no restriction on residence for less than four months.

From the beginning of the 6th year, all quantitative limits applicable to nationals of the other Member States shall be abolished.

2. For a maximum period of 2 years after the entry into force of the Swiss-EC Agreement on the free movement of persons, the Member States may maintain the controls on the priority of workers integrated into the regular labour market and wage and working conditions applicable to nationals of other Member States, including the persons providing services referred to in Article 5. Before the end of the first year, the Committee referred to in Article 14 (hereinafter the "Committee") shall consider whether these restrictions need to be maintained. The Council may curtail the maximum period. The controls on the priority of workers integrated into the regular labour market shall not apply to providers of services liberalised under Annexes P, Q and R in so far as it covers the provision of services.
3. Upon entry into force of the Swiss-EC Agreement on the free movement of persons, and until the end of the 5th year, each year Switzerland shall reserve, within its overall quotas, for employed and self-employed persons of the other Member States, at least 300 new residence permits valid for a period equal to, or exceeding, one year and 200 valid for more than four months and less than one year. If the agreed quota should not suffice, arrangements will be made by the Council.
4. The number of new residence permits issued by Switzerland to employed and self-employed persons of the other Member States may not be limited to fewer than 300 per year valid for a period equal to, or exceeding, one year and 200 per year valid for more than four months and less than one year.
5. The transitional provisions of paragraphs 1 to 4, and in particular those of paragraph 2 concerning the priority of workers integrated into the regular labour market and controls on wage and working conditions, shall not apply to employed and self-employed persons who, at the time of the entry into force of the Swiss-EC Agreement on

the free movement of persons, are authorised to pursue an economic activity in the territory of the Member States. Such persons shall in particular enjoy occupational and geographical mobility. The holders of residence permits valid for less than one year shall be entitled to have their permits renewed; the exhaustion of quantitative limits may not be invoked against them. The holders of residence permits valid for a period equal to, or exceeding, one year shall automatically be entitled to have their permits extended. Such employed and self-employed persons shall therefore enjoy the rights to free movement accorded to established persons in the basic provisions of this Annex, and in particular Article 7 thereof, from its entry into force.

6. Switzerland shall regularly and promptly forward to the Council any useful statistics and information, including measures implementing paragraph 2. A Member State may request a review of the situation.
7. No quantitative limits may be applied to frontier workers.
8. The transitional provisions on social security and the retrocession of unemployment insurance contributions are laid down in Protocols 1, 2 and 3 to Appendix 2.

Article 11

Processing of appeals

1. The persons covered by this Annex shall have a right of appeal to the competent authorities of the Member State concerned in respect of the application of the provisions of this Annex.
2. Appeals must be processed within a reasonable period of time.
3. Persons covered by this Annex shall have the opportunity to appeal to the competent national judicial body in respect of decisions on appeals, or the absence of a decision within a reasonable period of time.

Article 12

More favourable provisions

This Annex shall not preclude any more favourable national provisions which may exist for both nationals of the Member States and their family members.

Article 13

Standstill

The Member States undertake not to adopt any further restrictive measures vis-à-vis each other's nationals in fields covered by this Annex.

Article 14

Committee on the movement of persons

1. The Council shall establish a Committee on the movement of persons, which shall be responsible for the management and proper application of the Annex. To that end it shall issue recommendations. It may set up working groups on the coordination of social security systems and on the mutual recognition of professional qualifications.
2. For the purposes of proper implementation of this Annex, the Member States shall regularly exchange information and, at the request of one Member State, shall hold consultations within the Committee.
3. The Council may decide to modify the Appendices 2 and 3 of this Annex.

Article 15

Safeguard measures

In the event of serious economic or social difficulties, the Committee shall meet, at the request of one Member State, to examine appropriate measures to remedy the situation. The Council may decide what measures to take within 60 days of the date of the request. This period may be extended by the Council. The scope and duration of such measures shall not exceed that which is strictly necessary to remedy the situation. Preference shall be given to measures that least disrupt the working of this Annex.

Article 16

Reference to Community law

1. In order to attain the objectives pursued by this Annex, the Member States shall take all measures necessary to ensure that rights and obligations equivalent to those contained in the legal acts of the European Community to which reference is made, as incorporated

in the EEA Agreement and in the Swiss – EC Agreement on the free movement of persons, are applied in relations between them.

2. Insofar as the application of this Annex involves common concepts of the legal instruments referred to in paragraph 1, account shall be taken of relevant case- law prior to 21 June 1999. In order to ensure the good functioning of this Annex, the Council shall, at the request of any Member State, determine the implications of case- law after 21 June 1999.

Article 17

Development of law

1. As soon as one Member State initiates the process of adopting a draft amendment to its domestic legislation, or as soon as there is a change in the case-law of authorities against whose decisions there is no judicial remedy under domestic law in a field governed by this Annex, it shall inform the other Member States through the Committee.
2. The Committee shall hold an exchange of views on the implications of such an amendment for the proper functioning of this Annex.

Article 18

Relationship to bilateral social security agreements

Unless otherwise provided for under Appendix 2, bilateral social security agreements between the Member States shall be suspended upon entry into force of this Annex, in so far as the latter covers the same subject matter.

Article 19

Relationship to bilateral agreements on double taxation

1. The provisions of bilateral agreements between the Member States on double taxation shall be unaffected by the provisions of this Annex. In particular, the provisions of this Annex shall not affect the double taxation agreements' definition of 'frontier workers'.
2. No provision of this Annex may be interpreted in such a way as to prevent the Member States from distinguishing, when applying the relevant provisions of their fiscal legislation, between taxpayers whose situations are not comparable, especially as regards their place of residence.

3. No provision of this Annex shall prevent the Member States from adopting or applying measures to ensure the imposition, payment and effective recovery of taxes or to forestall tax evasion under their national fiscal legislation or agreements aimed at preventing double taxation between the Member States, or any other tax arrangements.

Article 20

Relationship to bilateral agreements on matters other than social security and double taxation

1. Notwithstanding the provisions of Articles 18 and 19, this Annex shall not affect bilateral agreements between Member States, such as those concerning private individuals, economic operators, cross-border co-operation or local frontier traffic, in so far as they are compatible with this Annex.
2. In the event of incompatibilities between such agreements and this Annex, the latter shall prevail.

Article 21

Acquired rights

In the event of termination or non-renewal, rights acquired by private individuals shall not be affected. The Member States shall settle by mutual agreement what action is to be taken in respect of rights in the process of being acquired.

ANNEX T
ARBITRATION (ART. 48)

Article 1

Establishment and functioning of the arbitral tribunal and the implementation of arbitral awards

1. The arbitral tribunal shall comprise three members.
2. In its written notification pursuant to Article 48 of this Convention, the Member State(s) referring the dispute to arbitration shall designate one member of the arbitral tribunal.
3. Within 15 days from the receipt of the notification referred to in paragraph 2, the Member State(s) to which it was addressed shall, in turn, designate one member.
4. Within 30 days from the receipt of the notification referred to in paragraph 2, the Member States concerned shall agree on the designation of a third member. The third member shall not be a national of the parties to the dispute, nor permanently reside in the territory of either Member State. The member thus appointed shall be the President of the arbitral tribunal.
5. If all three members have not been designated or appointed within 30 days from the receipt of the notification referred to in paragraph 2, the necessary designations shall be made, at request of either party to the dispute, by the President of the International Court of Justice applying the criteria of paragraphs 3 and 4. If the President is unable to act under this paragraph or is a national of a party to the dispute, the designations shall be effected by the next senior member of the Court who is neither unable to act nor a national of a Member State.
6. Unless otherwise agreed between the parties to the dispute, and subject to Article 48 of the Convention and this Annex, the Optional Rules for Arbitrating Disputes between Two States of the Permanent Court of Arbitration (PCA), effective 20 October 1992, shall apply.

7. The arbitral tribunal shall take its decisions by majority vote. Minority opinions shall not be disclosed.
8. A Member State which is not a party to the dispute, on delivery of a written notice to the disputing parties, shall be entitled to make written submissions to the arbitral tribunal, to receive written submissions of the disputing parties, attend all hearings and make oral submissions.
9. The arbitral award shall be rendered within six months of the date at which the President of the arbitral tribunal was appointed. This period can be extended by a maximum of three additional months, if the parties to the dispute so agree.
10. The expenses of the arbitral tribunal, including the remuneration of its members, shall be borne by the parties to the dispute in equal shares. Fees and expenses payable to members of an arbitral tribunal established under these Articles will be subject to schedules established by the Council and in force at the time of the establishment of the arbitral tribunal.

Article 2

Implementation of the arbitral award

1. On receipt of the arbitral award, the parties to the dispute shall agree on the implementation of the arbitral award, which, unless they decide otherwise by common accord, shall conform with the determinations and recommendations of the arbitral tribunal. The parties to the dispute shall notify the other Member States of any agreed resolution of the dispute.
2. Wherever possible, the resolution shall be non-implementation or removal of a measure not conforming with this Convention or, failing such a resolution, compensation.
3. In case of disagreement as to the existence or consistency of a measure implementing the arbitral award with the recommendations of the arbitral tribunal, such dispute shall be decided by the same arbitral tribunal before compensation can be sought or suspension of benefits can be applied in accordance with Article 3 below.
4. The complaining Member State may not initiate arbitration under the preceding paragraph before a period of 12 months has expired following the rendering of the award pursuant to paragraph 3 of Article 48. The award of the tribunal referred to in the preceding paragraph shall normally be rendered within three months of the request for arbitration.

Article 3

Non-implementation – suspension of benefits

1. If the arbitral tribunal, in accordance with paragraph 3 of Article 48, has determined that a measure is inconsistent with the obligations of this Convention, and the Member State complained against has not reached agreement with any complaining Member State on a mutually satisfactory resolution within 30 days of receiving the arbitral award, or if no implementing measures have been taken, such complaining Member State or Member States may:
   (a) seek compensation through an agreement with the Member State complained against; or
   (b) suspend the application to the Member State complained against of benefits of equivalent effect until such time as the disputing Member States have reached agreement on a resolution of the dispute.
2. Upon written request of any party to the dispute delivered to the other Member State or Member States, the same arbitral tribunal shall be reconvened to determine whether the level of benefits suspended by a Member State pursuant to paragraph 1 is of equivalent effect.
3. The proceedings of the arbitral tribunal shall be conducted in accordance with paragraph 2 of Article 1 above. The arbitral tribunal shall present its determination within 60 days after the date of the request referred to in paragraph 2 or such other period as the parties to the dispute may agree.

INDEX

ABOUT THE AUTHOR

Georges Baur is a Senior Research Fellow specialising in European law and international trade law at the Liechtenstein-Institute. He received his doctorate in law from the University of Zurich before being admitted to the bar. Prior to joining the Liechtenstein-Institute in 2018, he advised the Liechtenstein Government on financial services issues and European law, was the Deputy Head of the Liechtenstein Mission to the EU and acted as Assistant Secretary General of EFTA. He also chaired the Scientific Board of the Liechtenstein-Institute until 2003. His research interests lie in European association law and other forms of international treaties as well as their institutional structures. His work also covers legal theory and its historical development. His current research focuses on the recent development of European external relations, particularly with view to the UK and EFTA, including the doctrinal aspects of their structural principles.

www.ingramcontent.com/pod-product-compliance
Ingram Content Group UK Ltd.
Pitfield, Milton Keynes, MK11 3LW, UK
UKHW021844100926
8556IPUK00019B/1049

9 781780 68656